Abner Daniel

by

Will N. Harben

Abner Daniel
by Will N. Harben

Copyright © 2023

All Rights reserved.

ISBN: 978-93-59950-33-4

Published by

DOUBLE 9 BOOKS
2/13-B, Ansari Road
Daryaganj, New Delhi – 110002
info@double9books.com
www.double9books.com
Tel. 011-40042856

ABOUT THE AUTHOR

Will N. Harben's novel "Abner Daniel: A Novel" has been released in the United States. The novel is set in the rural South during the post-Civil War Reconstruction era and chronicles the moving tale of its title character, Abner Daniel. Abner is a hardworking and humble farmer from a small Southern town. The story of the book follows his life as he faces the challenges of changing times and the economic and social turmoil of the postwar South. The reader is given a view of the intricacies of life in the American South during this time period, including concerns of race, class, and economic hardship, through Abner's experiences. As the story progresses, Abner Daniel becomes a symbol of tenacity and persistence in the face of hardship. He is a guy of strong values who navigates the South's altering social and cultural landscape with elegance and integrity. Will N. Harben's novel depicts the South during a pivotal moment in its history in a vivid and authentic manner. "Abner Daniel" is not only a riveting character study, but also a mirror of the region's greater socioeconomic developments. It's a fascinating look at the human spirit and the timeless principles of dignity and perseverance.

CONTENTS

CHAPTER I

THE young man stood in the field road giving directions to a robust negro who was ploughing the corn, which, in parallel rows, stretched on to the main road a quarter of a mile distant. The negro placed the point of his ploughshare a few inches from the first stalk of corn, wound the line around his wrist, and clucked to his horse. With a jangling jerk of the trace-chains the animal lunged ahead: the polished ploughshare cut into the mellow soil and sped onward, curling the gray earth like shavings, and uprooting and burying the tenacious crab-grass and succulent purslane.

It was a beautiful day. The sun was shining brightly, but the atmosphere had dropped a dim veil over the near-by mountain. Even the two-storied farm-house, with its veranda and white columns, to which the field road led up a gradual slope, showed only its outlines. However, Alan Bishop, as he steadied his gaze upon the house, saw the figure of an elderly woman come out of the gate and with a quick step hurry down to him. It was his mother; she was tall and angular, and had high cheek-bones and small blue eyes. She had rather thin gray hair, which was wound into a knot behind her head, and over it she wore only a small red breakfast shawl which she held in place by one of her long hands.

"Alan," she said, panting from her brisk walk, "I want you to come to the house right off. Mr. Trabue has come to see yore pa again an' I can't do a thing with 'im."

"Well, what does he want with him?" asked the young man. His glance was on the ploughman and his horse. They had turned the far end of the corn-row and were coming back, only the nodding head of the animal being visible beyond a little rise.

"He's come to draw up the papers fer another land trade yore pa's makin'. He's the lawyer fer the Tompkins estate. Yore pa tried to buy the land a yeer ago, but it wasn't in shape to dispose of. Oh, Alan, don't you see he's goin' to ruin us with his fool notions? Folks all about are a-laughin' at him fer buyin' so much useless mountain-land. I'm powerful afeered his mind is wrong."

"Well, mother, what could I do?" Alan Bishop asked impatiently. "You know he won't listen to me."

"I reckon you can' t stop 'im," sighed the woman, "but I wish you'd come on to the house. I knowed he was up to some 'n'. Ever'day fer the last week he's been ridin' up the valley an' rollin' and tumblin' at night an' chawin' ten times as much tobacco as he ort. Oh, he's goin' to ruin us! Brother Abner says he is buyin' beca'se he thinks it's goin' to advance in value, but sech property hain't advanced a speck sence I kin remember, an' is bein' sold ever' yeer fer tax money."

"No, it's very foolish of him," said the young man as the two turned towards the house. "Father keeps talking about the fine timber on such property, but it is entirely too far from a railroad ever to be worth anything. I asked Rayburn Miller about it and he told me to do all I could to stop father from investing, and you know he's as sharp a speculator as ever lived; but it's his money."

There was a paling fence around the house, and the enclosure was alive with chickens, turkeys, geese, ducks, and peafowls. In the sunshine on the veranda two pointers lay sleeping, but at the sound of the opening gate they rose, stretched themselves lazily, and gaped.

"They are in the parlor," said Mrs. Bishop, as she whisked off her breakfast shawl. "Go right in, I 'll come in a minute. I want to see how Linda is makin' out with the churnin'. La! I feel like it's a waste o' time to do a lick o' work with him in thar actin' like a child. Ef we both go in together it 'll look like we've concocked somethin', but we must stop 'im ef we kin."

Alan went into the parlor on the left of the wide, uncarpeted hall. The room had white plastered walls, but the ceiling was of boards planed by hand and painted sky blue. In one corner stood a very old piano with pointed, octagonal legs and a stool with hair-cloth covering. The fireplace was wide and high, and had a screen made of a decorated window-shade tightly pasted on a wooden frame. Old man Bishop sat near a window, and through his steel-framed nose-glasses was carefully reading a long document written on legal-cap paper. He paid no attention to the entrance of his son, but the lawyer, a short, fat man of sixty-five with thick black hair that fell below his coat-collar, rose and extended his hand.

"How's Alan?" he asked, pleasantly. "I saw you down in the field as I come along, but I couldn't catch your eye. You see I'm out after some o' your dad's cash. He's buying hisse'f rich. My Lord! if it ever *does* turn his way he 'll scoop in enough money to set you and your sister up for life. Folks tell me he owns mighty near every stick of timber-land in the Cohutta Valley, and what he has he got at the bottom figure."

"If it ever turns his way," said Alan; "but do you see any prospect of it's ever doing so, Mr. Trabue?" The lawyer shrugged his shoulders. "I never bet on another man's trick, my boy, and I never throw cold water on the plans of a speculator. I used to when I was about your age, but I saw so many of 'em get rich by paying no attention to me that I quit right off. A man ought to be allowed to use his own judgment." Old Bishop was evidently not hearing a word of this conversation, being wholly absorbed in studying the details of the deed before him. "I reckon it's all right," he finally said. "You say the Tompkins children are all of age?"

"Yes, Effie was the youngest," answered Trabue, "and she stepped over the line last Tuesday. There's her signature in black and white. The deed's all right. I don't draw up any other sort."

Alan went to his father and leaned over him. "Father," he said, softly, and yet with firmness, "I wish you'd not act hastily in this deal. You ought to consider mother's wishes, and she is nearly distracted over it."

Bishop was angry. His massive, clean-shaven face was red. "I'd like to know what I'd consult her fer," he said. "In a matter o' this kind a woman's about as responsible as a suckin' baby."

Trabue laughed heartily. "Well, I reckon it's a good thing your wife didn't hear that or she'd show you whether she was responsible or not. I couldn't have got the first word of that off my tongue before my wife would 'a' knocked me clean through that wall."

Alfred Bishop seemed not to care for levity during business hours, for he greeted this remark only with a frown. He scanned the paper again and said: "Well, ef thar's any flaw in this I reckon you 'll make it right."

"Oh yes, I 'll make any mistake of mine good," returned Trabue. "The paper's all right."

"You see," said Alan to the lawyer, "mother and I think father has already more of this sort of property than he can carry, and—"

"I wish you and yore mother'd let my business alone," broke in Bishop, firing up again. "Trabue heer knows I've been worryin' 'im fer the last two months to get the property in salable shape. Do you reckon after he gets it that away I want to listen to yore two tongues a-waggin' in open opposition to it?"

Trabue rubbed his hands together. "It really don't make a bit of difference to me, Alan, one way or the other," he said, pacifically. "I'm only acting as attorney for the Tompkins estate, and get my fee whether there's a transfer or not. That's where I stand in the matter."

"But it's not whar I stand in it, Mr. Trabue," said a firm voice in the doorway. It was Mrs. Bishop, her blue eyes flashing, her face pale and rigid. "I think I've got a right—and a big one—to have a say-so in this kind of a trade. A woman 'at 's stayed by a man's side fer thirty odd yeer an' raked an' scraped to he'p save a little handful o' property fer her two children has got a right to raise a rumpus when her husband goes crooked like Alfred has an' starts in to bankrupt 'em all jest fer a blind notion o' his'n."

"Oh, thar you are!" said Bishop, lifting his eyes from the paper and glaring at her over his glasses. "I knowed I'd have to have a knock-down-an'-drag-out fight with you 'fore I signed my name, so sail in an' git it over. Trabue's got to ride back to town."

"But whar in the name o' common-sense is the money to come from?" the woman hurled at her husband, as she rested one of her bony hands on the edge of the table and glared at him. "As I understand it, thar's about five thousand acres in this piece alone, an' yo're a-payin' a dollar a acre. Whar's it a-comin' from, I'd like to know? Whar's it to come from?"

Bishop sniffed and ran a steady hand over his short, gray hair. "You see how little she knows o' my business," he said to the lawyer. "Heer she's raisin' the devil an' Tom Walker about the trade an' she don't so much as know whar the money's to come from."

"How *was* I to know?" retorted the woman, "when you've been tellin' me fer the last six months that thar wasn't enough in the bank to give the house a coat o' fresh paint an' patch the barn roof."

"You knowed I had five thousand dollars wuth o' stock in the Shoal River Cotton Mills, didn't you?" asked Bishop, defiantly, and yet with the manner of a man throwing a missile which he hoped would fall lightly.

"Yes, I knowed that, but—" The woman's eyes were two small fires burning hungrily for information beyond their reach.

"Well, it happens that Shoal stock is jest the same on the market as ready money, up a little to-day an' down to-morrow, but never varyin' more'n a fraction of a cent on the dollar, an' so the Tompkins heirs say they'd jest as lieve have it, an' as I'm itchin' to relieve them of the'r land, it didn't take us long to come together."

If he had struck the woman squarely in the face, she could not have shown more surprise. She became white to the lips, and with a low cry turned to her son. "Oh, Alan, don't—don't let 'im do it, it's all we have left that we can depend on! It will ruin us!"

"Why, father, surely," protested Alan, as he put his arm around his mother, "surely you can't mean to let go your mill investment which is paying fifteen per cent, to put the money into lands that may never advance in value and always be a dead weight on your hands! Think of the loss of interest and the taxes to be kept up. Father, you must listen to—"

"Listen to nothin'," thundered Bishop, half rising from his chair. "Nobody axed you two to put in. It's my business an' I'm a-goin' to attend to it. I believe I'm doin' the right thing, an' that settles it."

"The right thing," moaned the old woman, as she sank into a chair and covered her face with her hands. "Mr. Trabue," she went on, fiercely, "when that factory stock leaves our hands we won't have a single thing to our names that will bring in a cent of income. You kin see how bad it is on a woman who has worked as hard to do fer her children as I have. Mr. Bishop always said Adele, who is visitin' her uncle's family in Atlanta, should have that stock for a weddin'-gift, ef she ever married, an' Alan was to have the lower half of this farm. Now what would we have to give the girl—nothin' but thousands o' acres o' hills, mountains an' gulches full o' bear, wild-cats, and catamounts—land that it ud break any young couple to hold on to— much less put to any use. Oh, I feel perfectly sick over it."

There was a heavy, dragging step in the hall, and a long, lank man of sixty or sixty-five years of age paused in the doorway. He had no beard except a tuft of gray hair on his chin, and his teeth, being few and far between, gave to his cheeks a hollow appearance. He was Abner Daniel, Mrs. Bishop's bachelor brother, who lived in the family.

"Hello!" he exclaimed, shifting a big quid of tobacco from one cheek to the other; "plottin' agin the whites? Ef you are, I 'll decamp, as the feller said when the bull yeerlin' butted 'im in the small o' the back. How are you, Mr. Trabue? Have they run you out o' town fer some o' yore legal rascality?"

"I reckon your sister thinks it's rascality that's brought me out to-day," laughed the lawyer. "We are on a little land deal."

"Oh, well, I 'll move on," said Abner Daniel. "I jest wanted to tell Alan that Rigg's hogs got into his young corn in the bottom jest now an' rooted up about as many acres as Pole Baker's ploughed all day. Ef they'd a-rooted in straight rows an' not gone too nigh the stalks they mought 'a' done the crap more good than harm, but the'r aim or intention, one or t'other, was bad. Folks is that away; mighty few of 'em root—when they root at all—fer anybody but the'rse'ves. Well, I 'll git along to my room."

"Don't go, brother Ab," pleaded his sister. "I want you to he'p me stand up fer my rights. Alfred is about to swap our cotton-mill stock fer some more wild mountain-land."

In spite of his natural tendency to turn everything into a jest—even the serious things of life—the sallow face of the tall man lengthened. He stared into the faces around him for a moment, then a slow twinkle dawned in his eye.

"I've never been knowed to take sides in any connubial tustle yet," he said to Trabue, in a dry tone. "Alf may not know what he's about right now, but he's Solomon hisse'f compared to a feller that will undertake to settle a dispute betwixt a man an' his wife—more especially the wife. Geewhilikins! I never shall forget the time old Jane Hardeway come heer to spend a week an' Alf thar an' Betsy split over buyin' a hat-rack fer the hall. Betsy had seed one over at Mason's, at the camp-ground, an' determined she'd have one. Maybe you noticed that fancy contraption in the hall as you come in. Well, Alf seed a nigger unloadin' it from a wagon at the door one mornin', an' when Betsy, in feer an' tremblin', told 'im what it was fer he mighty nigh had a fit. He said his folks never had been above hangin' the'r coats an' hats on good stout nails an' pegs, an' as fer them umbrella-pans to ketch the drip, he said they was fancy spit-boxes, an' wanted to know ef she expected a body to do the'r chawin' an' smokin' in that windy hall. He said it jest should not stand thar with all them prongs an' arms to attack unwary folks in the dark, an' he toted it out to the buggy-shed. That got Betsy's dander up an' she put it back agin the wall an' said it ud stay thar ef she had to stand behind it an' hold it in place. Alf wasn't done yet; he 'lowed ef they was to have sech a purty trick as that on the hill it had to stay in the best room in the house, so he put it heer in the parlor by the piano. But Betsy took it back two or three times an' he larnt that he was a-doin' a sight o' work fer nothin', an' finally quit totin' it about. But that ain't what I started in to tell. As I was a-sayin', old Jane Hardeway thought she'd sorter put a word in the dispute to pay fer her board an' keep, an' she told Betsy that it was all owin' to the way the Bishops was raised that Alf couldn't stand to have things nice about 'im. She said all the Bishops she'd ever knowed had a natural stoop that they got by livin' in cabins with low roofs. She wasn't spreadin' 'er butter as thick as she thought she was—ur maybe it was the sort she was spreadin'—fer Betsy blazed up like the woods afire in a high wind. It didn't take old Jane long to diskiver that thar was several breeds o' Bishops out o' jail, an' she spent most o' the rest o' her visit braggin' on some she'd read about. She said the name sounded like the start of 'em had been religious an' substanch."

"Brother Abner," whined Mrs. Bishop, "I wisht you'd hush all that foolishness an' help me 'n the children out o' this awful fix. Alfred always would listen to you."

"Well," and the old man smiled, and winked at the lawyer, "I 'll give you both all the advice I kin. Now, the Shoal River stock is a good thing right now; but ef the mill was to ketch on fire an' burn down thar'd be a loss. Then as fer timber-land, it ain't easy to sell, but it mought take a start before another flood. I say it mought, an' then agin it moughtn't. The mill mought burn, an' then agin it moughtn't. Now, ef you-uns kin be helped by this advice you are welcome to it free o' charge. Not changin' the subject, did you-uns know Mrs. Richardson's heffer's got a calf? I reckon she won't borrow so much milk after hers gits good."

Trabue smiled broadly as the gaunt man withdrew; but his amusement was short-lived, for Mrs. Bishop began to cry, and she soon rose in despair and left the room. Alan stood for a moment looking at the unmoved face of his father, who had found something in the last clause of the document which needed explanation; then he, too, went out.

CHAPTER II

ALAN found his uncle on the back porch washing his face and hands in a basin on the water-shelf. The young man leaned against one of the wooden posts which supported the low roof of the porch and waited for him to conclude the puffing, sputtering operation, which he finally did by enveloping his head in a long towel hanging from a wooden roller on the weather-boarding.

"Well," he laughed, "yore uncle Ab didn't better matters in thar overly much. But what could a feller do? Yore pa's as bull-headed as a young steer, an' he's already played smash anyway. Yore ma's wastin' breath; but a woman seems to have plenty of it to spare. A woman' s tongue's like a windmill—it takes breath to keep it a-goin', an' a dead calm ud kill her business."

"It's no laughing matter, Uncle Ab," said Alan, despondently. "Something must have gone wrong with father's judgment. He never has acted this way before."

The old man dropped the towel and thrust his long, almost jointless fingers into his vest pocket for a horn comb which folded up like a jack-knife. "I was jest a-wonderin'," as he began to rake his shaggy hair straight down to his eyes—"I was jest a-wonderin' ef he could 'a' bent his skull in a little that time his mule th'owed 'im agin the sweet-gum. They say that often changes a body powerful. Folks do think he's off his cazip on the land question, an' now that he's traded his best nest-egg fer another swipe o' the earth's surface, I reckon they 'll talk harder. But yore pa ain't no fool; no plumb idiot could 'a' managed yore ma as well as he has. You see I know what he's accomplished, fer I've been with 'em ever since they was yoked together. When they was married she was as wild as a buck, an' certainly made our daddy walk a chalk-line; but Alfred has tapered 'er down beautiful. She didn't want this thing done one bit, an' yet it is settled by this time"—the old man looked through the hall to the front gate—"yes, Trabue's unhitchin'; he's got them stock certificates in his pocket, an' yore pa has the deeds in his note-case. When this gits out, moss-backs from heer clean to Gilmer 'll be trapsin' in to dispose o' land at so much a front foot."

"But what under high heaven will he do with it all?"

"Hold on to it," grinned Abner, "that is, ef he kin rake an' scrape enough together to pay the taxes. Why, last yeer his taxes mighty nigh floored 'im, an' the expenses on this county he's jest annexed will push 'im like rips; fer now, you know, he 'll have to do without the income on his factory stock; but he thinks he's got the right sow by the yeer. Before long he may yell out to us to come he'p 'im turn 'er loose, but he's waltzin' with 'er now."

At this juncture Mrs. Bishop came out of the dining-room wiping her eyes on her apron.

"Mother," said Alan, tenderly, "try not to worry over this any more than you can help."

"Your pa's gettin' old an' childish," whimpered Mrs. Bishop. "He's heerd somebody say timber-land up in the mountains will some day advance, an' he forgets that he's too old to get the benefit of it. He's goin' to bankrupt us."

"Ef I do," the man accused thundered from the hall, as he strode out, "it 'll be my money that's lost—money that I made by hard work."

He stood before them, glaring over his eye-glasses at his wife. "I've had enough of yore tongue, my lady; ef I'd not had so much to think about in thar jest now I'd 'a' shut you up sooner. Dry up now—not another word! I'm doin' the best I kin accordin' to my lights to provide fer my children, an' I won't be interfered with."

No one spoke for a moment. However, Mrs. Bishop finally retorted, as her brother knew she would, in her own time.

"I don't call buyin' thousands o' acres o' unsalable land providin' fer anything, except the pore-house," she fumed.

"That's beca'se you don't happen to know as much about the business as I do," said Bishop, with a satisfied chuckle, which, to the observant Daniel, sounded very much like exultation. "When you all know what I know you 'll be laughin' on t'other sides o' yore mouths."

He started down the steps into the yard as if going to the row of bee-hives along the fence, but paused and came back. He had evidently changed his mind. "I reckon," he said, "I 'll jest *have* to let you all know about this or I won't have a speck o' peace from now on. I didn't tell you at fust beca'se nobody kin keep a secret as well as the man it belongs to, an' I was afeerd it ud leak out an' damage my interests; but this last five thousand acres jest about sweeps all the best timber in the whole Cohutta section, an' I mought as well let up. I reckon you all know that ef—I say *ef*—my land was nigh a railroad it ud be low at five times what I paid fer it, don't you? Well, then!

The long an' short of it is that I happen to be on the inside an' know that a railroad is goin' to be run from Blue Lick Junction to Darley. It 'll be started inside of the next yeer an' 'll run smack dab through my property. Thar now, you know more'n you thought you did, don't you?"

The little group stared into his glowing face incredulously.

"A railroad is to be built, father?" exclaimed Alan.

"That's what I said."

Mrs. Bishop's eyes flashed with sudden hope, and then, as if remembering her husband's limitations, her face fell.

"Alfred," she asked, sceptically, "how does it happen that you know about the railroad before other folks does?"

"How do I? That's it now—how do I?" and the old man laughed freely. "I've had my fun out o' this thing, listenin' to what every crank said about me bein' cracked, an' so on; but I was jest a-lyin' low waitin' fer my time."

"Well, I 'll be switched!" ejaculated Abner Daniel, half seriously, half sarcastically. "Geewhilikins! a railroad! I've always said one would pay like rips an' open up a dern good, God-fersaken country. I'm glad you are a-goin' to start one, Alfred."

Alan's face was filled with an expression of blended doubt and pity for his father's credulity. "Father," he said, gently, "are you sure you got your information straight?"

"I got it from headquarters." The old man raised himself on his toes and knocked his heels together, a habit he had not indulged in for many a year. "It was told to me confidentially by a man who knows all about the whole thing, a man who is in the employ o' the company that's goin' to build it."

"Huh!" the exclamation was Abner Daniel's, "do you mean that Atlanta lawyer, Perkins?"

Bishop stared, his mouth lost some of its pleased firmness, and he ceased the motion of his feet.

"What made you mention his name?" he asked, curiously.

"Oh, I dunno; somehow I jest thought o' him. He looks to me like he mought be buildin' a railroad ur two."

"Well, that's the man I mean," said Bishop, more uneasily.

Somehow the others were all looking at Abner Daniel, who grunted suddenly and almost angrily.

"I wouldn't trust that skunk no furder'n I could fling a bull by the tail."

"You say you wouldn't?" Bishop tried to smile, but the effort was a facial failure.

"I wouldn't trust 'im nuther, brother Ab," chimed in Mrs. Bishop. "As soon as I laid eyes on 'im I knowed he wouldn't do. He's too mealy-mouthed an' fawnin'. Butter wouldn't melt in his mouth; he bragged on ever'thing we had while he was heer. Now, Alfred, what we must git at is, what was his object in tellin' you that tale."

"Object?" thundered her husband, losing his temper in the face of the awful possibility that her words hinted at. "Are you all a pack an' passle o' fools? If you must dive an' probe, then I'll tell you he owns a slice o' timber-land above Holley Creek, j'inin' some o' mine, an' so he let me into the secret out o' puore good will. Oh, you all cayn't skeer me; I ain't one o' the skeerin' kind."

But, notwithstanding this outburst, it was plain that doubt had actually taken root in the ordinarily cautious mind of the crude speculator. His face lengthened, the light of triumph went out of his eyes, leaving the shifting expression of a man taking desperate chances.

Abner Daniel laughed out harshly all at once and then was silent. "What's the matter?" asked his sister, in despair.

"I was jest a-wonderin'," replied her brother.

"You are?" said Bishop, angrily. "It seems to me you don't do much else."

"Folks 'at wonders a lot ain't so apt to believe ever'thing they heer," retorted Abner. "I was just a-wonderin' why that little, spindle-shanked Peter Mosely has been holdin' his head so high the last week or so. I'll bet I could make a durn good guess now."

"What under the sun's Peter Mosely got to do with my business?" burst from Bishop's impatient lips.

"He's got a sorter roundabout connection with it, I reckon," smiled Abner, grimly. "I happen to know that Abe Tompkins sold 'im two thousand acres o' timber-land on Huckleberry Ridge jest atter yore Atlanta man spent the day lookin' round in these parts."

Bishop was no fool, and he grasped Abner's meaning even before it was quite clear to the others.

"Looky heer," he said, sharply, "what do you take me fur?"

"I'ain't tuck you fer nothin'," said Abner, with a grin. "Leastwise, I'ain't tuck you fer five thousand dollars' wuth o' cotton-mill stock. To make a long story short, the Atlanta jack-leg lawyer is akin to the Tompkins family some way. I don't know exactly what kin, but Joe Tompkins's wife stayed at Perkins's house when she was down thar havin' er spine straightened. I'd bet a new hat to a ginger-cake that Perkins never owned a spoonful o' land up heer, an' that he's jest he'pin' the Tompkins folks on the sly to unload some o' the'r land, so they kin move West, whar they've always wanted to go. Peter Mosely is a man on the watch-out fer rail soft snaps, an' when Perkins whispered the big secret in his yeer, like he did to you, he started out on a still hunt fer timbered land on the line of the proposed trunk line due west vy-ah Lickskillet to Darley, with stop-over privileges at Buzzard Roost, an' fifteen minutes fer hash at Dog Trot Springs. Then, somehow or other, by hook or crook—mostly crook—Abe Tompkins wasn't dodgin' anybody about that time; Peter Mosely could 'a' run agin 'im with his eyes shut on a dark night. I was at Neil Fulmore's store when the two met, an' ef a trade was ever made quicker betwixt two folks it was done by telegraph an' the paper was signed by lightnin'. Abe said he had the land an' wouldn't part with it at any price ef he hadn't been bad in need o' money, fer he believed it was chuck-full o' iron ore, soapstone, black marble, an' water-power, to say nothin' o' timber, but he'd been troubled so much about cash, he said, that he'd made up his mind to let 'er slide an' the devil take the contents. I never seed two parties to a deal better satisfied. They both left the store with a strut. Mosely's strut was the biggest, fer he wasn't afeerd o' nothin'. Tompkins looked like he was afeerd Mosely ud call 'im back an' want to rue."

"You mean to say—" But old Bishop seemed unable to put his growing fear into words.

"Oh, I don't know nothin' fer certain," said Abner Daniel, sympathetically; "but ef I was you I'd go down to Atlanta an' see Perkins. You kin tell by the way he acts whether thar's anything in his railroad story or not; but, by gum, you ort to know whar you stand. You've loaded yorese'f from hind to fore quarters, an' ef you don't plant yore feet on some'n you 'll go down."

Bishop clutched this proposition as a drowning man would a straw. "Well, I will go see 'im," he said. "I 'll go jest to satisfy you. As fer as I'm concerned, I know he wasn't tellin' me no lie; but I reckon you all never 'll rest till you are satisfied."

He descended the steps and crossed the yard to the barn. They saw him lean over the rail fence for a moment as if in troubled thought, and then he seemed to shake himself, as if to rid himself of an unpleasant mental burden, and passed through the little sagging gate into the stable to feed his horses. It was now noon. The sun was shining broadly on the fields, and ploughmen were riding their horses home in their clanking harnesses.

"Poor father," said Alan to his uncle, as his mother retired slowly into the house. "He seems troubled, and it may mean our ruin—absolute ruin."

"It ain't no triflin' matter," admitted Daniel. "Thar's no tellin' how many thousand acres he may have bought; he's keepin' somethin' to hisse'f. I remember jest when that durn skunk of a lawyer put that flea in his yeer. They was at Hanson's mill, an' talked confidential together mighty nigh all mornin'. But let's not cross a bridge tell we git to it. Let's talk about some'n else. I hain't never had a chance to tell you, but I seed that gal in town yesterday, an' talked to 'er."

"Did you, Uncle Ab?" the face of the young man brightened. His tone was eager and expectant.

"Yes, I'd hitched in the wagon-yard an' run into Hazen's drug-store to git a box o' axle-grease, an' was comin' out with the durn stuff under my arm when I run upon 'er a-settin' in a buggy waitin' to git a clerk to fetch 'er out a glass o' sody-water. She recognized me, an' fer no other earthly reason than that I'm yore uncle she spoke to me as pleasin' as a basket o' chips. What was I to do? I never was in such a plight in my life. I'd been unloadin' side-meat at Bartow's warehouse, an' was kivered from head to foot with salt and grease. I didn't have on no coat, an' the seat o' my pants was non est—I don't think thar was any est about 'em, to tell the truth; but I knowed it wouldn't be the part of a gentleman to let 'er set thar stretchin' 'er neck out o' socket to call a clerk when I was handy, so I wheeled about, hopin' an' prayin' ef she did look at me she'd take a fancy to the back o' my head, an' went in the store an' told 'em to git a hustle on the'r-se'ves. When I come out, she hauled me up to ax some questions about when camp-meetin' was goin' to set in this yeer, and when Adele was comin' home. I let my box o' axle-grease drap, an' it rolled like a wagon-wheel off duty, an' me after it, bendin'—*bendin'* of all positions—heer an' yan in the most ridiculous way. I tell you I'd never play croquet ur leapfrog in them pants. All the way home I thought how I'd disgraced you."

"Oh, you are all right, Uncle Ab," laughed Alan. "She's told me several times that she likes you very much. She says you are genuine—genuine through and through, and she's right."

"I'd ruther have her say it than any other gal I know," said Abner. "She's purty as red shoes, an', ef I'm any judge, she's genuwine too. I've got another idee about 'er, but I ain't a-givin' it away jest now."

"You mean that she—"

"No," and the old man smiled mischievously, "I didn't mean nothin' o' the sort. I wonder how on earth you could 'a' got sech a notion in yore head. I'm goin' to see how that black scamp has left my cotton land. I 'll bet he hain't scratched it any deeper'n a old hen would 'a' done lookin' fer worms."

CHAPTER III

THE next morning at breakfast Alfred Bishop announced his intention of going to Atlanta to talk to Perkins, and incidentally to call on his brother William, who was a successful wholesale merchant in that city.

"I believe I would," said Mrs. Bishop. "Maybe William will tell you what to do."

"I'd see Perkins fust," advised Abner Daniel. "Ef I felt shore Perkins had buncoed me I'd steer cleer o' William. I'd hate to heer 'im let out on that subject. He's made his pile by keepin' a sharp lookout."

"I hain't had no reason to think I have been lied to," said Bishop, doggedly, as he poured his coffee into his saucer and shook it about to cool. "A body could hear his death-knell rung every minute ef he'd jest listen to old women an' —"

"Old bachelors," interpolated Abner. "I reckon they *are* alike. The longer a man lives without a woman the more he gits like one. I reckon that's beca'se the man 'at lives with one don't see nothin' wuth copyin' in 'er, an' vice-a-versy."

Mrs. Bishop had never been an appreciative listener to her brother's philosophy. She ignored what he had just said and its accompanying smile, which was always Abner's subtle apology for such observations.

"Are you goin' to tell Adele about the railroad?" she asked.

"I reckon I won't tell 'er to git up a' excursion over it, "fore the cross-ties is laid," retorted Bishop, sharply, and Abner Daniel laughed—that sort of response being in his own vein.

"I was goin' to say," pursued the softly treading wife, "that I wouldn't mention it to 'er, ef—ef—Mr. Perkins ain't to be relied on, beca'se she worries enough already about our pore way o' livin' compared to her uncle's folks. Ef she knowed how I spent last night she'd want to come back. But I ain't a-goin' to let brother Ab skeer me yet. It is jest too awful to think about. What on earth would we do? What would we, I say?"

That afternoon Bishop was driven to Darley by a negro boy who was to bring the buggy back home. He first repaired to a barber-shop, where he was shaved, had his hair cut, and his shoes blacked; then he went to the station half an hour before time and impatiently walked up and down the platform till the train arrived.

It was six o'clock when he reached Atlanta and made his way through the jostling crowd in the big passenger depot out into the streets. He had his choice of going at once to the residence of his brother, on Peachtree Street, the most fashionable avenue of the city, or looking up Perkins in his office. He decided to unburden his mind by at once calling on the lawyer, whose office was in a tall building quite near at hand.

It was the hour at which Perkins usually left for home, but the old planter found him in.

"Oh, it's you, Mr. Bishop," he said, suavely, as he rose from his desk in the dingy, disordered little room with its single window. He pushed a chair forward. "Sit down; didn't know you were in town. At your brother's, I reckon. How are the crops up the road? Too much rain last month, I'm afraid."

Bishop sank wearily into the chair. He had tired himself out thinking over what he would say to the man before him and with the awful contemplation of what the man might say to him.

"They are doin' as well as can be expected," he made answer; but he didn't approve of even that platitude, for he was plain and outspoken, and hadn't come all that distance for a mere exchange of courtesies. Still, he lacked the faculty to approach easily the subject which had grown so heavy within the last twenty-four hours, and of which he now almost stood in terror.

"Well, that's good," returned Perkins. He took up a pen as he resumed his seat, and began to touch it idly to the broad nail of his thumb. He was a swarthy man of fifty-five or sixty, rather tall and slender, with a bald head that sloped back sharply from heavy, jutting brows, under which a pair of keen, black eyes shone and shifted. "Come down to see your daughter," he said. "Good thing for her that you have a brother in town. By-the-way, he's a fine type of a man. He's making headway, too; his trade is stretching out in all directions—funny how different you two are! He seems to take to a swallow-tail coat and good cigars like a duck to water, while you want the open sky above you, sweet-smelling fields around, an' fishing, hunting, sowing, reaping, and chickens—fat, juicy ones, like your wife fried when I was there. And her apple-butter! Ice-cream can' t hold a candle to it."

"I 'lowed I'd see William 'fore I went back," said Bishop, rather irrelevantly, and, for the lack of something else to do, he took out his eye-glasses and perched them on his sharp nose, only, on discovering the inutility of the act, to restore them clumsily to his pocket. He was trying to persuade himself, in the silence that followed, that, if the lawyer had known of his trade with the Tompkins heirs, he would naturally have alluded to it. Then, seeing that Perkins was staring at him rather fixedly, he said—it was a verbal plunge: "I bought some more timber-land yesterday!"

"Oh, you did? That's good." Perkins's eyes fluttered once or twice before his gaze steadied itself on the face of the man before him. "Well, as I told you, Mr. Bishop, that sort of a thing is a good investment. I reckon it's already climbing up a little, ain't it?"

"Not much yet." It struck Bishop that he had given the lawyer a splendid opportunity to speak of the chief cause for an advance in value, and his heart felt heavier as he finished. "But I took quite a slice the last time—five thousand acres at the old figure, you know—a dollar a acre."

"You don't say! That *was* a slice."

Bishop drew himself up in his chair and inhaled a deep breath. It was as if he took into himself in that way the courage to make his next remark.

"I got it from the Tompkins estate."

"You don't say. I didn't know they had that much on hand."

There was a certain skill displayed in the lawyer's choice of questions and observations that somehow held him aloof from the unlettered man, and there was, too, something in his easy, bland manner that defied the open charge of underhand dealing, and yet Bishop had not paid out his railroad fare for nothing. He was not going back to his home-circle no wiser than when he left it. His next remark surprised himself; it was bluntness hardened by despair.

"Sence I bought the land I've accidentally heerd that you are some kin o' that family."

Perkins started slightly and raised his brows.

"Oh yes; on my wife's side, away off, some way or other. I believe the original Tompkins that settled there from Virginia was my wife's grandfather. I never was much of a hand to go into such matters."

The wily lawyer had erected as strong a verbal fence as was possible on such short notice, and for a moment it looked as if Bishop's frankness would not attempt to surmount it; but it did, in a fashion.

"When I heerd that, Perkins, it was natural fer me to wonder why you, you see—why you didn't tell *them* about the railroad."

The sallow features of the lawyer seemed to stiffen. He drew himself up coldly and a wicked expression flashed in his eyes.

"Take my advice, old man," he snarled, as he threw down his pen and stared doggedly into Bishop's face, "stick to your farming and don't waste your time asking a professional lawyer questions which have no bearing on your business whatever. Now, really, do I have to explain to you my personal reasons for not favoring the Tompkins people with a—I may say— any piece of information?"

Bishop was now as white as death; his worst suspicions were confirmed; he was a ruined man; there was no further doubt about that. Suddenly he felt unable to bridle the contemptuous fury that raged within him.

"I think I know *why* you didn't tell 'em," was what he hurled at the lawyer.

"You think you do."

"Yes, it was beca'se you knowed no road was goin' to be built. You told Pete Mosely the same tale you did me, an' Abe Tompkins unloaded on 'im. That's a way you have o' doin' business."

Perkins stood up. He took his silk hat from the top of his desk and put it on. "Oh yes, old man," he sneered, "I'm a terribly dishonest fellow; but I've got company in this world. Now, really, the only thing that has worried me has been your unchristian act in buying all that land from the Tompkins heirs at such a low figure when the railroad will advance its value so greatly. Mr. Bishop, I thought you were a good Methodist."

"Oh, you kin laugh an' jeer all you like," cried Bishop, "but I can handle you fer this."

"You are not as well versed in the law as you are in fertilizers, Mr. Bishop," sneered the lawyer. "In order to make a case against me, you'd have to publicly betray a matter I told to you in confidence, and then what would you gain? I doubt if the court would force me to explain a private matter like this where the interests of my clients are concerned. And if the court did, I could simply show the letters I have regarding the possible construction of a railroad in your section. If you remember rightly, I did not say the thing was an absolute certainty. On top of all this, you'd be obliged to prove collusion between me and the Tompkins heirs over a sale made by their attorney, Mr. Trabue. There is one thing certain, Mr. Bishop, and that is that you have forfeited your right to any further confidence in this matter.

If the road is built you 'll find out about it with the rest of your people. You think you acted wisely in attacking me this way, but you have simply cut off your nose to spite your face. Now I have a long car-ride before me, and it's growing late."

Bishop stood up. He was quivering as with palsy. His voice shook and rang like that of a madman.

"You are a scoundrel, Perkins," he said—"a dirty black snake in the grass. I want to tell you that."

"Well, I hope you won't make any charge for it."

"No, it's free." Bishop turned to the door. There was a droop upon his whole body. He dragged his feet as he moved out into the unlighted corridor, where he paused irresolutely. So great was his agony that he almost obeyed an impulse to go back and fall at the feet of Perkins and implore his aid to rescue him and his family from impending ruin. The lawyer was moving about the room, closing his desk and drawing down the window-shade. Up from the street came the clanging of locomotive bells under the car-shed, the whir of street-cars, the clatter of cabs on the cobble-stones.

"It's no use," sighed Bishop, as he made his way down-stairs. "I'm ruined—Alan an' Adele hain't a cent to their names, an' that devil—" Bishop paused on the first landing like an animal at bay. He heard the steady step of Perkins on the floor above, and for a moment his fingers tingled with the thought of waiting there in the darkness and choking the life out of the subtle scoundrel who had taken advantage of his credulity.

But with a groan that was half a prayer he went on down the steps and out into the lighted streets. At the first corner he saw a car which would take him to his brother's, and he hastened to catch it.

William Bishop's house was a modern brick structure, standing on a well-clipped lawn which held a gothic summer-house and two or three marble statues. It was in the best portion of the avenue. Reaching it, the planter left the car and approached the iron gate which opened on to the granite steps leading up the terrace. It was now quite dark and many pedestrians were hurrying homeward along the sidewalks. Obeying a sudden impulse, the old man irresolutely passed by the gate and walked farther up the street. He wanted to gain time, to think whether it would be best for him in his present state of mind to meet those fashionable relatives—above all, his matter-of-fact, progressive brother.

"Somehow I don't feel one bit like it," he mused. "I couldn't tell William. He'd think I wanted to borrow money an' ud git skeerd right off. He always was afeerd I'd mismanage. An' then I'd hate to sp'ile Adele's visit, an' she could tell thar was some'n wrong by me bein' heer in sech a flurry. I reckon I *do* show it. How could a body he'p it? Oh, my Lord, have mercy! It's all gone, all—all me'n Betsy has saved."

He turned at the corner of his brother's property and slowly retraced his halting steps to the gate, but he did not pause, continuing his way back towards the station. A glance at the house showed that all the lower rooms were lighted, as well as the big prismatic lamp that hung over the front door. Bishop saw forms in light summer clothing on the wide veranda. "I 'll bet that tallest one is Sis," he said, pathetically. "I jest wish I could see 'er a little while. Maybe it ud stop this awful hurtin' a little jest to look at 'er an' heer 'er laugh like she always did at home. She'd be brave; she wouldn't cry an' take on; but it would hurt 'er away down in 'er heart, especially when she's mixin' with sech high-flyers an' money-spenders. Lord, what 'll I do fer cash to send 'er next month? I'm the land-porest man in my county."

As he went along he passed several fashionable hotels, from which orchestral music came. Through the plate-glass windows he saw men and women, amid palms and flowers, dining in evening dress and sparkling jewels.

Reaching the station, he inquired about a train to Darley, and was told that one left at midnight. He decided to take it, and in the mean time he would have nothing to occupy him. He was not hungry; the travel and worry had killed his appetite; but he went into a little café across the street from the depot and ordered a sandwich and a cup of coffee. He drank the coffee at a gulp, but the food seemed to stick in his throat. After this he went into the waiting-room, which was thronged with tired women holding babies in their arms, and roughly clad emigrants with packs and oil-cloth bags. He sat in one of the iron-armed seats without moving till he heard his train announced, and then he went into the smoking-car and sat down in a corner.

He reached Darley at half-past three in the morning and went to the only hotel in the place. The sleepy night-clerk rose from his lounge behind the counter in the office and assigned him to a room to which a colored boy, vigorously rubbing his eyes, conducted him. Left alone in his room, he sat down on the edge of his bed and started to undress, but with a sigh he stopped.

"What's the use o' me lyin' down almost at daybreak?" he asked himself. "I mought as well be on the way home. I cayn't sleep nohow."

Blowing out his lamp, he went down-stairs and roused the clerk again. "Will I have to pay fer that bed ef I don't use it?" he questioned.

"Why, no, Mr. Bishop," said the clerk.

"Well, I believe I 'll start out home."

"Is your team in town?" asked the clerk.

"The team I'm a-goin' to use is. I'm goin' to foot it. I've done the like before this."

"Well, it's a purty tough stretch," smiled the clerk. "But the roads are good."

CHAPTER IV

IT was a little after sunrise; the family had just left the breakfast-table when Bishop walked in; his shoes and trousers were damp with dew and covered with the dust of the road. His wife saw him entering the gate and called out to him from the hall:

"Well, I declare! Didn't you go to Atlanta?"

He came slowly up the steps, dragging his feet after him. He had the appearance of a man beaten by every storm that could fall upon a human being.

"Yes, I went," he said, doggedly. He passed her and went into the sitting-room, where his brother-inlaw stood at the fireplace lighting his pipe with a live coal of fire on the tip of a stick. Abner Daniel looked at him critically, his brows raised a little as he puffed, but he said nothing. Mrs. Bishop came in behind her husband, sweeping him from head to foot with her searching eyes.

"You don't mean to tell me you walked out heer this mornin'," she cried. "Lord have mercy!"

"I don't know as I've prepared any set speech on the subject," said her husband, testily; "but I walked. I could 'a' gone to a livery an' ordered out a team, but I believe thar's more'n one way o' wearin' sackcloth an' ashes, an' the sooner I begin the better I 'll feel." Abner Daniel winked; the scriptural allusion appealed to his fancy, and he smiled impulsively.

"That thar is," he said. "Thar's a whole way an' a half way. Some folks jest wear it next to the skin whar it don't show, with broadcloth ur silk on the outside. They think ef it scratches a little that 'll satisfy the Lord an' hoodwink other folks. But I believe He meant it to be whole hog or none."

Mrs. Bishop was deaf to this philosophy. "I don't see," she said, in her own field of reflection—"I don't see, I say, how you got to Atlanta; attended to business; seed Adele; an' got back heer at sunrise. Why, Alfred—"

But Bishop interrupted her. "Have you all had prayers yet?"

"No, you know we hain't," said his wife, wondering over his strange manner. "I reckon it can pass jest this once, bein' as you are tired an' hain't had nothin' to eat."

"No, it can't pass, nuther; I don't want to touch a mouthful; tell the rest of 'em to come in, an' you fetch me the Book."

"Well!" Mrs. Bishop went out and told the negro woman and her daughter to stop washing the dishes and go in to prayer. Then she hurried out to the back porch, where Alan was oiling his gun.

"Something's happened to yore pa," she said. "He acts queer, an' says sech strange things. He walked all the way from Darley this morning, an' now wants to have prayers 'fore he touches a bite o' breakfast. I reckon we are ruined."

"I'm afraid that's it," opined her son, as he put down his gun and followed her into the sitting-room. Here the two negroes stood against the wall. Abner Daniel was smoking and Bishop held the big family Bible on his quivering knees.

"Ef you mean to keep it up," Abner was saying, argumentatively, "all right an' good; but I don't believe in sudden spurts o' worship. My hosses is hitched up ready to haul a load o' bark to the tannery, an' it may throw me a little late at dinner; but ef you are a-goin' to make a daily business of it I'm with you."

"I'm a-goin' to be regular from now on," said Bishop, slowly turning the leaves of the tome. "I forgot whar I read last."

"You didn't finish about Samson tyin' all them foxes' tails together," said Abner Daniel, as he knocked the hot ashes from his pipe into the palm of his hand and tossed them into the chimney. "That sorter interested me. I wondered how that was a-goin' to end. I'd hate to have a passle o' foxes with torches to the'r tails turned loose in my wheat jest 'fore cuttin' time. It must 'a' been a sight. I wondered how that was a-goin' to end."

"You 'll wonder how *yo're* a-goin' to end if you don't be more respectful," said his sister.

"Like the foxes, I reckon," grinned Abner, "with a eternal torch tied to me. Well, ef I am treated that away, I 'll go into the business o' destruction an' set fire to everything I run across."

"Ain' t you goin' to tell us what you did in Atlanta 'fore you have prayer?" asked Mrs. Bishop, almost resentfully.

"No, I hain't!" Bishop snapped. "I 'll tell you soon enough. I reckon I won't read this mornin'; let's pray."

They all knelt reverently, and yet with some curiosity, for Bishop often suited his prayers to important occasions, and it struck them that he might now allude to the subject bound up within him.

"Lord, God Almighty," he began, his lower lip hanging and quivering, as were his hands clasped in the seat of his chair, "Thou knowest the struggle Thy creatures are makin' on the face of Thy green globe to live up to the best of the'r lights an' standards. As I bend before Thee this mornin' I realize how small a bein' I am in Thy sight, an' that I ort to bow in humble submission to Thy will, an' I do. For many yeers this family has enjoyed Thy bounteous blessings. We've had good health, an' the influence of a Bible-readin', God-fearin' community, an' our childern has been educated in a way that raised 'em head an' shoulders above many o' the'r associates an' even blood kin. I don't know exactly whar an' how I've sinned; but I know I have displeased Thee, fer Thy scourge has fallen hard an' heavy on my ambitions. I wanted to see my boy heer, a good, obedient son, an' my daughter thar in Atlanta, able to hold the'r heads up among the folks they mix with, an' so I reached out. Maybe it was forbidden fruit helt out by a snake in the devil's service. I don't know—Thou knowest. Anyways, I steered my course out o' the calm waters o' content an' peace o' soul into the whirlpool rapids o' avarice an' greed. I'lowed I was in a safe haven an' didn't dream o' the storm-clouds hangin' over me till they bust in fury on my head. Now, Lord, my Father, give them hearts of patience an' forgiveness fer the blunders of Thy servant. What I done, I done in the bull-headed way that I've always done things; but I meant good an' not harm. These things we ask in the name o' Jesus Christ, our blessed Lord an' Master. Amen."

During the latter part of the prayer Mrs. Bishop had been staring at her husband through her parted fingers, her face pale and agitated, and as she rose her eyes were glued to his face.

"Now, Alfred," she said, "what are you goin' to tell us about the railroad? Is it as bad as brother Ab thought it would be?"

Bishop hesitated. It seemed as if he had even then to tear himself from the clutch of his natural stubbornness. He looked into all the anxious, waiting faces before he spoke, and then he gave in.

"Ab made a good guess. Ef I'd 'a' had his sense, or Alan' s, I'd 'a' made a better trader. It's like Ab said it was, only a sight wuss—a powerful sight wuss!"

"Wuss?" gasped his wife, In fresh alarm. "How could it be wuss? Why, brother Ab said—"

"I never have told you the extent o' my draim's," went on Bishop in the current of confession. "I never even told Perkins yesterday. Fust an' last I've managed to rake in fully twenty thousand acres o' mountain-land. I was goin' on what I'lowed was a dead-shore thing. I secured all I could lay my hands on, an' I did it in secret. I was afeerd even to tell you about what Perkins said, thinkin' it mought leak out an' sp'ile my chances."

"But, father," said Alan, "you didn't have enough money to buy all that land."

"I got it up"—Bishop's face was doggedly pale, almost defiant of his overwhelming disaster—"I mortgaged this farm to get money to buy Maybry and Morton's four thousand acres."

"The farm you was going to deed to Alan?" gasped his wife. "You didn't include that?"

"Not in *that* deal," groaned Bishop. "I swapped that to Phil Parsons fer his poplar an' cypress belt." The words seemed to cut raspingly into the silence of the big room. Abner Daniel was the only one who seemed unmoved by the confession. He filled his pipe from the bowl on the mantel-piece and pressed the tobacco down with his forefinger; then he kicked the ashes in the chimney till he uncovered a small five coal. He eyed it for a moment, then dipped it up in the shovel, rolled it into his pipe, and began to smoke.

"So I ain't a-goin' to git no yeerly pass over the new road," he said, his object being to draw his brother-in-law back to Perkins's action in the matter.

"Perkins was a-lyin' to me," answered Bishop. "He hain't admitted it yet; but he was a-lyin'. His object was to he'p the Tompkins sell out fer a decent price, but he can' t be handled; he's got me on the hip."

"No," said Abner. "I'd ruther keep on swappin' gold dollars fer mountain-land an' lettin' it go fer taxes 'an to try to beat a lawyer at his own game. A court-house is like the devil's abode, easy to git into, no outlet, an' nothin' but scorch while you are thar."

"Hush, fer the name o' goodness!" cried Mrs. Bishop, looking at her husband. "Don't you see he's dyin' from it? Are you all a-goin' to kill 'im? What does a few acres o' land ur debts amount to beside killin' a man 'at's been tryin' to help us all? Alfred, it ain't so mighty awful. You know it ain't! What did me 'n' you have when we started out but a log-house boarded up on the outside? an' now we've got our childern educated an' all of us in good health. I railly believe it's a sin agin God's mercy fer us to moan an' fret under a thing like this."

"That's the talk," exclaimed Abner Daniel, enthusiastically. "Now you are gittin' down to brass tacks. I've always contended—"

"For God's sake, don't talk that way!" said Bishop to his wife. "You don't mean a word of it. You are jest a-sayin' it to try to keep me from seein' what a fool I am."

"You needn't worry about me, father," said Alan, firmly. "I am able to look out for myself an' for you and mother. It's done, and the best thing to do is to look at it in a sensible way. Besides, a man with twenty thousand acres of mountain-land paid for is not broken, by a long jump."

"Yes, I'm gone," said Bishop, a wavering look of gratitude in his eye as he turned to his son. "I figured on it all last night. I can't pay the heavy interest an' come out. I was playin' for big stakes an' got left. Thar's nothin' to do but give up. Me buyin' so much land has made it rise a little, but when I begin to try to sell I won't be able to give it away."

"Thar's some'n in that," opined Abner Daniel, as he turned to leave the room. "I reckon I mought as well go haul that tan-bark. I reckon you won't move out 'fore dinner."

Alan followed him out to the wagon.

"It's pretty tough, Uncle Ab," he said. "I hadn't the slightest idea it was so bad."

"I wasn't so shore," said Daniel. "But I was jest a-thinkin' in thar. You've got a powerful good friend in Rayburn Miller. He's the sharpest speculator in North Georgia; ef I was you, I'd see him an' lay the whole thing before him. He 'll be able to give you good advice, an' I'd take it. A feller that's made as much money as he has at his age won't give a friend bad advice."

"I thought of him," said Alan; "but I am a little afraid he will think we want to borrow money, and he never lets out a cent without the best security."

"Well, you needn't be afeerd on that score," laughed the old man, as he reached up on the high wagon-seat for his whip. "I once heerd 'im say that business an' friendship wouldn't mix any better'n oil an' water."

CHAPTER V

THE following Saturday Alan went to Darley, as he frequently did, to spend Sunday. On such visits he usually stayed at the Johnston House, a great, old-fashioned brick building that had survived the Civil War and remained untouched by the shot and shell that hurtled over it during that dismal period when most of the population had "refugeed farther south." It had four stories, and was too big for the town, which could boast of only two thousand inhabitants, one-third of whom were black. However, the smallness of the town was in the hotel's favor, for in a place where no one would have patronized a second-class hotel, opposition would have died a natural death. The genial proprietor and his family were of the best blood, and the Johnston House was a sort of social club-house, where the church people held their affairs and the less serious element gave dances. To be admitted to the hotel without having to pay for one's dinner was the hallmark of social approval. It was near the ancient-looking brick car-shed under which the trains of two main lines ran, and a long freight warehouse of the same date and architecture. Around the hotel were clustered the chief financial enterprises of the town—its stores, post-office, banks, and a hall for theatrical purposes. Darley was the seat of its county, and another relic of the days before the war was its court house. The principal sidewalks were paved with brick, which in places were damp and green, and sometimes raised above their common level by the undergrowing roots of the sycamore-trees that edged the streets.

In the office of the hotel, just after registering his name, Alan met his friend Rayburn Miller, for whose business ability, it may be remembered, Abner Daniel had such high regard. He was a fine-looking man of thirty-three, tall and of athletic build; he had dark eyes and hair, and a ruddy, out-door complexion.

"Hello," he said, cordially. "I thought you might get in to-day, so I came round to see. Sorry you've taken a room. I wanted you to sleep with me to-night. Sister's gone, and no one is there but the cook. Hello, I must be careful. I'm drumming for business right under Sanford's nose."

"I 'll make you stay with me to make up for it," said Alan, as the clerk behind the counter laughed good-naturedly over the allusion to himself.

"Blamed if I don't think about it," said Miller. "Come round to the office. I want to talk to you. I reckon you've got every plough going such weather as this."

"Took my horse out of the field to drive over," said Alan, as they went out and turned down to a side street where there was a row of law offices, all two-roomed buildings, single-storied, built of brick, and bearing battered tin signs. One of these buildings was Miller's, which, like all its fellows, had its door wide open, thus inviting all the lawyers in the "row" and all students of law to enter and borrow books or use the ever-open desk.

Rayburn Miller was a man among ten thousand in his class. Just after being graduated at the State University he was admitted to the bar and took up the practice of law. He could undoubtedly have made his way at this alone, had not other and more absorbing talents developed within him. Having had a few thousand dollars left him at his father's death, he began to utilize this capital in "note shaving," and other methods of turning over money for a handsome profit furnished by the unsettled conditions, the time, and locality. He soon became an adept in many lines of speculation, and as he was remarkably shrewd and cautious, it is not to be wondered at that he soon accumulated quite a fortune.

"Take a seat," he said to Alan, as they went into the office, and he threw himself into the revolving-chair at his littered desk. "I want to talk to you. I suppose you are in for some fun. The boys are getting up a dance at the hotel and they want your dollar to help pay the band. It's a good one this time. They've ordered it from Chattanooga. It will be down on the seven-thirty-five. Got a match?"

Alan had not, and Miller turned his head to the open door. An old negro happened to be passing, with an axe on his shoulder.

"Heigh, there, Uncle Ned!" Miller called out.

The negro had passed, but he heard his name called and he came back and looked in at the door.

"Want me, Marse Rayburn?"

"Yes, you old scamp; get me a match or I'll shoot the top of your head off."

"All right, suh; all right, Marse Rayburn!"

"You ought to know him," said Miller, with a smile, as the negro hurried into the adjoining office. "His wife cooks for Colonel Barclay; he might tell you if Miss Dolly's going to-night, but I know she is. Frank Hillhouse checked her name off the list, and I heard him say she'd accepted. By-the-way, that fellow will do to watch. I think he and the Colonel are pretty thick."

"Will you never let up on that?" Alan asked with a flush.

"I don't know that I shall," laughed Rayburn. "It seems so funny to see you in love, or, rather, to see you think you are."

"I have never said I was," said Alan, sharply.

"But you show it so blamed plain," said Miller.

"Heer 'tis, Marse Rayburn. Marse Trabue said you could have a whole box ef you'd put up wid sulphur ones."

Miller took the matches from the outstretched hand and tossed a cigar to Alan. "Say, Uncle Ned," he asked, "do you know that gentleman?" indicating Alan with a nod of his head.

A quizzical look dawned in the old negro's eyes, and then he gave a resounding guffaw and shook all over.

"I reckon I know his hoss, Marse Rayburn," he tittered.

"That's a good one on you, Alan," laughed Miller. "He knows your 'hoss.'I 'll have to spring that on you when I see you two together."

As the negro left the office Mr. Trabue leaned in the doorway, holding his battered silk hat in his hand and mopping his perspiring face.

He nodded to Alan, and said to Miller: "Do you want to write?"

"Not any more for you, thanks," said Miller. "I have the back-ache now from those depositions I made out for you yesterday."

"Oh, I don't mean that," the old lawyer assured him, "but I had to borrow yore ink just now, and seein' you at yore desk I thought you might need it."

"Oh, if I do," jested Miller, "I can buy another bottle at the book-store. They pay me a commission on the ink I furnish the row. They let me have it cheap by the case. What stumps me is that you looked in to see if I needed it. You are breaking the rule, Mr. Trabue. They generally make me hunt for my office furniture when I need it. They've borrowed everything I have except my iron safe. Their ignorance of the combination, its weight, and their confirmed laziness is all that saved it."

When the old lawyer had gone the two friends sat and smoked in silence for several minutes. Alan was studying Miller's face. Something told him that the news of his father's disaster had reached him, and that Miller was going to speak of it. He was not mistaken, for the lawyer soon broached the subject.

"I've been intending to ride out to see you almost every day this week," he said, "but business has always prevented my leaving town."

"Then you have heard—"

"Yes, Alan, I'm sorry, but it's all over the country. A man's bad luck spreads as fast as good war news. I heard it the next day after your father returned from Atlanta, and saw the whole thing in a flash. The truth is, Perkins had the cheek to try his scheme on me. I'm the first target of every scoundrel who has something to sell, and I've learned many of their tricks. I didn't listen to all he had to say, but got rid of him as soon as I could. You must not blame the old man. As I see it now, it was a most plausible scheme, and the shame of it is that no one can be handled for it. I don't think the Tompkins heirs knew anything of Perkins's plans at all, except that he was to get a commission, perhaps, if the property was sold. Trabue is innocent, too—a cat's-paw. As for Perkins, he has kept his skirts clear of prosecution. Your father will have to grin and bear it. He really didn't pay a fabulous price for the land, and if he were in a condition to hold on to it for, say, twenty-five years, he might not lose money; but who can do that sort of thing? I have acres and acres of mountain-land offered me at a much lower figure, but what little money I've made has been made by turning my capital rapidly. Have you seen Dolly since it happened?"

"No, not for two weeks," replied Alan. "I went to church with her Sunday before last, and have not seen her since. I was wondering if she had heard about it."

"Oh yes; she's heard it from the Colonel. It may surprise you, but the thing has rubbed him the wrong way."

"Why, I don't understand," exclaimed Alan. "Has he—"

"The old man has had about two thousand acres of land over near your father's purchases, and it seems that he was closely watching all your father's deals, and, in spite of his judgment to the contrary, Mr. Bishop's confidence in that sort of real-estate has made him put a higher valuation on his holdings over there. So you see, now that your father's mistake is common talk, he is forced to realize a big slump, and he wants to blame some one for it. I don't know but that your father or some one else made him an offer for his land which he refused. So you see it is only natural for him to be disgruntled."

"I see," said Alan. "I reckon you heard that from Miss Dolly?"

Miller smoked slowly.

"Yes" — after a pause — "I dropped in there night before last and she told me about it. She's not one of your surface creatures. She talks sensibly on all sorts of subjects. Of course, she's not going to show her heart to me, but she couldn't hide the fact that your trouble was worrying her a good deal. I think she'd like to see you at the ball to-night. Frank Hillhouse will give you a dance or two. He's going to be hard to beat. He's the most attentive fellow I ever run across. He's got a new buggy — a regular hug-me-tight — and a high-stepping Kentucky mare for the summer campaign. He 'll have some money at his father's death, and all the old women say he's the best catch in town because he doesn't drink, has a Sunday-school class, and will have money. We are all going to wear evening-suits to-night. There are some girls from Rome visiting Hattie Alexander, and we don't want them to smell hay in our hair. You know how the boys are; unless all of us wear spike-tails no one will, so we took a vote on it and we 'll be on a big dike. There 'll be a devilish lot of misfits. Those who haven't suits are borrowing in all directions. Frank Buford will rig out in Colonel Day's antebellum toggery. Did you bring yours?"

"It happens to be at Parker's shop, being pressed," said Alan.

"I've had three in the last six years," laughed Miller. "You know how much larger Todd Selman is than I am; he bursted one of mine from collar to waist last summer at the Springs, and sweated so much that you could dust salt out of it for a month afterwards. I can't refuse 'em, God bless 'em! Jeff Higgins married in my best Prince Albert last week and spilled boiled custard on it; but he's got a good wife and a fair job on a railroad in Tennessee now. I'd have given him the coat, but he'd never have accepted it, and been mad the rest of his life at my offer. Parker said somebody had tried to scrape the custard off with a sharp knife, and that he had a lot of trouble cleaning it. I wore the coat yesterday and felt like I was going to be married. Todd must have left some of his shivers in it I reckon that's as near as I 'll ever come to the hitching-post."

Just then a tall, thin man entered. He wore a rather threadbare frock-coat, unevenly bound with braid, and had a sallow, sunken, and rather long face. It was Samuel Craig, one of the two private bankers of the town. He was about sixty years of age and had a pronounced stoop.

"Hello!" he said, pleasantly; "you young bloods are a-goin' to play smash with the gals' hearts to-night, I reckon. I say go it while you are young. Rayburn, I want to get one of them iron-clad mortgage-blanks. I've got a feller that is disposed to wiggle, an' I want to tie 'im up. The inventor of that form is a blessing to mankind."

"Help yourself," smiled Miller. "I was just telling Mr. Trabue that I was running a stationery store, and if I was out of anything in the line I'd order it for him."

The banker laughed good-humoredly as he selected several of the blanks from the drawer Rayburn had opened in the desk.

"I hope you won't complain as much of hard times as Jake Pitner does," he chuckled. "I passed his store the other day, where he was standin' over some old magazines that he'd marked down.

"'How's trade?' I asked 'im. 'It's gone clean to hell,' he said, and I noticed he'd been drinking. 'I 'll give you a sample of my customers,' he went on. 'A feller from the mountains come in jest now an' asked the price of these magazines. I told him the regular price was twenty-five cents apiece, but I'd marked 'em down to five. He looked at 'em for about half a hour an' then said he wasn't goin' out o' town till sundown an' believed he'd take one if I'd read it to him.'"

Craig laughed heartily as he finished the story, and Alan and Miller joined in.

"I want you to remember that yarn when you get to over-checkin' on me," said Craig, jestingly. "I was just noticing this morning that you have drawn more than your deposit."

"Over-checked?" said Miller. "You 'll think I have when all my checks get in. I mailed a dozen to-day. They 'll slide in on you in about a week and you 'll telegraph *Bradstreet's* to know how I stand. This is a *fine* banker," Miller went on to Alan. "He twits me about over-checking occasionally. Let me tell you something. Last year I happened to have ten thousand dollars on my hands waiting for a cotton factory to begin operations down in Alabama, and as I had no idea when the money would be called for I placed it with his nibs here 'on call.' Things got in a tangle at the mill and they kept waiting, and our friend here concluded I had given it to him."

"I thought you had forgotten you had it," said Craig, with another of his loud, infectious laughs.

"Anyway," went on Miller, "I got a sudden order for the amount and ran in on him on my way from the post-office. I made out my check and stuck it under his nose. Great Scott! you ought to have seen him wilt. I don't believe he had half of it in the house, but he had ten million excuses. He kept me waiting two days and hustled around to beat the band. He thought I was going to close him up."

"That was a close shave," admitted Craig. "Never mind about the over-checking, my boy; keep it up, if it will help you. You are doing altogether too much business with the other bank to suit me, anyway."

CHAPTER VI

THE young people assembled slowly at the dance that evening. Towards dark it had begun raining, and according to custom two livery-stable carriages, called "hacks," were engaged to convey all the couples to and from the hotel. There was no disputing over who should have the first use of the vehicles, for the young ladies who had the reputation of getting ready early on such occasions were gone after first, and those who liked to take their time in making preparations were left till later.

Everything in life is relative, and to young people who often went to even less pretentious entertainments this affair was rather impressive in its elegance. Lamps shone everywhere, and bunches of candles blazed and sputtered in nooks hung about with evergreens. The girls were becomingly attired in light evening-gowns, and many of them were good-looking, refined, and graceful. All were soft-spoken and easy in their manners, and either wore or carried flowers. The evening-suits of the young men were well in evidence, and more noticeable to the wearers themselves than they would have been to a spectator used to conventional style of dress. They could be seen in all stages of inadaptability to figures too large or too small, and even after the dance began there were several swaps, and a due amount of congratulation on the improvement from the appreciative fair sex. The young lady accompanying each young man had pinned a small bouquet on his lapel, so that it would have been impossible to tell whether a man had a natural taste for flowers or was the willing victim to a taste higher than his own.

Rayburn Miller and Alan sat smoking and talking in the room of the latter till about half-past nine o' clock, and then they went down. As a general rule, young men were expected to escort ladies to dances, when the young men went at all; but Alan was often excused from so doing on account of living in the country, and Miller had broken down every precedent in that respect and never invited a girl to go with him. He atoned for this shortcoming by contributing most liberally to every entertainment given by the young people, even when he was out of town. He used to say he liked to graze and nibble at such things and feel free to go to bed or business at will.

As the two friends entered the big parlor, Alan espied the girl about whom he had been thinking all day. She was seated in one of the deep, lace-curtained windows behind the piano. Frank Hillhouse was just presenting to her a faultlessly attired travelling salesman. At this juncture one of the floor-managers with a white rosette on his lapel called Miller away to ask his advice about some details, and Alan turned out of the parlor into the wide corridor which ran through the house. He did this in obedience to another unwritten law governing Darley's social intercourse—that it would be impolite for a resident gentleman to intrude himself upon a stranger who had just been introduced to a lady. So he went down to the ground floor and strolled into the office. It was full of tobacco smoke and a throng of men, some of whom were from the country and others from the town, drawn to the hotel by the festivities. From the office a door opened into a bar and billiard room, whence came the clicking of ivory balls and the grounding of cues. Another door led into the large dining-room, which had been cleared of its tables that it might be used for dancing. There was a sawing of fiddles, the twanging of guitars, the jingle of tambourines, and the groaning of a bass-viol. The musicians, black and yellow, occupied chairs on one of the tables, which had been placed against the wall, and one of the floor-managers was engaged in whittling paraffine-candles over the floor and rubbing it in with his feet. Seeing what he was doing, some of the young men, desirous of trying their new patent-leather pumps, came in and began to waltz singly and in couples.

When everything was in readiness the floor-managers piloted the dancers down-stairs. From the office Alan saw them filing into the big room and taking seats in the chairs arranged against the walls on all sides. He saw Frank Hillhouse and Dolly Barclay sit down near the band; the salesman had disappeared. Alan threw his cigar away and went straight to her.

"Oh, here you are," laughed Frank Hillhouse, as Alan shook hands with her. "I told Miss Dolly coming on that the west wind would blow you this way, and when I saw Ray Miller just now I knew you'd struck the town."

"It wasn't exactly the wind," replied Alan. "I'm afraid you will forget me if I stay on the farm all the time."

"We certainly are glad to have you," smiled Miss Barclay.

"I knew she'd say that—I knew it—I knew it," said Hillhouse. "A girl can always think of nicer things to say to a feller than his rival can. Old Squire Trabue was teasing me the other day about how hard you was to beat, Bishop, but I told him the bigger the war the more victory for somebody; and, as the feller said, I tote fair and am above board."

Alan greeted this with an all but visible shudder. There was much in his dignified bearing and good appearance to commend him to the preference of any thinking woman, especially when contrasted to Hill-house, who was only a little taller than Dolly, and was showing himself even at a greater disadvantage in his unrefined allusions to his and Alan' s attentions to her. Indeed, Alan was sorry for the spectacle the fellow was making of himself, and tried to pass it over.

"I usually come in on Saturdays," he explained.

"That's true," said Dolly, with one of her rare smiles.

"Yes"—Hillhouse took another header into forbidden waters—"he's about joined your church, they tell me."

Alan treated this with an indulgent smile. He did not dislike Hillhouse, but he did not admire him, and he had never quite liked his constant attentions to Miss Barclay. But it was an acknowledged fact among the society girls of Darley that if a girl refused to go out with any young man in good standing it was not long before she was left at home oftener than was pleasant. Dolly was easily the best-looking girl in the room; not, perhaps, the most daintily pretty, but she possessed a beauty which strength of character and intellect alone could give to a face already well featured. Even her physical beauty alone was of that texture which gives the beholder an agreeable sense of solidity. She was well formed, above medium height, had a beautiful neck and shoulders, dark-gray eyes, and abundant golden-brown hair.

"May I see your card?" asked Alan. "I came early to secure at least one."

At this Frank Hillhouse burst out laughing and she smiled up at Alan. "He's been teasing me all evening about the predicament I'm in," she explained. "The truth is, I'm not going to dance at all. The presiding elder happened in town to-day, on his way through, and is at our house. You know how bitter he is against church-members dancing. At first mamma said I shouldn't come a step; but Mr. Hillhouse and I succeeded in getting up a compromise. I can only look on. But my friends are having pity on me and filling my card for what they call stationary dances."

Alan laughed as he took the card, which was already almost filled, and wrote his name in one of the blank spaces. Some one called Hillhouse away, and then an awkward silence fell upon them. For the first time Alan noticed a worried expression on her face, now that it was in repose, but it lighted up again when she spoke.

"You have no button-hole bouquet," she said, noticing his bare lapel. "That's what you get for not bringing a girl. Let me make you one."

"I wish you would," he said, thoughtfully, for as she began to search among her flowers for some rosebuds and leaves he noted again the expression of countenance that had already puzzled him.

"Since you are so popular," he went on, his eyes on her deft fingers, "I'd better try to make another engagement. I'd as well confess that I came in town solely to ask you to let me take you to church tomorrow evening."

He saw her start; she raised her eyes to his almost imploringly, and then she looked down. He saw her breast heave suddenly as with tightened lips she leaned forward to pin the flowers on his coat. The jewels in her rings flashed under his eyes; there was a delicate perfume in the air about her glorious head. He had never seen her look so beautiful before. He wondered at her silence at just such a moment. The tightness of her lips gave way and they fell to trembling when she started to speak.

"I hardly know what to say," she began. "I—I—you know I said the presiding elder was at our house, and—"

"Oh, I understand," broke in Alan; "that's all right. Of course, use your own—"

"No, I must be plain with you," she broke in, raising a pair of helpless, tortured eyes to his; "you will not think I had anything to do with it. In fact, my heart is almost broken. I'm very, very unhappy."

He was still totally at sea as to the cause of her strange distress. "Perhaps you'd rather not tell me at all," he said, sympathetically; his tone never had been so tender. "You need not, you know."

"But it's a thing I could not keep from you long, anyway," she said, tremulously. "In fact, it is due you—an explanation, I mean. Oh, Alan, papa has taken up the idea that we—that we like each other too much, and—"

The life and soul seemed to leave Alan's face.

"I understand," he heard himself saying; "he does not want me to visit you any more."

She made no reply; he saw her catch a deep breath, and her eyes went down to her flowers. The music struck up. The mulatto leader stood waving his fiddle and calling for "the grand march" in loud, melodious tones. There was a scrambling for partners; the young men gave their left arms to the ladies and merrily dragged them to their places.

"I hope you do not blame me—that you don't think that I—" but the clatter and clamor ingulfed her words.

"No, not at all," he told her; "but it's awful—simply awful I I know you are a true friend, and that's some sort of comfort."

"And I always shall be," she gulped. "You must try not to feel hurt. You know my father is a very peculiar man, and has an awful will, and nobody was ever so obstinate."

Then Alan' s sense of the great injustice of the thing rose up within him and his blood began to boil. "Perhaps I ought to take my name off your card," he said, drawing himself up slightly; "if he were to hear that I talked to you to-night he might make it unpleasant for you."

"If you do I shall never—*never forgive you*," she answered, in a voice that shook. There was, too, a glistening in her eyes, as if tears were springing. "Wouldn't that show that you harbored ill-will against me, when I am so helpless and troubled?"

"Yes, it would; and I shall come back," he made answer. He rose, for Hillhouse, calling loudly over his shoulder to some one, was thrusting his bowed arm down towards her.

"I beg your pardon," he said to Dolly. "I didn't know they had called the march. We've got some ice-cream hid out up-stairs, and some of us are going for it. Won't you take some, Bishop?"

"No, thank you," said Alan, and they left him.

CHAPTER VI

ALAN made his way along the wall, out of the track of the promenaders, into the office, anxious to escape being spoken to by any one. But here several jovial men from the mountains who knew him intimately gathered around him and began to make laughing remarks about his dress.

"You look fer the world like a dirt-dauber." This comparison to a kind of black wasp came from Pole Baker, a tall, heavily built farmer with an enormous head, thick eyebrows, and long, shaggy hair. He lived on Bishop's farm, and had been brought up with Alan. "I 'll be derned ef you ain't nimble on yore feet, though. I've seed you cut the pigeon-wing over on Mossy Creek with them big, strappin' gals 'fore you had yore sights as high as these town folks."

"It's that thar vest that gits me," said another. "I reckon it's cut low so you won't drap saft victuals on it; but I guess you don't do much eatin' with that collar on. It don't look like yore Adam's-apple could stir a peg under it."

With a good-natured reply and a laugh he did not feel, Alan hurried out of the office and up to his room, where he had left his lamp burning. Rayburn Miller's hat and light overcoat were on the bed. Alan sat down in one of the stiff-backed, split-bottom chairs and stared straight in front of him. Never in his life had he suffered as he was now suffering. He could see no hope ahead; the girl he loved was lost to him. Her father had heard of the foolhardiness of old man Bishop, and, like many another well-meaning parent, had determined to save his daughter from the folly of marrying a penniless man, who had doubtless inherited his father's lack of judgment and caution.

There was a rap on the closed door, and immediately afterwards Rayburn Miller turned the knob and came in. His kindly glance swept the face of his friend, and he said, with forced lightness:

"I was doing the cake-walk with that fat Howard girl from Rome when I saw you leave the room. She can' t hide the fact that she is from a city of ten thousand population. She kept calling my attention to what our girls had on and sniggering. She's been to school in Boston and looked across the ocean from there. You know I don't think we lead the world, but it makes me fighting mad to have our town sneered at. When she was making so much fun of the girls' dresses, I came in an inch of asking her if she was a dressmaker. By God, I did! You remember," Miller went on lightly, as if he had divined Alan' s misery and was trying to cheer him up—"you remember how Percy Lee, Hamilton's shoe-clerk, hit back at that Savannah girl. She was stopping in this house for a month one summer, and he called on her and took her driving several times; but one day she let herself out. 'Everything is so different up here, Mr. Lee,' she giggled. 'Down home, girls in good society never receive young men in your business.'It was a lick between the eyes; but old North Georgia was ready for it. 'Oh,' said Percy, whose mother's blood is as blue as indigo, 'the Darley girls draw the line, too; I only get to go with hotel girls.'"

Alan looked up and smiled, but his face seemed frozen. Miller sat down, and an awkward silence fell for several minutes. It was broken by the lawyer.

"I don't want to bore you, old man," he said, "but I just had to follow you. I saw from your looks as you left the ballroom that something was wrong, and I am afraid I know what it is."

"You think you do?" asked Alan, flashing a glance of surprise upward.

"Yes. You see, Colonel Barclay is a rough, outspoken man, and he made a remark the other day which reached me. I wasn't sure it was true, so I didn't mention it; but I reckon my informant knew what he was talking about."

Alan nodded despondently. "I asked her to go to church with me to-morrow night. She was awfully embarrassed, and finally told me of her father's objections."

"I think I know what fired the old devil up," said Miller.

"You do?"

"Yes, it was that mistake of your father's. As I told you, the Colonel is as mad as a wet hen about the whole thing. He's got a rope tied to every nickel he's got, and he intends to leave Dolly a good deal of money. He thinks Frank Hillhouse is just the thing; he shows that as plain as day. He noticed how frequently you came to see Dolly and scented danger ahead, and simply put his foot down on it, just as fathers have been doing ever since the Flood. My dear boy, you've got a bitter pill to take, but you've got to swallow it like a man. You've reached a point where two roads fork. It is for you to decide which one you 'll take."

Alan made no reply. Rayburn Miller lighted a cigar and began to smoke steadily. There was a sound of boisterous laughter in a room across the corridor. It had been set aside as the dressing-room for the male revellers, and some of them were there, ordering drinks up from the bar. Now and then from below came muffled strains of music and the monotonous shuffling of feet.

"It's none of my business," Miller burst out, suddenly; "but I'm friend enough of yours to feel this thing like the devil. However, I don't know what to say. I only wish I knew how far you've gone into it."

Alan smiled mechanically.

"If you can' t look at me and see how far I've gone you are blind," he said.

"I don't mean that," replied Miller. "I was wondering how far you had committed yourself—oh, damn it!—made love, and all that sort of thing."

"I've never spoken to her on the subject," Alan informed him, gloomily.

"Good, good! Splendid!"

Alan stared in surprise.

"I don't understand," he said. "She knows—that is, I think she knows how I feel, and I have hoped that—"

"Never mind about that," interrupted Miller, laconically. "There is a chance for both of you if you 'll turn square around like sensible human beings and look the facts in the face."

"You mean—"

"That it will be stupid, childish idiocy for either or both of you to let this thing spoil your lives."

"I don't understand you."

"Well, you will before I'm through with you, and I 'll do you up brown. There are simply two courses open to you, my boy. One is to treat Colonel Barclay's wishes with dignified respect, and bow and retire just as any European gentleman would do when told that his pile was too small to be considered."

"And the other?" asked Alan, sharply.

"The other is to follow in the footsteps of nearly every sentimental fool that ever was born, and go around looking like a last year's bird's-nest, looking good for nothing, and being good for nothing; or, worse yet, persuading the girl to elope, and thus angering her father so that he will cut her out of what's coming to her and what is her right, my boy. She may be willing to live on a bread-and-water diet for a while, but she 'll lose flesh and temper in the long run. If you don't make as much money for her as you cause her to lose she 'll tell you of it some day, or at least let you see it, an' that's as long as it's wide. You are now giving yourself a treatment in self-hypnotism, telling yourself that life has not and cannot produce a thing for you beyond that particular pink frock and yellow head. I know how you feel. I've been there six different times, beginning with a terrible long first attack and dwindling down, as I became inoculated with experience, till now the complaint amounts to hardly more than a momentary throe when I see a fresh one in a train for an hour's ride. I can do you a lot of good if you 'll listen to me. I 'll give you the benefit of my experience."

"What good would your devilish experience do me?" said Alan, impatiently.

"It would fit any man's case if he'd only believe it. I've made a study of love. I've observed hundreds of typical cases, and watched marriage from inception through protracted illness or boredom down to dumb resignation or sudden death. I don't mean that no lovers of the ideal, sentimental brand are ever happy after marriage, but I do believe that open-eyed courtship will beat the blind sort all hollow, and that, in nine cases out of ten, if people were mated by law according to the judgment of a sensible, open-eyed jury, they would be happier than they now are. Nothing ever spoken is truer than the commandment, 'Thou shalt have no other God but me.'Let a man put anything above the principle of living right and he will be miserable. The man who holds gold as the chief thing in life will starve to death in its cold glitter, while a pauper in rags will have a laugh that rings with the music of immortal joy. In the same way the man who declares that only one woman is suited to him is making a god of her—raising her to a seat that won't support her dead, material weight. I frankly believe that the glamour of love is simply a sort of insanity that has never been correctly named and treated because so many people have been the victims of it."

"Do you know," Alan burst in, almost angrily, "when you talk that way I think you are off. I know what's the matter with you; you have simply frittered away your heart, your ability to love and appreciate a good woman. Thank Heaven! your experience has not been mine. I don't see how you could ever be happy with a woman. I couldn't look a pure wife in the face and remember all the flirtations you've indulged in—that is, if they were mine."

"There you go," laughed Miller; "make it personal, that's the only way the average lover argues. I am speaking in general terms. Let me finish.

Take two examples: first, the chap crazily in love, who faces life with the red rag of his infatuation—his girl. No parental objection, everything smooth, and a car-load of silverware—a clock for every room in the house. They start out on their honeymoon, doing the chief cities at the biggest hotels and the theatres in the three-dollar seats. They soon tire of themselves and lay it to the trip. Every day they rake away a handful of glamour from each other, till, when they reach home, they have come to the conclusion that they are only human, and not the highest order at that. For a while they have a siege of discontent, wondering where it's all gone. Finally, the man is forced to go about his work, and the woman gets to making things to go on the backs of chairs and trying to spread her trousseau over the next year, and they begin to court resignation. Now if they had not had the glamour attack they would have got down to business sooner, that's all, and they would have set a better example to other plungers. Now for the second illustration. Poverty on one side, boodle on the other; more glamour than in other case, because of the gulf between. They get married—they have to; they've inherited the stupid idea that the Lord is at the bottom of it and that the glamour is His smile. Like the other couple, their eyes are finally opened to the facts, and they begin to secretly wonder what it's all about; the one with the spondoolix wonders harder than the one who has none. If the man has the money, he will feel good at first over doing so much for his affinity; but if he has an eye for earthly values—and good business men have—there will be times when he will envy Jones, whose wife had as many rocks as Jones. Love and capital go together like rain and sunshine; they are productive of something. Then if the woman has the money and the man hasn't, there's tragedy—a slow cutting of throats. She is irresistibly drawn with the rest of the world into the thought that she has tied herself and her money to an automaton, for such men are invariably lifeless. They seem to lose the faculty of earning money—in any other way. And as for a proper title for the penniless young idiot that publicly advertises himself as worth enough, in himself, for a girl to sacrifice her money to live with him—well, the unabridged does not furnish it. Jack Ass in bill-board letters would come nearer to it than anything that occurs to me now. I'm not afraid to say it, for I know you'd never cause any girl to give up her fortune without knowing, at least, whether you could replace it or not."

Alan rose and paced the room. "That," he said, as he stood between the lace curtains at the window, against which the rain beat steadily—"that is why I feel so blue. I don't believe Colonel Barclay would ever forgive her, and I'd die before I'd make her lose a thing."

"You are right," returned Miller, relighting his cigar at the lamp, "and he'd cut her off without a cent. I know him. But what is troubling me is that you may not be benefited by my logic. Don't allow this to go any further. Let her alone from to-night on and you 'll find in a few months that you are resigned to it, just like the average widower who wants to get married six months after his loss. And when she is married and has a baby, she 'll meet you on the street and not care a rap whether her hat's on right or not. She 'll tell her husband all about it, and allude to you as her first, second, or third fancy, as the case may be. I have faith in your future, but you've got a long, rocky row to hoe, and a thing like this could spoil your usefulness and misdirect your talents. If I could see how you could profit by waiting I'd let your flame burn unmolested; but circumstances are agin us."

"I'd already seen my duty," said Alan, in a low tone, as he came away from the window. "I have an engagement with her later, and the subject shall be avoided."

"Good man!" Miller's cigar was so short that he stuck the blade of his penknife through it that he might enjoy it to the end without burning his fingers. "That's the talk! Now I must mosey on down-stairs and dance with that Miss Fewclothes from Rome—the one with the auburn tresses, that says 'delighted' whenever she is spoken to."

Alan went back to the window. The rain was still beating on it. For a long time he stood looking out into the blackness. The bad luck which had come to his father had been a blow to him; but its later offspring had the grim, cold countenance of death itself. He had never realized till now that Dolly Barclay was so much a part of his very life. For a moment he almost gave way to a sob that rose and struggled within him. He sat down again and clasped his hands before him in dumb self-pity. He told himself that Rayburn Miller was right, that only weak men would act contrary to such advice. No, it was over—all, all over.

CHAPTER VIII

AFTER the dance Frank Hillhouse took Dolly home in one of the drenched and bespattered hacks. The Barclay residence was one of the best-made and largest in town. It was an old-style Southern frame-house, painted white, and had white-columned verandas on two sides. It was in the edge of the town, and had an extensive lawn in front and almost a little farm behind.

Dolly's mother had never forgotten that she was once a girl herself, and she took the most active interest in everything pertaining to Dolly's social life. On occasions like the one just described she found it impossible to sleep till her daughter returned, and then she slipped up-stairs, and made the girl tell all about it while she was disrobing. To-night she was more alert and wide-awake than usual. She opened the front door for Dolly and almost stepped on the girl's heels as she followed her up-stairs.

"Was it nice?" she asked.

"Yes, very," Dolly replied. Reaching her room, she turned up the low-burning lamp, and, standing before a mirror, began to take some flowers out of her hair. Mrs. Barclay sat down on the edge of the high-posted mahogany bed and raised one of her bare feet and held it in her hand. She was a thin woman with iron-gray hair, and about fifty years of age. She looked as if she were cold; but, for reasons of her own, she was not willing for Dolly to remark it.

"Who was there?" she asked.

"Oh, everybody."

"Is that so? I thought a good many would stay away because it was a bad night; but I reckon they are as anxious to go as we used to be. Then you all did have the hacks?"

"Yes, they had the hacks." There was a pause, during which one pair of eyes was fixed rather vacantly on the image in the mirror; the other pair, full of impatient inquiry, rested alternately on the image and its maker.

"I don't believe you had a good time," broke the silence, in a rising, tentative tone.

"Yes, I did, mother."

"Then what's the matter with you?" Mrs. Barclay's voice rang with impatience. "I never saw you act like you do to-night, never in my life."

"I didn't know anything was wrong with me, mother."

"You act queer; I declare you do," asserted Mrs. Barclay. "You generally have a lot to say. Have you and Frank had a falling out?"

Dolly gave her shoulders a sudden shrug of contempt.

"No, we got along as well as we ever did."

"I thought maybe he was a little mad because you wouldn't dance to-night; but surely he's got enough sense to see that you oughtn't to insult brother Dill-beck that way when he's visiting our house and everybody knows what he thinks about dancing."

"No, he thought I did right about it," said Dolly.

"Then what in the name of common-sense is the matter with you, Dolly? You can' t pull the wool over my eyes, and you needn't try it."

Dolly faced about suddenly.

"I reckon you 'll sit there all night unless I tell you all about it," she said, sharply. "Mother, Alan Bishop was there."

"You don't say!"

"Yes, and asked me to let him take me to church to-morrow evening."

"Oh, he did?"

"Yes, and as I didn't want father to insult him, I—"

"You told him what your pa said?"

"No, I just told him father didn't want me to receive him any more. Heaven knows, that was enough."

"Well, that was the best thing for you to do." Mrs. Barclay took a deep breath, as if she were inhaling a delicious perfume. "It's much better than to have him plunge in here some day and have your father break out like he does in his rough way. What did Alan say?"

"He said very little; but he looked it. You ought to have seen him. Frank came up just about that time and invited me to have some ice-cream, and I had to leave him. He was as white as a sheet. He had made an engagement with me to sit out a dance, and he didn't come in the room again till that dance was called, and then he didn't even mention it. He acted so peculiarly,

I could see it was nearly killing him, but he wouldn't let me bring up the subject again. I came near doing it; but he always steered round it."

"He's a sensible young man," declared Mrs. Barclay. "Any one can see that by looking at him. He's not responsible for his father's foolhardy venture, but it certainly leaves him in a bad fix as a marrying man. He's had bad luck, and he must put up with the consequences. There are plenty of girls who have no money or prospects who would be glad to have him, but—"

"Mother," broke in Dolly, as if she had been listening to her own troubled thoughts rather than her mother's words; "he didn't act as if he wanted to see me alone. The other couples who had engagements to talk during that dance were sitting in windows and out-of-the-way corners, but he kept me right where I was, and was as carefully polite as if we had just been introduced. I was sorry for him and mad at the same time. I could have pulled his ears."

"He's sensible, very sensible," said Mrs. Barclay, in a tone of warm admiration. "A man like that ought to get along, and I reckon he will do well some day."

"But, mother," said Dolly, her rich, round voice rising like a wave and breaking in her throat, "he may never think about me any more."

"Well, that really would be best, dear, under the circumstances."

"Best?" Dolly blurted out. "How can you say that, when—when—"

"Dolly, you are not really foolish about him, are you?" Mrs. Barclay's face dropped into deeper seriousness.

Dolly looked away and was silent for a moment; then she faltered: "I don't know, mother, I—I'm afraid if I keep on feeling like I do now I 'll never get over it."

"Ah, but you 'll not keep on feeling like you do now," consoled the older woman. "Of course, right now, just after seeing how hard he took it, you will kind o' sympathize with him and want to help him; but that will all pass away. I remember when I was about your age I had a falling out with Will Despree—a young man my father didn't like because his grandfather had been an overseer. And, do you know, I thought I would actually kill myself. I refused to eat a bite and threatened to run away with Will. To this day I really don't know what I would have done if your grandfather hadn't scared him away with a shot-gun. Will kept writing notes to me. I was afraid to answer them, but my father got hold of one and went after him on a fast horse. Will's family heard what was up and they kept him out in the swamp for a few days, and then they sent him to Texas. The whole Despree family took it up and talked scand'lous about us."

"And you soon got over it, mother?" asked Dolly, almost in a tone of dismay.

"Well," said Mrs. Barclay, reflectively, "Will acted the fool so terribly; he wasn't out in Texas three months before he sent back a marked paper with an article in it about his engagement to the daughter of a rich man who, we found out afterwards, used to keep a livery-stable; then I reckon hardly any girl would keep caring for a boy when his folks was telling such lies about her family."

Dolly was staring studiously at the speaker.

"Mother," she asked, "don't you believe in real love?"

Mrs. Barclay laughed as if highly amused. "I believe in a different sort to the puppy love I had for that boy. Then after that there was another young man that I thought more of, if anything, than I did of Will; but he was as poor as Job's turkey, and my folks was all crazy for me 'n' your pa, who I'd never seen, to get married. I held out against the idea, just like you are doing with Frank, I reckon; but when your pa come with his shiny broadcloth coat and spotted silk vest—no, it was satin, I think, with red spots on it—and every girl in town was crazy to catch him, and there was no end of reports about the niggers he owned and his high connection;— well, as I say, it wasn't a week before I was afraid he'd see Joe Tinsley and hear about me 'n' him. My father was in for the match from the very jump, and so was your pa's folks. He put up at our house with his nigger servant and didn't want to go about town much. I reckon I was pleased to have him pick me out, and so we soon fixed it up. Lordy, he only had to mention Joe Tinsley to me after we got married to make me do anything he wanted. To this day he throws him up to me, for Joe never did amount to anything. He tried to borrow money from your pa after you was born. The neighbors had to feed his children."

"But you loved father, didn't you?" Dolly breathed, in some relief over what she thought was coming.

"Well, I can' t say I did," said Mrs. Barclay. "We had a terrible time getting used to one another's ways. You see, he'd waited a good while, and was some older than I was. After a while, though, we settled down, and now I'm awful glad I let my father manage for me. You see, what your pa had and what my father settled on me made us comfortable, and if a couple is that it's a sight more than the pore ones are."

Abner Daniel | 53

Dolly stood before her mother, close enough to touch her. Her face wore an indescribable expression of dissatisfaction with what she had heard.

"Mother, tell me one thing," she said. "Did you ever let either of those boys—the two that you didn't marry, I mean—kiss you?"

Mrs. Barclay stared up at her daughter for an instant and then her face broke into a broad smile of genuine amusement. She lowered her head to her knee and laughed out.

"Dolly Barclay, you are *such* a fool!" she said, and then she laughed again almost immoderately, her face in her lap.

"I know what *that* means," said Dolly, in high disgust. "Mother, I don't think you can do me any good. You'd better go to bed."

Mrs. Barclay rose promptly.

"I think I'd better, too," she said. "It makes your pa awful mad for me to sit up this way. I don't want to hear him rail out like he always does when he catches me at it."

After her mother had gone, Dolly sat down on her bed. "She never was in love," she told herself. "Never, never, never! And it is a pity. She never could have talked that way if she had really loved anybody as much as—" But Dolly did not finish what lay on her tongue. However, when she had drawn the covers up over her the cold tears rose in her eyes and rolled down on her pillow as she thought of Alan Bishop's brave and dignified suffering.

"Poor fellow!" she said. "Poor, dear Alan!"

CHAPTER IX

THERE is a certain class of individuals that will gather around a man in misfortune, and it differs very little, if it differs at all, from the class that warms itself in the glow of a man' s prosperity. It is made up of human failures, in the first instance, congratulating themselves on not being alone in bad luck; in the second, desirous of seeing how a fortunate man would look and act and guessing at his feelings. From the appearance of Bishop's home for the first fortnight after his return from Atlanta, you would have thought that some one was seriously ill in the house or that some general favorite had returned to the family after a long absence.

Horses were hitched to the fence from the front gate all the way round to the side entrance. The mountain people seemed to have left their various occupations to subtly enjoy the spectacle of a common man like themselves who had reached too far after forbidden fruit and lay maimed and torn before them. It was a sort of feast at which the baser part of their spiritual natures was fed, and, starved as they were, it tasted good. Many of them had never aspired to bettering their lot even with small ventures such as buying Jersey cows at double the value of common cattle when it was reported that the former gave four times as much milk and ate less, and to these cautious individuals Bishop's visible writhing was sweet confirmation of their own judgment.

Their disapproval of the old man's effort to hurry Providence could not have been better shown than in the failure of them all to comment on the rascally conduct of the Atlanta lawyer; they even chuckled over that part of the incident. To their minds Perkins was a sort of far-off personification of a necessary evil—who, like the devil himself, was evidently created to show mortals their limitations. They were not going to say what the lawyer had a right to do or should avoid doing, for they didn't pretend to know; but they did know what their old neighbor ought to have done, and if they didn't tell him so to his face they would let him see it by their actions. Yes, Bishop was a different thing altogether. He belonged to them and theirs. He led in their meetings, prayed in public, and had till now headed the list in all charitable movements.

The Reverend Charles B. Dole, a tall, spare man of sixty, who preached the first, second, third, and fourth Sundays of each month in four different meetinghouses within a day's ride of Bishop's, came around as the guest of the farm-house as often as his circuit would permit. He was called the "fightin' preacher," because he had had several fearless hand-to-hand encounters with certain moonshiners whose conduct he had ventured to call ungodly, because unlawful.

On the second Saturday after Bishop's mishap, as Dole was to preach the next day at Rock Crest meetinghouse, he rode up as usual and turned his horse into the stable and fed him with his own hands. Then he joined Abner Daniel on the veranda. Abner had seen him ride up and purposely buried his head in his newspaper to keep from offering to take the horse, for Abner did not like the preacher "any to hurt," as he would have put it.

Dole did not care much for Abner either. They had engaged in several doctrinal discussions in which the preacher had waxed furious over some of Daniel's views, which he described as decidedly unorthodox. Daniel had kept his temper beautifully and had the appearance of being amused through it all, and this Dole found harder to forgive than anything Abner had said.

"You all have had some trouble, I heer, sence I saw you last," said the preacher as he sat down and began to wipe his perspiring brow with a big handkerchief.

"Well, I reckon it mought be called that," Abner replied, as he carefully folded his newspaper and put it into his coat-pocket. "None of us was expectin' of it an' it sorter bu'sted our calculations. Alf had laid out to put new high-back benches in Rock Crest, an' new lamps an' one thing another, an' it seems to me"—Abner wiped his too facile mouth—"like I heerd 'im say one day that you wasn't paid enough fer yore thunder, an' that he'd stir around an' see what could be done." Abner's eyes twinkled. "But lawsy me! I reckon ef he kin possibly raise the scads to pay the tax on his investment next yeer he 'll do all the Lord expects."

"Huh, I reckon!" grunted Dole, irritated as usual by Abner's double meaning. "I take it that the Lord hain't got much to do with human speculations one way or other."

"Ef I just had that scamp that roped 'im in before me a minute I'd fix 'im," said Abner. "Do you know what denomination Perkins belongs to?"

"No, I don't," Dole blurted out, "an' what's more, I don't care."

"Well, I acknowledge it sorter interests me," went on our philosopher, in an inscrutable tone, "beca'se, brother Dole, you kin often trace a man' s good ur bad doin' s to his belief in Bible matters. Maybe you don't remember Jabe Lynan that stold Thad Wilson's stump-suckin' hoss an' was ketched an' put up. I was at the court-house in Darley when he received his sentence. His wife sent me to 'im to carry his pipe an' one thing or other—a pair o' socks an' other necessary tricks—a little can o' lye-soap, fer one thing. She hadn't the time to go, as she said she had a patch o' young corn to hoe out. I found 'im as happy as ef he was goin' off on a excursion. He laughed an' 'lowed it ud be some time 'fore he got back, an' I wondered what could 'a' made him so contented, so I made some inquiries on that line. I found that he was a firm believer in predestination, an' that what was to be was foreordained. He said that he firmly believed he was predestinated to go to the coal-mines fer hoss-stealin', an' that life was too short to be kickin' agin the Lord's way o' runnin' matters; besides, he said, he'd heerd that they issued a plug o'.tobacco a week to chawin' prisoners, an' he could prove that he was one o' that sort ef they'd look how he'd ground his jaw-teeth down to the gums."

"Huh!" grunted Dole again, his sharp, gray eyes on Abner's face, as if he half believed that some of his own theories were being sneered at. It was true that he, being a Methodist, had not advocated a belief in predestination, but Abner Daniel had on more than one occasion shown a decided tendency to bunch all stringent religious opinions together and cast them down as out of date. When in doubt in a conversation with Abner, the preacher assumed a coldness on the outside that was often not consistent with the fires within him. "I don't see what all that's got to do with brother Bishop's mistake," he said, frigidly, as he leaned back in his chair.

"It sets me to wonderin' what denomination Perkins belongs to, that's all," said Abner, with another smile. "I know in reason he's a big Ike in some church in Atlanta, fer I never knowed a lawyer that wasn't foremost in that way o' doin' good. I 'll bet a hoe-cake he belongs to some highfalutin crowd o' worshippers that kneel down on saft cushions an' believe in scoopin' in all they kin in the Lord's name, an' that charity begins at home. I think that myse'f, brother Dole, fer thar never was a plant as hard to git rooted as charity is, an' a body ought to have it whar they kin watch it close. It 'll die a heap o' times ef you jest look at it, an' it mighty nigh always has bad soil ur a drougth to contend with."

Just then Pole Baker, who has already been introduced to the reader, rode up to the fence and hitched his horse. He nodded to the two men on the veranda, and went round to the smoke-house to get a piece of bacon Bishop had promised to sell him on credit.

"Huh!" Dole grunted, and he crossed his long legs and swung his foot up and down nervously. He had the look of a man who was wondering why such insufferable bores as Abner should so often accompany a free dinner. He had never felt drawn to the man, and it irritated him to think that just when his mental faculties needed rest, Abner always managed to introduce the very topics which made it necessary for him to keep his wits about him.

"Take that feller thar," Abner went on, referring to Baker. "He's about the hardest customer in this county, an' yet he's bein' managed right now. He's got a wife an' seven children an' is a holy terror when he gits drunk. He used to be the biggest dare-devil moonshiner in all these mountains; but Alan kept befriendin' 'im fust one way an' another tell he up one day an' axed Alan what he could do fer 'im. Alan ain't none o' yore shoutin' kind o' Christians. He shakes a nimble toe at a shindig when he wants to, an' knows the ace from a ten-spot; but he gits thar with every claw in the air when some 'n' has to be done. So, when Pole axed 'im that, Alan jest said, as quiet as ef he was axin' 'im fer a match to light a cigar, 'Quit yore moonshinin', Pole.' That was all he said. Pole looked 'im straight in the eye fer a minute, an' then said:

"'The hell you say! By God, Alan Bishop, you don't mean that!'

"'Yes, I do, Pole,' said Alan, 'quit! Quit smack off!'

"'You ax that as a favor?' said Pole.

"'Yes, as a favor,' said Alan, 'an' you are a-goin' to do it, too.'

"Then Pole begun to contend with 'im. 'You are a-axin' that beca'se you think I 'll be ketched up with,' he said; 'but I tell you the' ain't no man on the face o' the earth that could find my still now. You could stand in two feet of the door to it all day an' not find it if you looked fer it with a spy-glass. I kin make bug-juice all the rest o' my life an' sell it without bein' ketched.'

"'I want you to give it up,' said Alan, an' Pole did. It was like pullin' an eye-tooth, but Pole yanked it out. Alan is workin' on 'im now to git 'im to quit liquor, but that ain't so easy. He could walk a crack with a gallon sloshin' about in 'im. Now, as I started to say, Alan 'ain't got no cut-and-dried denomination, an' don't have to walk any particular kind o' foot-log to do his work, but it's a-goin' on jest the same. Now I don't mean no reflection on yore way o' hitchin' wings on folks, but I believe you could preach yore sermons—sech as they are—in Pole Baker's yeers till Gabriel blowed his lungs out, an' Pole ud still be moonshinin'. An' sometimes I think that sech fellers as Alan Bishop ort to be paid fer what they do in betterin' the world. I don't see why you fellers ort always to be allowed to rake in the jack-pot unless you'd accomplish more'n outsiders, that jest turn the'r hands to the job at odd times."

Dole drew himself up straight and glared at the offender.

"I think that is a rather personal remark, brother Daniel," he said, coldly.

"Well, maybe it is," returned Abner; "but I didn't mean fer it to be. I've heerd you praise up certain preachers fer the good they was a-doin', an' I saw no harm in mentionin' Alan's method. I reckon it's jest a case o' the shoe bein' on another foot. I was goin' to tell you how this misfortune o' Alf's had affected Pole; he's been like a crazy man ever since it happened. It's been all Alan could do to keep 'im from goin' to Atlanta an' chokin' the life out o' Perkins. Pole got so mad when he wouldn't let 'im go that he went off cussin' 'im fer all he was worth. I wonder what sort of a denomination a man ud fit into that 'll cuss his best friends black an' blue beca'se they won't let 'im fight fer 'em. Yes, he 'll fight, an' ef he ever does jine the ranks above he 'll do the work o' ten men when thar's blood to spill. I seed 'im in a row once durin' election when he was leggin' fer a friend o' his'n; he stood right at the polls an' wanted to slug every man that voted agin 'im. He knocked three men's teeth down the'r throats an' bunged up two more so that they looked like they had on false-faces."

Here the preacher permitted himself to laugh. Being a fighting man himself, his heart warmed towards a man who seemed to be born to that sort of thing.

"He looks like he could do a sight of it," was his comment.

At this juncture the subject of the conversation came round the house, carrying a big piece of bacon wrapped in a tow grain-bag.

"Say thar, Pole," Abner called out to the long, lank fellow. "We are a-goin' to have preachin' at Rock Crest to-morrow; you'd better have a shirt washed an' hung out to dry. They are a-beatin' the bushes fer yore sort."

Pole Baker paused and brushed back his long, thick hair from his heavy eyebrows.

"I've been a-waitin' to see ef meetin' ever'd do you any good, Uncle Ab," he laughed. "They tell me the more you go the wuss you git to be. Neil Filmore said t'other day ef you didn't quit shootin' off yore mouth they'd give you a trial in meetin'."

Abner laughed good-naturedly as he spat over the edge of the veranda floor to the ground.

"That's been talked, I know, Pole," he said, "but they don't mean it. They all know how to take my fun. But you come on to meetin'; it will do you good."

"Well, maybe I will," promised Pole, and he came to the steps, and, putting his bacon down, he bent towards them.

"It's a powerful hard matter to know exactly what's right an' what's wrong, in some things," he said. "Now looky heer." Thrusting his hand down into the pocket of his trousers he drew out a piece of quartz-rock with a lump of yellow gold about the size of a pea half embedded in it. "That thar's puore gold. I got it this away: A feller that used to be my right bower in my still business left me when I swore off an' went over to Dalonega to work in them mines. T'other day he was back on a visit, an' he give me this chunk an' said he'd found it. Now I know in reason that he nabbed it while he was at work, but I don't think I'd have a right to report it to the minin' company, an' so I'm jest obleeged to receive stolen goods. It ain't wuth more'n a dollar, they tell me, an' I'll hang on to it, I reckon, ruther'n have a laborin' man discharged from a job. I'm tryin' my level best to live up to the line now, an' I don't know how to manage sech a thing as that. I've come to the conclusion that no harm will be done nohow, beca'se miners ain't too well paid anyway, an' ef I jest keep it an' don't git no good out of it, I won't be in it any more'n ef I'd never got hold o' the blamed thing."

"But the law, brother Baker," said Dole, solemnly; "without the law we'd be an awful lot o' people, an' every man ort to uphold it. Render the things that are Caesar's unto Caesar."

Pole's face was blank for a moment, and Abner came to his rescue with a broad smile and sudden laugh.

"I reckon you don't remember him, Pole," he said. "He's dead. He was a nigger that used to belong to old man Throgmartin in the cove. He used to be sech an awful thief during slavery days that it got to be a common sayin' that everything lyin' round mought as well be his'n, fer he'd take it sooner ur later, anyways."

"I've heerd o' that nigger," said Pole, much to the preacher's disgust, which grew as Pole continued: "Well, they say a feller that knows the law is broke an' don't report it is as guilty as the man who does the breakin'. Now, Mr. Dole, you know how I come by this nugget, an' ef you want to do your full duty you'll ride over to Dalonega an' report it to the right parties. I can't afford the trip."

Abner laughed out at this, and then forced a serious look on his face. "That's what you railly ort to do, brother Dole," he said. "Them Cæsars over thar ud appreciate it."

Then Mrs. Bishop came out to shake hands with the preacher, and invited him to go to his room to wash his face and hands. As the tall man followed his hostess away, Abner winked slyly at Pole and laughed under his long, scrawny hand.

"Uncle Ab, you ort to be killed," smiled Pole. "You've been settin' heer the last half-hour pokin' fun at that feller, an' you know it. Well, I'm goin' on home. Sally's a-goin' to fry some o' this truck fer me, an' I'm as hungry as a bear."

A few minutes after he had gone, Dole came out of his room and sat down in his chair again. "That seems to be a sorter bright young man," he remarked.

"As bright as a new dollar," returned Abner, in a tone of warm admiration. "Did you notice that big, wedge-shaped head o' his'n? It's plumb full o' brains. One day a feller come down to Filmore's store. He made a business o' feelin' o' heads an' writin' out charts at twenty-five cents apiece. He didn't waste much time on the rest o' the scabs he examined; but when he got to Pole's noggin he talked fer a good hour. I never heerd the like. He said ef his talents had been properly directed Pole ud 'a' made a big public man. He said he hadn't run across sech a head in a month o' Sundays. He was right, you bet, an' every one o' the seven brats Pole's got is jest as peert as he is. They are a-growin' up in idleness an' rags, too. I wisht I could meet some o' them dum big Yankees that are a-sendin' the'r money down heer an' buildin' fine schools to educate niggers an' neglectin' the'r own race beca'se it fit agin 'em. You cayn't hardly beat larnin' into a nigger's head, an' it ud be only common-sense to spend money whar it ud do the most good. I 'ain't got nothin' agin a nigger bein' larnt to read an' write, but I cayn't stomach the'r bein' forced ahead o' deservin' white folks sooner 'n the Lord counted on. Them kind o' Yankees is the same sort that makes pets o' dogs, an' pampers 'em up when pore white children is in need o' food an' affection."

"Pole looks like he had natural capacity," said Dole. He was fond of conversing with Abner on any topic except that of religious matters.

"He'd make a bang-up detective," laughed Abner. "One day I was at Filmore's store. Neil sometimes, when he's rushed, gits Pole to clerk fer 'im, beca'se he's quick at figures. It happened that Pole had the store to 'imse'f one day when Neil had gone off to cut down a bee-tree with a passle o' neighbors, an' a triflin' feller come in an' begun to nose about. An' when Pole's back was turned to weigh up some cotton in the seed he stole a pocket-book out o' the show-case. I reckon Pole didn't like his looks much nohow, fer as soon as the skunk had gone he begun to look about to see ef he'd tuck anything. All at once he missed the pocket-book, an' told Neil that night that he was mighty nigh shore the feller lifted it, but he couldn't railly swear to it. About a week after that he seed the same feller comin' down the road headed fer the store on his gray mule. Me 'n' Neil was both thar an' Pole hustled us in the back room, an' told us to stay thar. He said he was a-goin' to find out ef the feller stold the book. Neil was afeerd of a row an' tried to prevent 'im, but he jest shoved us back an' shet the door on us. Neil got 'im a crack in the partition an' I found me a knothole.

"The feller hitched an' come in an' said howdy-do, an' started to take a cheer nigh the door, but Pole stopped 'im.

"'Come heer to the show-case,' ses he; 'I want to show you some 'n'.' The feller went, an' I seed Pole yank out the box 'at had the rest o' the pocket-books in it. 'Look y'heer,' Pole said, in a loud, steady voice—you could 'a' heerd 'im clean to the creek—'look y'heer. The regular price o' these books is fifty cents; that's what we sell 'em fer; but you've got to run yore hand down in yore pocket an' give me a dollar fer one quicker'n you ever made a trade in yore life.'

"'What in the hell do you mean?' the feller said.

"'I mean exactly what I said, an' you are a-losin' time.' said Pole, talkin' louder an' louder. 'The price is fifty cents; but you got to gi'me a dollar fer one. Haul 'er out, my friend; haul 'er out! It 'll be the cheapest thing you ever bought in yore life.'

"The feller was as white as a sheet. He gulped two or three times 'fore he spoke, then he said: 'I know what you think; you think I took one t'other day when I was lookin' in the show-case; but you are mistaken.'

"'I never said a word about you takin' one,' Pole yelled at 'im, 'but you'd better yank out that dollar an' buy one; you need it.'

"The feller did it. I heerd the money clink as he laid it on the glass an' I knowed he was convicted.

"'They are only wuth fifty cents,' he said, kinder faint-like.

"'Yo're a liar,' Pole yelled at 'im, 'fer you've jest paid a dollar fer one on yore own accord. Now I 'll jest give you two minutes to straddle that mule. Ef you don't I 'll take you to the sheriff myself, you damned thief.

"'I've always done my tradin' heer,' said the feller, thinkin' that ud sorter pacify Pole, but he said: 'Yes, an' yore stealin', too, I reckon, you black-livered jailbird. Git out, git out!'

"Me 'n' Neil come in when the feller'd gone, but Pole was actually too mad to speak. 'He got off too durned light,' he said, after a while. 'I could 'a' sold 'im a big bill o' goods at a hundred per cent, profit, fer he had plenty o' money. Now he's ridin' off laughin' at me.'"

CHAPTER X

NEIL FILMORE'S store was about half a mile from Bishop's house, at the crossing of the Darley road and another leading into East Tennessee. Alan had gone down there one day to engage white labor to work in his growing cotton, negroes being scarce, owing to the tendency of that race to flock into the towns. With the aid of Pole Baker, who was clerking that day for Filmore, he soon employed the men he wanted and started to walk back home. On the way he was overtaken by his uncle, who was returning from Darley in his wagon.

"Hold on thar," the old man called out; "ef you are a-goin' home I'll rest yore legs."

Alan smiled as he climbed up into the seat by the old man.

"I shall certainly appreciate it," he said. "I'm tired out to-day."

"I sorter thought you looked flabbergasted," returned Abner, as he swung his whip over the backs of his sleek horses. "Well, I reckon I could afford to give you a ride. I hauled that cuss Dole three miles goin' t'other way. He had the cheek to yell at me from Habbersham's gin-house an' axed me ef I'd haul 'im. Then he kept me waitin' till he'd helt prayer an' read to the family."

"You don't seem to like him," said Alan. "I've noticed that for some time."

"I reckon I don't to any great extent," said Abner, clucking to his tired horses; "but it ain't raily to my credit. A feller's wrong som 'er's, Alan, that allows hisse'f to hate anything the Lord ever made. I've struggled agin that proposition fer twenty-five yeer. All this talk about the devil makin' the bad an' the Lord the good is talk through a hat. Bad things was made 'fore the devil ever jumped from his high estate ur he'd never preferred a fork to a harp. I've tuck notice, too, that the wust things I ever seed was sometimes at the root o' the best. Manure is a bad thing, but a cake of it will produce a daisy bigger 'n any in the field. Dole makes me gag sometimes; but as narrer as he is twixt the eyes, he may do some good. I reckon that hell-fire sermon he give us last August made some of the crowd sweat out a little o' the'r meanness. I'd 'a' been more merciful on sech a hot day, though. He mought 'a' reserved that harangue fer some cold day in December when the stove-flues wouldn't work. Ef I'd 'a' been a-goin' tell about future torment that hot day I'd 'a' said that every lost soul was made to set on a cake o' ice in a windy spot through all eternity, an' I'd 'a' started out by singin' 'On Greenland's Icy Mountain.' But that ain't what I axed you to git in my wagon fer."

"You didn't intend to try to convert me, then?"

"No, I didn't, fer you are jest my sort of a Christian—better'n me, a sight, fer you don't shoot off yore bazoo on one side or t'other, an' that's the habit I'm tryin' to quit. Ef I could hold in when Dole gits to spoutin' I'd be a better man. I think I 'll do better now. I've got a tenpenny nail in my pocket an' whenever he starts in I'm goin' to bite it an' keep my holt on it till he stops. Yes, you are jest my sort of a Christian. You believe in breathin' fresh air into yore windpipe, thankin' God with a clear eye an' a good muscle, an' takin' what He gives you an' axin' 'Im to pass more ef it's handy. You know the Lord has sent you a invite to His table, an' you believe in eatin' an' drinkin' an' makin' merry, jest like you'd have a body do that was stoppin' over night with you. Yes, I wanted to say some 'n' else to you. As I got to the widder Snowden's house, a mile this side o' Darley, she came out an' axed me ef I'd object to deliverin' a couple o' smoke-cured hams to a feller in town that had ordered 'em. Of course that's what a' old bach' like me 's heer fer, so I let 'er fling 'em in the back end."

The speaker paused and smiled knowingly, and Alan noticed that he slowed his horses up by drawing firmly on the reins as if he feared that their arrival at the farm-house might interrupt what he had to say.

"Well," said Alan, "you delivered the hams?"

"Yes." Abner was looking straight ahead of him. "They was fer Colonel Seth Barclay. I driv' up to the side gate, after I'd helloed in front till I was hoarse, an' who do you reckon come trippin' out o' the dinin'-room?

It was *her*. Ef you hain't never ketched 'er off'n her guard round the house, you've missed a treat. Durned ef I don't like 'er better without a hat on than with all the fluffy flamdoodle that gals put on when they go out. She was as neat as a new pin, an' seemed powerful glad to see me. That made me bless the widder Snowden fer sendin' me thar. She said the cook was off som 'er's, an' that old nigger Ned, the stable-man, was in the garden-patch behind the house, so she was thar by 'erse'f. She actually looked like she wanted to tote in the hams 'erse'f ruther'n bother me; but you bet my old bones hopped off'n this seat quicker'n you could say Jack Robinson with yore mouth open. I was afeerd my team wouldn't stand, fer fellers was a-scootin' by on bicycles; but I tuck the hams to the back porch an' put 'em on a shelf out'n re'ch o' the dogs. Then I went back to my wagon. She follered me to the fence, an' I noticed that some 'n' was wrong with 'er. She looked so funny, an' droopy about the mouth, an' kept a-talkin' like she was afeerd I'd fly off. She axed all about Adele an' how she was a-makin' out down in Atlanta, an' said she'd heerd that Sis was mighty popular with the young men, an' from that she axed about my craps an' the meetin' goin' on at Big Bethel. Finally she got right white about the mouth, an' said, kinder shaky, that she was afeerd you was mad about some 'n' her pa'd said about you, an' I never seed a woman as nigh cryin' as she was without doin' of it.

"I told 'er I was at the fust of it; but I'd noticed how worried you've looked heer of late, an' so I told 'er I'd been afeerd some 'n' had come betwixt you two. Then she put her head down on the top rail o' the fence an' helt it thar fer a good minute. After a while she looked up an' told me all about it an' ended by axin' me ef I thought she was to blame in the matter. I told 'er no; but her old skunk of a daddy had acted sech a fool that I couldn't hold in. I reckon I told 'er jest about what I thought o' him an' the more I raked up agin 'im the better she seemed pleased. I tried to pin' er down to what she'd be willin' to do in a pinch ef her pa continued to hold out agin you, but she was too sharp to commit 'erse'f. It jest looked like she wanted to make up with you an' didn't want no row nuther."

The horses stopped to drink at a clear stream of water which ran across the road on a bed of brown pebbles. The bridles were too tight to allow them to lower their heads, so Alan went out on the heavy tongue between the pair and unfastened the reins. When he had regained his seat he told the old man in detail all that had happened at the dance at the hotel, ending with the advice he had received from Rayburn Miller.

"I don't know about that," Abner said. "Maybe Miller could call a halt like that an' go on like nothin' had happened. I don't say he could nur couldn't; but it's fool advice. You mought miss it, an' regret it to yore dyin' day."

Alan looked at him in some surprise; he had hardly expected just that stand on the part of a confirmed old bachelor like his uncle. The old man's glance swept dreamily over the green fields on either side of the road across which the red rays of the setting sun were streaming. Then he took a deep breath and lowered the reins till they rested on the backs of the horses.

"My boy," he began, "I'm a good mind to tell you some 'n' that I hain't mentioned fer mighty nigh forty yeer. I don't believe anything but my intrust in that town gal an' you would make me bring it up. Huh! Ray Miller says you kin pass 'er over jest as ef you'd never seed 'er, does he? An' go on an' pick an' choose agin. Huh! I wasn't as old as you are by five yeer when the one I'm talkin' about passed away, jest a week after me 'n' her 'd come to a understandin'. I've seed women, women, women, sence I seed 'er corpse that day amongst all that pile o' wild flowers that old an' young fetched from the woods whar me 'n' 'er used to walk, but ef I live to be as old as that thar hill I 'll never forget my feelin'. I kin see 'er right now as plain as I did then, an' sometimes my heart aches as bad. I reckon you know now why I never got married. Folks has poked a lots o' fun at me, an' I tuck it as it was intended, but a lots o' times what they said made me suffer simply awful. They've picked out this un an' that un, from spring chickins to hags o' all ages, shapes, an' sizes; but the very thought o' givin' anybody her place made me sick. Thar never was but one fer me. I may be a fool, but I believe I was intended fer her. Shucks! Sech skip-abouts as Miller may talk sech bosh as that, but it's because the Lord never give 'em the glory o' the other thing. It larnt me the truth about the after-life; I know thar's a time to come, an' a blessed one, ur the Lord never would 'a' give me that taste of it. She's som 'er's out o' harm's way, an' when me 'n' her meet I 'll not have a wrinkle, an' I 'll be able to walk as spry an' hopeful as I did when she was heer. Thar ort to be punishment reserved fer hard-headed fools that separate lovin' young folks beca'se one ur t'other hain't jest so many dollars tied in a rag. Don't you listen to Miller. I don't say you ort to plunge right in an' make the old man mad; but don't give up. Ef she's what I think she is, an' she sees you ain't a-goin' to run after no fresh face, she 'll stick to you like the bark on a tree. The wait won't hurt nuther one of you, either. My wait ain't a-hurtin' me, an' yore'n won't you. I never seed a young woman I liked better 'n I do the one you selected, an' I've sent up many a petition that you'd both make it all right."

The old man raised his reins and clucked to his horses.

"Uncle Ab," said Alan, "you've made a better man of me. I've had a lot of trouble over this, but you make me hope. I've tried to give her up, but I simply cannot do it."

"She ain't a-goin' to give you up, nuther," replied Abner; "that's the purty part about it. Thar ain't no give up in 'er. She ain't that sort. She's goin' to give that daddy o' her'n a tussle."

CHAPTER XI

ONE morning early in July, as Alan was passing Pole Baker's cabin, on his way to Darley, Pole's wife came out to the fence and stopped him. She was a slender, ill-clad woman, who had once been pretty, and her face still had a sort of wistful attractiveness that was appealing to one who knew what she had been through since her marriage.

"Are you goin' to town, Mr. Alan?" she asked, nervously.

"Yes, Mrs. Baker," Alan answered. "Is there anything I can do for you?"

She did not reply at once, but came through the little gate, which swung on wooden hinges, and stood looking up at him, a thin, hesitating hand on his bridle-rein.

"I'm afeerd some 'n' s happened to Pole," she faltered. "He hain't been home fer two whole days an' nights. It's about time fer 'im to spree agin, an' I'm powerful afeerd he's in trouble. I 'lowed while you was in town that you mought inquire about 'im, an' let me know when you come back. That ud sorter free my mind a little. I didn't close my eyes all last night."

"I 'll do all I can, Mrs. Baker," Alan promised. "But you mustn't worry; Pole can take care of himself, drunk or sober. I 'll be back to-night."

Alan rode on, leaving the pathetic figure at the gate looking after him. "I wonder," he mused, "what Uncle Ab would say about love that has that sort of reward. Poor woman! Pole was her choice, and she has to make the best of it. Perhaps she loves the good that's in the rascal."

He found Rayburn Miller at his desk, making out some legal document. "Take a seat," said Miller, "I 'll be through in a minute. What's the news out your way?" he asked, as he finished his work and put down his pen.

"Nothing new, I believe," said Alan. "I've been away for two days. Not having anything else to do, I made it my business to ride over every foot of my father's big investment, and, to tell you the truth, I've come to you with a huge idea. Don't laugh; I can't help it. It popped in my head and sticks, that's all."

"Good. Let me have it."

"Before I tell you what it is," said Alan, "I want you to promise not to ridicule me. I'm as green as a gourd in business matters; but the idea has hold of me, and I don't know that even your disapproval will make me let it loose."

"That's a good way to put it," laughed Miller. "The idea has hold of you and you can't let it loose. It applies more closely to investments than anything else. Once git into a deal and you are afraid to let it go—like the chap that held the calf and called for help."

"Well, here it is," said Alan. "I've made up my mind that a railroad can—and shall—be built from these two main lines to my father's lumber bonanza." Miller whistled. A broad smile ingulfed the pucker of his lips, and then his face dropped into seriousness. A look almost of pity for his friend's credulity and inexperience came into his eyes.

"I must say you don't want a little thing, my boy," he said, indulgently. "Remember you are talking to a fellow that has rubbed up against the moneyed world considerable for a chap raised in the country. The trouble with you, Alan, is that you have got heredity to contend with; you are a chip off the old block in spite of your belonging to a later generation. You have inherited your father's big ideas. You are a sort of Colonel Sellers, who sees millions in everything you look at."

Alan' s face fell, but there remained in it a tenacious expression that won Miller's admiration even while he deplored it. There was, too, a ring of confidence in the young farmer's tone when he replied:

"How much would a railroad through that country, eighteen miles in length, cost?"

"Nothing but a survey by an expert could answer that, even approximately," said the lawyer, leaning back in his creaking chair. "If you had the right of way, a charter from the State, and no big tunnels to make nor long bridges to build, you might, I should say, construct the road alone—without locomotives and rolling-stock generally—for a little matter of one hundred and fifty thousand. I don't know; I'm only guessing; but it wouldn't fall under that estimate."

"I didn't think it would," replied Alan, growing more enthusiastic. "Now then, if there *was* a railroad to my father's property, how much would his twenty thousand acres be worth?"

Miller smiled again and began to figure on a scrap of paper with a pencil. "Oh, as for that," he said, "it would really be worth—standing uncut, unsawn, including a world of tan-bark—at least twenty-five dollars an acre, say a clear half million for it all. Oh, I know it looks as plain as your nose on your face; things always do on paper. It looks big and it shines; so does a spider-web in the sunshine to a fly; but you don't want to be no fly, my boy; and you don't want any spider-webs—on the brain, anyway."

Alan stood up and walked to the door and back; finally he shrugged his broad shoulders. "I don't care what you say," he declared, bringing his hand down firmly on Miller's desk. "It will pay, as sure as I'm alive. There's no getting around the facts. It will take a quarter of a million investment to market a half-million-dollar bunch of timber with the land thrown in and the traffic such a road would secure to help pay expenses. There are men in the world looking for such opportunities and I'm going to give somebody a chance."

"You have not looked deep enough into it, my boy," mildly protested Miller. "You haven't figured on the enormous expense of running such a road and the dead loss of the investment after the lumber is moved out. You'd have a railroad property worth a quarter of a million on your hands. I can't make you see my position. I simply say to you that I wouldn't touch a deal like that with a ten-foot pole."

Alan laughed good-naturedly as he laid his hand on his friend's shoulder. "I reckon you think I'm off," he said, "but sooner or later I'm going to put this thing through. Do you hear me? I 'll put it through if it takes ten years to do it. I want to make the old man feel that he has not made such a fool of himself; I want to get even with the Thompson crowd, and Perkins, and everybody that is now poking fun at a helpless old man. I shall begin by raising money some way or other to pay taxes, and hold on to every inch of the ground."

Miller's glance fell before the fierce fire of Alan's eyes, and for the first time his tone wavered.

"Well," he said, "you may have the stuff in you that big speculators are made of, and I may simply be prejudiced against the scheme on account of your father's blind plunging, and what some men would call over-cautiousness on my part. I may be trying to prevent what you really ought to do; but I am advising you as a friend. I only know *I* would be more cautious. Of course, you may try. You'd not lose in doing that; in fact, you'd gain experience. I should say that big dealers in lumber are the men you ought to see first. They know the values of such investments, and they are reaching out in all directions now. They have cleaned up the timber near the railroads."

CHAPTER XII

MILLER accompanied Alan to the door. Old Trabue stood in front of his office in his shirt-sleeves, his battered silk hat on the back part of his head. He was fanning himself with a palm-leaf fan and freely using his handkerchief on his brow. He bowed cordially to Alan and came towards him.

"I want to ask you," he began, "as Pole Baker any way of raisin' money?"

"Not that I know of," laughed Alan. "I don't know whether he's got a clear title to the shirt on his back. He owes everybody out our way. My father is supplying him on time now."

"That was my impression," said Trabue. "He wanted me to defend 'im the other day, but he couldn't satisfy me about the fee, an' I let him go. He first said he could give me a lien on a mule, but he finally admitted that it wasn't his."

"He's not in trouble, is he?" exclaimed Alan, suddenly recalling Mrs. Baker's uneasiness.

Trabue looked at Miller, who stood leaning in the doorway, and laughed. "Well, I reckon he might call it that. That chap owned the town two days ago. He got blind, stavin' drunk, an' wanted to whip us from one end o' the place to the other. The marshals are afraid of 'im, for they know he 'll shoot at the drop of a hat, an' the butt of it was stickin' out o' his hippocket in plain sight. Was you thar, Rayburn? Well, it was better 'n a circus. Day before yesterday thar was a sort o' street temperance lecturer in front o' the Johnston House, speakin' on a dry-goods box. He had a lot o' gaudy pictures illustratin' the appearance of a drinkin' man' s stomach an' liver, compared to one in a healthy condition. He was a sort of a snide faker, out fer what he could git dropped in a hat, an' Pole was sober enough to git on to his game. Pole stood thar with the rest, jest about able to stand, an' that was all. Finally, when the feller got warmed up an' got to screechin', Pole begun to deny what he was sayin'. As fast as he'd make a statement Pole would flatly deny it. The feller on the box didn't know what a tough customer he had to handle or he'd 'a' gone slow. As it was, he p'inted a finger o' scorn at Pole an' helt 'im up fer a example. Pole wasn't sober by a long shot, but you'd 'a' thought he was, fer he was as steady as a post. He kept grinnin', as cool as a cucumber, an' sayin', 'Now you know yo' re a-lyin', stranger—jest a-lyin' to get a few dimes drapped in yore hat. You know nobody's stomach don't look like that durn chromo. You never seed inside of a drinkin' man, an' yo' re the biggest liar that ever walked the earth.' This made the crowd laugh at the little, dried-up feller, an' he got as mad as Old Nick. He begun to tell Pole his liver was swelled from too much whiskey, an' that he'd bet he was jest the sort to beat his wife. Most of us thought that ud make Pole jump on 'im, but he seemed to enjoy naggin' the feller too much to sp'ile it by a fight. A nigger boy had been carryin' round a bell and a sign advertisin' Webb's auction sale, an' stopped to see the fun. Pole heerd the tinkle of the bell, an' tuck it an' begun to ring it in the lecturer's face. The harder the feller spoke the harder Pole rung. It was the damnedest racket ever heerd on a public square. Part of the crowd—the good church folks—begun to say it was a disgrace to the town to allow a stranger to be treated that away, sence thar was no law agin public speakin' in the streets. They was in fer callin' a halt, but all the rest—the drinkin' men, an' I frankly state I was one—secretly hoped Pole would ring 'im down. When the pore devil finally won I felt like yellin' hooray, fer I glory in the pluck even of a dare-devil, if he's a North Georgian an' white. The lecturer had to stop without his collection, an' went off to the council chamber swearin' agin the town fer allowin' him to be treated that away. Thar wasn't anything fer the mayor to do but order Pole's arrest, but it took four men—two regulars and two deputized men—to accomplish it.

"The trial was the richest thing I ever attended. Pole had sobered up jest enough to be witty, an' he had no more respect fer Bill Barrett's court than he had fer the lecturer's platform. Him an' Barrett used to fish an' hunt together when they was boys, an' Pole kept callin' him Bill. It was Bill this an' Bill that; an' as Barrett had only been in office a month, he hardly knew how to rise to his proper dignity, especially when he saw the crowd was laughin' at his predicament. When I declined to defend 'im, Pole attempted to read the law on the case to Barrett an' show whar he was right. Barrett let 'im talk because he didn't know how to stop 'im, an' Pole made the best defence I ever heerd from a unlettered man. It kept the crowd in a roar. For a while I swear it looked like Pole was goin' to cleer hisse'f, but Barrett had to do his duty, an' so he fined Pole thirty dollars, or in default thereof to break rock on the streets fer ten days. You ort to 'a' heerd Pole snort. 'Looky heer, Bill!' he said, 'you know as well as yo're a-settin' cocked up thar, makin' folks say 'yore honor' ever' breath they draw, that I ain't a-goin' to break no rock in that br'ilin' sun fer ten day 'ca'se I beat that skunk at his own game!'

"You 'll have to do it if you don't pay out," Barrett told 'im.

"'Well, I jest won't pay out, an' I won't break rock nuther,' Pole said. 'You've heerd about the feller that could lead a hoss to water but couldn't make 'im drink, hain't you? Well, I'm the hoss.'

"Yesterday was Pole's fust day on the street. They put a ball an' chain to one of his ankles an' sent 'im out with the nigger gang, but all day yesterday an' to-day he hain't worked a lick. He's as stubborn as a mule. Thar's been a crowd around 'im all the time. You kin see 'im standin' up as straight as a post in the middle of the street from one end of it to the other. I'm sorter sorry fer 'im; he looks like he's ashamed at bottom, but don't want to give in. The funniest thing about the whole thing is that Pole seems to know more about the law than the mayor. He says unless they force him to work in the specified ten days they can't hold him any longer, an' that if they attempt to flog 'im he 'll kill the first man that lays hands on him. I think Bill Barrett likes him too well to have 'im whipped, an' the whole town is guyin' him, an' axin' 'im why he don't make Pole set in."

Alan went down the street to see Pole. He found him seated on a large stone, a long-handled rock-hammer at his feet. He looked up from under his broad-brimmed hat, and a crestfallen look came into his big, brown eyes.

"I'm sorry to see this, Pole," said Alan.

Pole stood up at his full height, the chain clanking as he rose. "They hain't treated me right about this matter, Alan Bishop," he said, half resentfully, half as if he recognized his own error. "Bill knows he hain't done the fair thing. I know I was full, but I jest wanted to have my fun. That don't justify him in puttin' me out heer with these niggers fer folks to gap' at, an' he knows it. He ain't a friend right. Me 'n' him has slep' together on the same pile o' leaves, an' I've let 'im pull down on a squirrel when I could 'a' knocket it from its perch; an' I've lent 'im my pointer an' gun many an' many a time. But he's showed what he is! He's got the wrong sow by the yeer, though, fer ef he keeps me heer till Christmas I 'll never crack a rock, unless I do it by accidentally step-pin' on it. Mark my words, Alan Bishop, thar 'll be trouble out o' this."

"Don't talk that way, Pole," said Alan. "You've broken the law and they had to punish you for it. If they hadn't they would have made themselves ridiculous. Why didn't you send me word you were in trouble, Pole?"

The fellow hung his head, and then he blurted out:

"Beca'se I knowed you would make a fool o' yorese'f an' try to pay me out. Damn it, Alan Bishop, this ain't no business o' yore'n!"

"I 'll make it my business," said Alan. "How much is your fine? You ought to have sent me word."

"Sent you hell, Alan Bishop," growled the prisoner. "When I send you word to he'p me out of a scrape that whiskey got me into I'll do it after I've decently cut my throat. I *say!*—when you've plead with me like you have to quit the durn stuff!"

At this point of the conversation Jeff Dukes, a man of medium size, dressed in dark-blue uniform, with a nickel-plated badge shaped like a shield and bearing the words "Marshal No. 2," came directly towards them from a stone-cutter's shop near by.

"Look heer, Bishop," he said, dictatorially, "whar'd you git the right to talk to that man?"

Alan looked surprised. "Am I breaking the law, too?"

"You are, ef you hain't got a permit from the mayor in yore pocket."

"Well, I have no permit," replied Alan, with a good-natured smile. "Have you got another ball an' chain handy?"

The officer frowned off his inclination to treat the matter as a jest. "You ort to have more sense than that," he said, crustily. "Pole's put out heer to work his time out, an' ef everybody in town is allowed to laugh an' joke with him he'd crack about as many rocks as you or me."

"You are a durn liar, Jeff Dukes," said Pole, angrily. "You are a-makin' that up to humiliate me furder. You know no law like that never was inforced. Ef I ever git you out in Pea Vine Destrict I'll knock a dent in that egg-shaped head o' yor'n, an' make them eyes look two ways fer Sunday. You know a gentleman like Alan Bishop wouldn't notice you under ordinary circumstances, an' so you trump up that excuse to git his attention."

The two men glared at each other, but Pole seemed to get the best of that sort of combat, for the officer only growled.

"You can insult a man when you are under arrest," he said, "beca'se you know I am under bond to keep the peace. But I'm not afeerd of you."

"They tell me you are afeerd o' sperits, though," retorted the prisoner. "They tell me a little nigger boy that was shot when a passle o' skunks went to whip his daddy fer vagrancy stands at the foot o' yore bed ever' night. Oh, I know what I'm a-talkin' about!"

"Yes, you know a lots," said the man, sullenly, as his eyes fell.

To avoid encouraging the disputants further, Alan walked suddenly away. The marshal took willing advantage of the opportunity and followed him.

"I could make a case agin you," he said, catching up, "but I know you didn't mean to violate the ordinance."

"No, of course I didn't," said Alan; "but I want to know if that fellow could be released if I paid his fine."

"You are not fool enough to do it, are you?"

"That's what I am."

"Have you got the money in yore pocket?" The officer was laughing, as if at a good joke.

"I have."

"Well"—the marshal laughed again as he swung his short club round by a string that fastened it to his wrist—"well, you come with me, an' I 'll show you a man that wants thirty dollars wuss than any man I know of. I don't believe Bill Barrett has slept a wink sence this thing happened. He 'll be tickled to death to git off so easy. The town has devilled the life out of him. He don't go by whar Pole's at work—I mean, whar he ain't at work—fer Pole yells at 'im whenever he sees 'im."

That night when Alan reached home he sent a servant over to tell Mrs. Baker that Pole was all right and that he'd be home soon. He had eaten his supper and had gone up-stairs to go to bed when he heard his name called outside. Going to a window and looking out, he recognized Pole Baker standing at the gate in the clear moonlight.

"Alan," he said, softly, "come down heer a minute. I want to see you."

Alan went down and joined him. For a moment Pole stood leaning against the fence, his eyes hidden by his broad-brimmed slouch hat.

"Did you want to see me, Pole?" Alan asked.

"Yes, I did," the fellow swallowed. He made a motion as if to reach out his hand, but refrained. Then he looked straight into Alan's face.

"I couldn't go to sleep till I'd said some 'n' to you," he began, with another gulp. "I laid down an' made a try at it, but it wasn't no go. I've got to say it. I'm heer to swear that ef God, or some 'n' else, don't show me a way to pay you back fer what you done to-day, I 'll never draw a satisfied breath. Alan Bishop, yo're a man, *God damn it!* a man from yore outside skin to the marrow o' yore bones, an' ef I don't find some way to prove what I think about you, I 'll jest burn up! I got into that trouble as thoughtless as I'd play a prank with my baby, an' then they all come down on me an' begun to try to drive me like a hog out'n a field with rocks an' sticks, an' the very Old Harry riz in me an' defied 'em. I reckon thar wasn't anything Bill could do but carry out the law, an' I knowed it, but I wasn't ready to admit it. Then you come along an' rendered a verdict in my favor when you needed the money you did it with. Alan, ef I don't show my appreciation, it 'll be beca'se I don't live long enough. You never axed me but one thing, an' that was to quit drinkin' whiskey. I'm goin' to make a try at it, not beca'se I think that 'll pay you back, but beca'se with a sober head I kin be a better friend to you ef the chance ever comes my way."

"I'm glad to hear you say that, Pole," replied Alan, greatly moved by the fellow's earnestness. "I believe you can do it. Then your wife and children—"

"Damn my wife an' children," snorted Pole. "It's *you* I'm a-goin' to work fer—*you*, I say!"

He suddenly turned through the open gate and strode homeward across the fields. Alan stood looking after him till his tall form was lost in the hazy moonlight, and then he went up to his bed.

Pole entered the open door of his cabin and began to undress as he sat on the side of his crude bedstead, made of unbarked poles fastened to the bare logs in one corner of the room. His wife and children slept on two beds on the other side of the room.

"Did you see 'im, Pole?" piped up Mrs. Baker from the darkness.

"Yes, I seed 'im. Sally, say, whar's that bottle o' whiskey I had the last time I was at home?"

There was an ominous silence. Out of it rose the soft breathing of the children. Then the woman sighed. "Pole, shorely you ain't a-goin' to begin agin?"

"No, I want to bu'st it into smithereens. I don't want it about—I don't want to know thar's a drap in the house. I've swore off, an' this time she sticks. Gi'me that bottle."

Another silence. Suddenly the woman spoke. "Pole, you've swore off as many times as a dog has fleas. Often when I feel bad an' sick when you are off, a drap o' whiskey makes me feel better. I don't want you to destroy the last bit in the house jest be-ca'se you've tuck this turn, that may wear off before daylight. The last time you emptied that keg on the ground an' swore off you got on a spree an' helt the baby over the well an' threatened to drap 'er in ef I didn't find a bottle, an' you'd 'a' done it, too."

Pole laughed softly. "I reckon yo're right, old gal," he said. "Besides, ef I can't—ef I ain't man enough to let up with a bottle in the house I won't do it without. But the sight or smell of it is hell itse'f to a lover of the truck. Ef I was to tell you what a little thing started me on this last spree you'd laugh. I went to git a shave in a barber shop, an' when the barber finished he soaked my face in bay-rum an' it got in my mustache. I kept smellin' it all mornin' an' tried to wipe it off, but she wouldn't wipe. All the time I kept walkin' up an' down in front o' Luke Sell-more's bar. Finally I said to myself: 'Well, ef you have to have a bar-room stuck under yore nose all day like a wet sponge, old man, you mought as well have one whar it 'll taste better, an' I slid up to the counter." The woman sighed audibly, but she made no reply. "Is Billy awake?" Pole suddenly asked.

"No, you know he ain't," said Mrs. Baker.

"Well, I want to take 'im in my bed." Pole stood out on the floor in the sheet of moonlight that fell through the open door.

"I wouldn't, Pole," said the woman. "The pore little feller's been toddlin' about after the others, draggin' bresh to the heap tell he's tired. He drapped to sleep at the table with a piece o' bread in his mouth."

"I won't wake 'im, God bless his little heart," answered Pole, and he reached down and took the limp child in his arms and pressed him against the side of his face. He carried him tenderly across the room and laid down with him. His wife heard him uttering endearing things to the unconscious child until she fell asleep.

CHAPTER XIII

IT was the second Sunday in July, and a bright, clear day. In that mountainous region the early mornings of dry summer days are delightfully cool and balmy. Abner Daniel was in his room making preparations to go to meeting at Rock Crest Church. He had put on one of his best white shirts, black silk necktie, doeskin trousers, flowered waistcoat, and long frock-coat, and was proceeding to black his shoes. Into an old pie-pan he raked from the back of the fireplace a quantity of soot and added to it a little water and a spoonful of sorghum molasses from a jug under his bed, stirring the mixture into a paste. This he applied to his shoes with a blacking-brush, rubbing vigorously until quite a decent gloss appeared. It was a thing poverty had taught him just after the war, and to which he still resorted when he forgot to buy blacking.

On his way to church, as he was crossing a broom-sedge field and steering for the wood ahead of him, through which a path made a short cut to Rock Crest Church, he overtook Pole Baker swinging along in his shirt-sleeves and big hat.

"Well, I 'll be bungfuzzled," Abner exclaimed, "ef you hain't got on a clean shirt! Church?"

"Yes, I 'lowed I would, Uncle Ab. I couldn't stay away. I told Sally it ud be the biggest fun on earth. She's a-comin' on as soon as she gits the childern ready. She's excited, too, an' wants to see how it 'll come out. She's as big a believer in you as I am, mighty nigh, an' she 'lowed, she did, that she'd bet you'd take hair an' hide off'n that gang 'fore they got good started."

Abner raised his shaggy eyebrows. If this was one of Pole's jokes it failed in the directness that usually characterized the jests of the ex-moonshiner.

"I wonder what yo' re a-drivin' at, you blamed fool," he said, smiling in a puzzled fashion.

Pole was walking in front, and suddenly wheeled about. He took off his hat, and, wiping the perspiration from his high brow with his forefinger, he cracked it into the broom-sedge like a whip.

"Looky' heer, Uncle Ab," he laughed, "what you givin' me?"

"I was jest tryin' to find out what you was a-givin' me," retorted the rural philosopher, a dry note of rising curiosity dominating his voice.

They had reached a rail fence which separated the field from the wood, and they climbed over it and stood in the shade of the trees. Pole stared at the old man incredulously. "By hunkley, Uncle Ab, you don't mean to tell me you don't know what that passle o' hill-Billies is a-goin' to do with you this mornin' at meetin'?"

Abner smiled mechanically. "I can't say I do, Pole. I'm at the fust of it, if thar is to be any—"

Pole slapped his thigh and gave vent to a loud guffaw that rang through the trees and was echoed back from a hidden hill-side.

"Well, what they *are* a-goin' to do with you 'll be a God's plenty. They are a-goin' to walk yore log, ur make you do it on all fours so they kin see you. You've made it hot fer them an' they are a-goin' to turn t'other cheek an' git a swipe at you. They are a-goin' to show you whar you come in—ur, ruther, whar you go out."

Abner's face was a study in seriousness. "You don't say!" he muttered. "I *did* notice that brother Dole kinder give our house a wide berth last night. I reckon he sorter hated to eat at the same table with a feller he was goin' to hit at to-day. Yes, Dole is at the bottom of it. I know in reason I pushed 'im too fur the last time he was heer, but when he rears back an' coughs up sanctimony like he was literally too full of it fer comfort, I jest cayn't hold in. Seems to me I kin jest close my eyes an' hit some spot in 'im that makes 'im wiggle like a tadpole skeered in shallow water. But maybe I mought 'a' got a better mark to fire at; fer this 'll raise no end of a rumpus, an' they may try to make me take back water, but I never did crawfish. I couldn't do that, Pole. No siree, I—I can' t crawfish."

Abner was a special object of regard as he and Pole emerged from the wood into the opening in front of the little unpainted meeting-house, where the men stood about among the buggies and horses, whittling, gossiping, and looking strange and fresh-washed in their clean clothes. But it was noticeable that they did not gather around him as had been their habit. His standing in that religious community was at stake; his continued popularity depended on the result of that day's investigation. Pole could afford to stand by him, and he did. They sat down on a log near the church door and remained silent till the cast-iron bell in the little belfry, which resembled

Abner Daniel | 79

a dog-kennel, was rattled vigorously as an announcement that the service was about to begin. They all scurried in like sheep. Abner went in last, with slow dignity and deliberation, leaving Pole in a seat near the door.

He went up the narrow aisle to his accustomed seat near the long-wood stove. Many eyes were on his profile and the back of his neck. Dole was seated in the arm-chair behind the preacher's stand, but somehow he failed to look at Abner as he entered, or even after he had taken his seat. He seemed busy making notes from the big Bible which lay across his lap. Abner saw Bishop and his wife come in and sit down, and knew from the glances they gave him that they had heard the news. Mrs. Bishop looked keenly distressed, but Bishop seemed to regard the matter only as a small, buzzing incident in his own troubled career. Besides, Abner was no blood relative of his, and Bishop had enough to occupy him in looking after the material interests of his own family without bothering about the spiritual welfare of a connection by marriage.

Dole stood up and announced a hymn, and read it from beginning to end in a mellow, sonorous voice. The congregation, all eying Abner, rose and sang it energetically; even Abner, who sang a fair bass of the rasping, guttural variety, popular in the mountains, found himself joining in, quite unconcerned as to his future right to do so. After this, Dole led in prayer, standing with both hands resting on the crude, unpainted stand, the sole ornament of which was a pitcher of water, a tumbler, and a glass lamp with a green paper shade on it. Abner remarked afterwards that Dole, in this prayer, used the Lord as a cat's-paw to hit at him. Dole told the Lord a few things that he had never had the courage to tell Daniel. Abner was a black sheep in a flock earnestly striving to keep itself white—a thing in human shape that soiled that with which it came in contact. He had the subtle tongue of the serpent that blasted the happiness of the primeval pair in the Garden of Eden. Under the cloak of wit and wisdom he was continually dropping poison into the beverages of earnest folk who had not the religious courage to close their ears. As a member of a consecrated body of souls, it was the opinion of many that Abner was out of place, but that was to be decided after careful investigation in the Lord's presence and after ample testimony pro and con had been submitted. Any one wishing to show that the offending member had a right to remain in good standing would be gladly listened to, even prayerfully. On the other hand, such members as had had their religious sensibilities wounded should feel that a most sacred duty rested on them to speak their minds. All this Dole said he trusted the

Lord would sanction and bless in the name of the Lord Jesus Christ, the Saviour and Director of all men.

Dole then started another hymn, and when it had been sung he announced that no sermon would be preached that day, as the important business in hand would consume all available time before the dinner-hour. Then he courageously faced Abner. His countenance was pale and determined, his tone perfunctory and sharp as a knife.

"I reckon, brother Daniel," he said, "that you have a idee who I've been talkin' about?"

Abner was slightly pale, but calm and self-possessed. The light of merriment, always kindled by contact with Dole, danced in his eyes. "I kinder 'lowed I was the one," he said, slowly, "an' I'm sorter curis to see who' ll speak an' what they 'll say. I 'll tell you now I ain't a-goin' to do myse'f jestice. I 'ain't been to a debatin' club sence I was a boy, but I 'll do my best."

Dole stroked his beard and consulted a scrap of paper in the palm of his hand. "Brother Throg-martin," he called out, suddenly, and a short, fat man on a bench behind Abner rose and cleared his throat.

"Now, brother Throgmartin," went on the preacher, "jest tell some o' the things you've heerd brother Daniel say that struck you as bein' undoctrinal an' unbecomin' a member of this body."

"Well, sir," Throgmartin began, in a thin, high voice that cut the profound silence in the room like a rusty blade, "I don't raily, in my heart o' hearts, believe that Ab—brother Daniel—has the right interpretation of Scriptur'. I remember, after you preached last summer about the sacred teachin' in regard to future punishment, that Ab—brother Daniel—an' me was walkin' home together. Ever' now an' then he'd stop in the road an' laugh right out sudden-like over what you'd contended."

"Oh, he did, did he?" Dole's face hardened. He couldn't doubt that part of the testimony, for it was distinctly Abner's method.

"Yes, sir," responded Throgmartin, sternly, "he 'lowed what you'd said was as funny to him as a circus clown's talk, an' that it was all he could do to hold in. He 'lowed ef you was to git up in a Darley church with sech talk as that they'd make you preach to niggers. He 'lowed he didn't believe hell was any hot place nohow, an' that he never could be made to believe that the Lord ud create folks an' then barbecue 'em alive through all eternity. He said it sorter turned his stomach to see jest a little lamb roasted at a big political gatherin', an' that no God he believed in would institute sech long torture as you spoke about when you brought up the mustard-seed p'int."

"He deliberately gives the lie to Holy Scripture, then," said Dole, almost beside himself with rage. "What else did he say of a blasphemous nature?"

"Oh, I hardly know," hesitated the witness, his brow wrinkled thoughtfully.

"Well," snarled Dole, "you hain't told half you said to me this mornin' on the way to meetin'. What was his remark about the stars havin' people on 'em ever' bit an' grain as worthy o' salvation as us all?"

"I disremember his exact words. Perhaps Ab—brother Daniel—will refresh my memory." Throg-martin was gazing quite respectfully at the offender. "It was at Billy Malone's log-rollin', you know, Ab; me 'n' you'd eat a snack together, an' you said the big poplar had strained yore side an' wanted to git it rubbed."

Abner looked straight at Dole. The corners of his big, honest mouth were twitching defiantly.

"I said, I think," he answered, "that no matter what some folks mought believe about the starry heavens, no man ever diskivered a big world with a tail to it through a spy-glass without bein' convinced that thar was other globes in the business besides jest this un."

Dole drew himself up straight and gazed broadly over his congregation. He felt that in the estimation of unimaginative, prosaic people like his flock Abner's defence would certainly fall.

"Kin I ax," he asked, sternly, "how you happen to think like you do?"

Abner grasped the back of the bench in front of him and pulled himself up, only to sink back hesitatingly into his seat. "Would it be out o' order fer me to stand?" he questioned.

Dole spread a hard, triumphant smile over the congregation. "Not at all, if it will help you to give a sensible answer to my question."

"Oh, I kin talk settin'," retorted the man on trial. "I jest didn't know what was right an' proper, an' I 'lowed I could hit that spit-box better standin' than I kin over brother Tarver's legs."

The man referred to quickly slid along the bench, giving Abner his place near the aisle, and Abner calmly emptied his mouth in the wooden box filled with sawdust and wiped his lips.

"I hardly know why I think like I do about other worlds," he answered, slowly, "unless it's beca'se I've always had the notion that the universe is sech a powerful, whoppin' big thing. Most folks believe that the spot they inhabit is about all thar is to creation, anyway. That's human natur'. About the biggest job I ever tackled was to drive a hungry cow from bad grass into a good patch. She wants to stay thar an' eat, an' that's about the way it is with folks. They are short-sighted. It makes most of 'em mad to tell 'em they kin better the'r condition. I've always believed that's the reason they make the bad place out so bad; they've made up the'r minds to live thar, an' they ain't a-goin' to misrepresent it. They are out o' fire-wood in this life an' want to have a good sweat in the next."

CHAPTER XIV

IT looked as if Dole thought he could get down to the matter better out of the pulpit, so he descended the steps on the side near Abner, and stood on the floor inside the altar railing.

"We didn't assemble heer to argue with brother Daniel," he informed the congregation, "fer that's evidently jest what he'd like. It would be raily kind of you all to consider what he's jest said as the product of a weak brain ruther 'n a bad heart. Brother Throgmartin, have you any other charges to prefer agin brother Daniel?" Dole looked as if he had already been apprised of the extent of the witness's testimony.

"That's all I keer to say," replied the man addressed, and he coughed.

Dole consulted the scrap of paper in his hand, and while he did so Abner stole a glance at Bishop and his wife. Mrs. Bishop had her handkerchief to her eyes as if she were crying, and her husband's face wore the impatient look of a man detained by trivialities.

"Brother Daniel," the preacher began, suddenly, "charges has been preferred agin you on the score that you are a profane man. What have you got to say on that line?"

Abner bent his head and spat down into the hopper-shaped box in the aisle.

"I hardly know, brother Dole," he said. "It's all owin' to what profanity is an' what it hain't. I don't know that I ever used but one word out o' the general run, an' that is 'dem.' I don't believe thar's any more harm in sayin' 'dem' than 'scat,' ur gruntin' when thar's no absolute call fer it. I don't know as anybody knows what it means. I don't. I've axed a number o' times, but nobody could tell me, so I knowed it wasn't patented anyway. Fer a long time I 'lowed nobody used it but me. I met a feller from up in Yankeedom that said 'darn,' an' another from out West that said 'dang,' so I reckon they are all three in a bunch."

At this juncture some one in the rear of the church laughed out, and the entire congregation turned its head. It was Pole Baker. He was red in the face, had his big hand pressed tightly over his mouth, and was bent over the bench towards the open doorway. Abner's eyes sparkled with appreciative merriment as he saw him, but he did not permit himself to smile. Dole could not hide his irritation, for Pole's unalloyed enjoyment had communicated itself to some of the less rigid members, and he felt that the reply which was stinging his tongue would fall less forcefully than if the incident hadn't happened.

He held up his hand to invoke silence and respect. "I believe such a word, to say the least, is unbecoming in a Christian, and I think the membership will back me up in it."

"I don't look at it that away," argued Abner. "I'd be above takin' the Lord's name in vain, but a little word that nobody cayn't find no fault with or tell its origin shorely is different."

"Well, that 'll be a matter to decide by vote."

Dole paused a moment and then introduced another topic.

"A report has gone round among the members that you said that red-handed murderer who killed a man over in Fannin' an' was hung, an' passed on without a single prayer fer pardon to his Maker—that he'd stand a chance fer redemption. In all my experience I've never heerd sech a dangerous doctrin' as that, brother Daniel—never, as I myself hope to be redeemed."

"I said he'd have a chance—I *thought*," said Abner. "I reckon I must 'a' got that idee from what Jesus said to the thief on the cross. You see, brother Dole, I believe the Almighty gives us all equal chances, an' I don't believe that feller in Fannin' had as good a opportunity to git his heart saftened as the feller did that was dyin' right alongside o' the great Redeemer o' the world. Nobody spoke a kind word to the Fannin' man; on the contrary, they was hootin' an' spittin' at 'im night an' day, an' they say the man he killed had pestered 'im all his life. Scriptur' says we ort to forgive a man seventy times seven, an' that is four hundred an' ninety. Why they didn't make it even five hundred I never could tell. An' yet you-uns try to make folks believe the Lord that made us, frail as we are an' prone to sin, won't forgive us once ef we happen to die sudden. Shucks! that doctrine won't hold water; it's hide-bound an' won't stretch one bit. It seems to me that the trouble with yore—"

"We haven't time to listen to a speech on the subject," interrupted the preacher, whose anger was inflamed by hearing Pole Baker sniggering. "If thar is anybody else that has anything to say we'd be glad to hear from 'em."

Then Mrs. Bishop rose, wiping her eyes. She was pale and deeply agitated. "I jest want to ax you all to be lenient with my pore brother," she began, her thin voice cracking under its strain. "I've predicted that he'd bring disrepute down on us with his ready tongue an' odd notions. I've tried an' tried to stop 'im, but it didn't do a bit o' good."

"It's very good of you to speak in his behalf," said Dole, as she sank back into her seat. "I'm sure the membership will do its duty, sister Bishop."

Then a little, meanly clad man behind Daniel stood up. It was Jasper Marmaduke, a ne 'er-do-well farmer, who had a large family, few friends, and no earthly possessions. He was greatly excited, and as white as if he were on trial for his life.

"I ain't no member," he began. "I know I ort to be, but I hain't. I don't know whether a outsider's got a right to chip into this or not, but it seems to me I 'll bu'st wide open ef I don't git up heer an' say as loud as I kin holler that Abner Daniel's the best man I ever seed, knowed, ur heerd tell of." Tears were on the man's face and his voice shook with emotion. "He's fetched food an' medicine over to my folks an' run after a doctor when all the rest o' humanity had turned the'r backs on us. He made me promise not to cheep it to a soul, but I'm a-goin' to tell it—tell it, ef he never speaks to me agin. I ain't no godly man, an' this thing's makin' me so mad I feel like throwin' rocks!" And with a sob bursting from him, Marmaduke strode from the church with a loud clatter of his untied shoes.

"Good! Good man!" spoke up Pole Baker, impulsively, unconscious of where he was. "Jas', yo're the right stuff." And then, in the dead silence that followed his ejaculation, Pole realized what he had said and lowered his head in red embarrassment, for Dole's fierce eyes were bearing down on him. The preacher's pent-up wrath burst; he was really more infuriated at the man who had just left the church, but he had to make an example of some one, and Pole had laid himself open to attack.

"This is no place fer rowdies," he snarled. "That outlaw back thar who has been continually disturbing these proceedings ort to be jailed. He's undertakin' to bring his violations of decency into the very house of God."

A vast surprise clutched the congregation, who, knowing Pole, scented trouble. And Pole did not disappoint them. With his flabby hat in his brawny grasp, Pole stood up, but his wife, who sat on the women's side across the aisle from him with her three eldest children, stepped to him and drew him back in his seat, sitting by him and whispering imploringly. Dole stared fiercely for a moment, and then, seeing that the disturbance was over, he shrugged his broad shoulders and applied himself to the business in hand.

"Is thar anybody else pro or con that ud like to be heerd?"

It was the widow Pellham, sitting well towards the front, who now rose. "I feel like Jas' Marmaduke does," she began, falteringly. Her hearers could not see her face, for she wore a black calico sunbonnet, and it was tilted downward. "I believe I 'll be committin' of a grievous sin ef I let my natural back'ard-ness keep me quiet. Abner Daniel was the fust, last, an' only pusson that made me see the true way into God's blessed sunshine out o' the pitch-black darkness that was over me. All of you, especially them livin' nigh me, knowed how I acted when my daughter Mary died. We'd lived together sence she was born, an' after her pa passed away she was all I had. Then God up an' tuck 'er. I tell you it made a devil out'n me. I liter'ly cussed my Maker an' swore revenge agin 'Im. I quit meetin' an' closed my door agin my neighbors. They all tried to show me whar I was wrong, but I wouldn't listen. Some nights I set up from dark till daylight without candle or fire, bemeanin' my God fer the way He'd done me. You remember, brother Dole, that you come a time or two an' prayed an' read, but I didn't budge out'n my cheer an' wouldn't bend a knee. Then that other little preacher, that was learnin' to preach, an' tuck yore place when you went off to bury yore mother—he come an' made a set at me, but every word he said made me wuss. I ordered *him* off the hill, an' told 'im ef he appeared agin I'd set my dog on 'im. I don't know why everybody made me so mad, but they did. The devil had me by the leg, an' was a-drag-gin' me as fast to his hole as a dog kin trot. But one mornin' Abner Daniel come over with that thar devilish twinkle in his eyes that ud make a cow laugh, an' begun to banter me to sell 'im the hay off'n my little neck o' land betwixt the creek an' the road. I kept tellin' 'im I didn't want to sell, but he kept a-com-in' an' a comin', with no end o' fool talk about this un an' that un, tell somehow I got to watchin' fer 'im, but still I wouldn't let nobody else in. Then one day, after I'd refused to sell an' told 'im I'd *give* 'im the hay, he growed serious an' said, ses he: 'Sister Pellham, I don't want the hay on that patch. I've been deliberately lyin'. I've been comin' over heer as a friend, to try to make you feel better.' Then he set in, an', as God is my highest judge, ef thar 'll be any more speritual talk on t'other shore it 'll be after Abner Daniel gits thar. He jest rolled me about in his hands like a piece o' wheat dough. He showed me what aileded me as plain as I could p'int out the top o' old Bald Mountain to you on a cleer day. He told me, I remember, that in grievin' like I was, I was sinnin' agin the Holy Ghost, an' jest as long as I did it I'd suffer wuss an' wuss as a penalty. He said it was a fight betwixt me an' my Maker an' that I was bound to be worsted. He said that when my Mary come into the world I couldn't tell whar she was from, nur why the Lord had fetched 'er, but I was jest pleased beca'se it suited me to be pleased, but, ses he, when she went back into the great mystery o' God's beautiful plan I wasn't satisfied beca'se it didn't suit me to be. He said it was downright selfishness, that had no part nur parcel in the kingdom o' heaven. He said to me, ses he, 'Sister, ef you 'll jest fer one minute make up yore mind that Mary is in better hands 'an she was in yor'n '—an' you kin bet yore bottom dollar she is—'you 'll feel as light as a feather. 'I had a tussle, but it come, God bless him! it come. It was jest like a great light had bu'sted over me. I fell down on my knees before 'im an' shouted an' shouted till I was as limp as a wet rag. I had always thought I was converted away back in the sixties when I was a gal, but I wasn't. I got my redemption that day under Abner Daniel's talk, an' I shall bless 'im an' sing his name on my dyin' bed. I don't want to entertain no spiteful feelin' s, but ef he goes out I 'll have to. I wouldn't feel right in no church too puore to fellowship with Abner Daniel."

"Good! Good woman!" shouted Pole Baker, as if he were at a political speaking. She sat down. The house seemed profoundly moved. People were thinking of the good things they had heard about Abner Daniel. However, the turn of affairs did not suit Dole, who showed decided anger. His eyes flashed as they rested on Pole Baker, who had offended him again.

"I shall have to ax that law-breaker back thar to leave the church," he said. "I think it's come to a purty pass ef strong, able-bodied church-members will set still an' allow the'r own house o' worship to be insulted by such a rascal as that one."

Pole rose; many thought he was going to leave, but to the surprise of all he walked deliberately up to the altar and laid his hand upon the railing.

"Looky' heer," he said, "they call you the fightin' preacher. They say you believe in hittin' back when yo' re hit. I'm heer to show you that ef I am a outlaw I ain't afeerd o' you, an' I ain't a-goin' to be abused by you when you are under the cloak o' this meetin'. When you say some 'n' you think is purty good you wink at some brother in the amen-corner an' he yells 'Amen 'loud enough to be heerd to the cross-roads. Then you go on as if nothin' had happened. What I said back thar was jest my way o' sayin' amen. Little Jas' Marmaduke hit you in a weak spot; so did what Mis' Pellham said, an' yo' re tryin' to take yore spite out on me. That won't work. I come heer to see fair play, an' I'm a-goin' to do it. Uncle Ab's a good man an' I'm heer to testify to it. He's come nigher—him an' Alan Bishop, that's a chip off'n 'im—to turn me into the right way than all the shoutin'-bees I ever attended, an' I've been to as many as thar are hairs on my head. I ain't bald, nuther. Now ef you want to have it out with me jest wait an' meet me outside, whar we 'll both have fair play."

Dole was quivering with rage. "I kin whip a dozen dirty scoundrels like you," he panted. "Men like you insult ministers, thinking they won't fight, but after meetin' I 'll simply wipe up the ground with you."

"All right, 'nough said!" and Pole sat down. There was silence for a moment. Dole's furious panting could be heard all over the room. Then Abner Daniel rose. A vast change had come over him. The light of quizzical merriment had faded from his face; nothing lay there except the shadows of deepest regret. "I've been wrong—wrong—*wrong!*" he said, loudly. "I'm dead wrong, ur Pole Baker never would 'a' wanted to fight, an' brother Dole wouldn't 'a' been driv' to lose his temper in the pulpit. I'm at the bottom o' all this rumpus that has kept you all from listenin' to a good sermon. You've not found me hard to git along with when I see my error, an' I promise that I 'll try from this day on to keep from shovin' my notions on folks that ain't ready fer 'em. I want to stay in the church. I think every sane man an' woman kin do good in a church, an' I want to stay in this un."

The confession was so unexpected, and furnished Dole with such an easy loop-hole for gracefully retiring from a most unpleasant predicament, that he actually beamed on the speaker.

"I don't think any more need be said," he smiled. "Brother Daniel has shown himself willing to do the right thing, an' I propose that the charges be dropped." Thereupon a vote was taken, and it went overwhelmingly in Abner's favor. After the benediction, which followed immediately, Pole Baker hurried across to Daniel. "I declare, you make me sick, Uncle Ab," he grumbled. "What on earth did you mean by takin' back-water? You had 'im whar the wool was short; he was white at the gills. You could 'a' mauled the life out'n 'im. Ef I'd—"

But Abner, smiling indulgently, had a watchful eye on Dole, and was moving forward to shake the preacher's outstretched hand.

"Well, I 'll be damned!" Pole grunted, half aloud and in high disgust, as he pushed his way through the crowd to the door.

Abner found him waiting for him near the hitch-ing-post, where he had been to untie Bishop's horse.

"I reckon," he said, "bein' as you got so mighty good yorese'f, 'at you think I acted wrong."

"Not any wuss'n I did, Pole," replied the old man, seriously. "My advice to you is to go to Dole an' tell 'im you are sorry."

"Sorry hell!"

"It ud be better fer you," half smiled Abner. "Ef you don't, some o' them hill-Billies 'll make a case at court agin you fer disturbin' public worship. Before a grand jury o' mossbacks a man with yore record ud not stand any better chance o' comin' cleer 'n a old bird-nest ud o' makin' good soup. When you was a-runnin' of yore still it made you powerful mad to have revenue men after you, didn't it? Well, this heer shebang is Dole's still, my boy, whar he claims to make good sperits out'n bad material, an' he's got a license, which is more 'n you could 'a' said."

"I reckon yo' re right," said Pole. "I 'll wait fer 'im."

CHAPTER XV

IN the middle of the following week some of the young people of Darley gave a picnic at Morley's Spring, a beautiful and picturesque spot about a mile below Bishop's farm. Alan had received an urgent invitation to join the party, and he rode down after dinner.

It was a hot afternoon, and the party of a dozen couples had scattered in all directions in search of cool, shady nooks. Alan was by no means sure that Miss Barclay would be there, but, if the truth must be told, he went solely with the hope of at least getting another look at her. He was more than agreeably surprised, for, just as he had hitched his horse to a hanging bow of an oak near the spring, Frank Hillhouse came from the tangle of wild vines and underbrush on a little hill-side and approached him.

"You are just the fellow I'm looking for," said Frank. "Miss Dolly's over there in a hammock, and I want to leave somebody with her. Old man Morley promised me the biggest watermelon in his patch if I'd come over for it. I won't be long."

"Oh, I don't care how long you are," smiled Alan. "You can stay all day if you want to."

"I thought you wouldn't mind," grinned Frank. "I used to think you were the one man I had to fight, but I reckon I was mistaken. A feller in love imagines everybody in creation is against him."

Alan made no reply to this, but hurried away to where Dolly sat, a new magazine in her hands and a box of candies on the grass at her feet. "I saw you riding down the hill," she said, with a pretty flush and no little excitement. "To tell the truth, I sent Frank after the melon when I recognized you. He's been threatening to go all the afternoon, but I insisted on it. You may be surprised, but I have a business message for you, and I would have made Frank drive me past your house on the way home if you hadn't come."

"Business," Alan laughed, merrily; he felt very happy in her presence under all her assurances of welcome. "The idea of your having a business message! That's really funny."

"Well, that's what it is; sit down." She made room for him in the hammock, and he sat beside her, his foolish brain in a whirl. "Why, yes, it is business; and it concerns you. I fancy it is important; anyway, it may take you to town to-night."

"You don't mean it," he laughed. She looked very pretty, in her light organdie gown and big rustic hat, with its wide, flowing ribbons.

"Yes, it is a message from Rayburn Miller, about that railroad idea of yours."

"Really? Then he told you about that?"

"Yes; he was down to see me last week. He didn't seem to think much of it then—but"—she hesitated and smiled, as if over the memory of something amusing—"he's been thinking of it since. As Frank and I drove through the main street this morning—Frank had gone in a store to get a basket of fruit—he came to me on his way to the train for Atlanta. He hadn't time to say much, but he said if you were out here to-day to tell you to come in town to-night without fail, so as to meet him at his office early in the morning. He 'll be back on the midnight train. I asked him if it was about the railroad, and he said it was—that he had discovered something that looked encouraging."

"I'm glad of that," said Alan, a thrill of excitement passing over him. "Rayburn threw cold water on my ideas the other day, and—"

"I know he did, and it was a shame," said Dolly, warmly. "The idea of his thinking he is the only man in Georgia with originality! Anyway, I hope it will come to something."

"I certainly do," responded Alan. "It's the only thing I could think of to help my people, and I am willing to stake all I have on it—which is, after all, nothing but time and energy."

"Well, don't you let him nor any one else discourage you," said the girl, her eyes flashing. "A man who listens to other people and puts his own ideas aside is unworthy of the brain God gave him. There is another thing"—her voice sank lower and her eyes sought the ground. "Rayburn Miller is a fine, allround man, but he is not perfect by any means. He talks freely to me, you know; he's known me since I was knee-high. Well, he told me—he told me of the talk he had with you at the dance that night. Oh, that hurt me—hurt me!"

"He told you that!" exclaimed Alan, in surprise. "Yes, and it actually disgusted me. Does he think all men ought to act on that sort of advice? He might, for he has made an unnatural man of himself, with all his fancies for new faces; but you are not that kind, Alan, and I'm sorry you and he are so intimate—not that he can influence you *much*, but he has already, *in a way*, and that has pained me deeply."

"He has influenced me?" cried Alan, in surprise. "I think you are mistaken."

"You may not realize it, but he has," said Dolly, with gentle and yet unyielding earnestness. "You see, you are so very sensitive that it would not be hard to make you believe that a young man ought not to keep on caring for a girl whose parents object to his attentions."

"Ah!" He had caught her drift.

There was a pause. At the foot of the hill a little brook ran merrily over the water-browned stones, and its monotonous lapping could be heard distinctly. Under the trees across the open some of the couples had drawn together and were singing:

"I see the boat go 'round the bend,
Good-bye, my lover, good-bye."

Dolly had said exactly what he had never hoped to hear her say, and the fact of her broaching such a subject in such a frank, determined way sent a glow of happiness all over him.

"I don't think," he began, thoughtfully, "that Rayburn or any man could keep me from"—he looked into her full, expectant eyes, and then plunged madly—"could keep me from caring for you, from loving you with all my heart, Dolly; but it really is a terrible thing to know that you are robbing a girl of not only the love of her parents but her rightful inheritance, when, when"—he hurried on, seeing that an impulse to speak was urging her to protest—"when you haven't a cent to your name, and, moreover, have a black eye from your father's mistakes."

"I knew that's what he'd said!" declared the girl, almost white with anger. "I knew it! Oh, Alan, Rayburn Miller might be able to draw back and leave a girl at such a time, but no man could that truly loves as—as I believe you love me. I have known how you have felt all this time, and it has nearly broken my heart, but I could not write to you when you had never even told me, what you have to-day. You must not let anybody or anything influence you, Alan. I'd rather be a poor man' s wife, and do my own work, than let a paltry thing like my father's money keep me from standing by the man I love."

Alan' s face was ablaze. He drew himself up and gazed at her, all his soul in his eyes. "Then I shall not give you up," he declared; "not for anything in the world. And if there is a chance in the railroad idea I shall work at it ten times as hard, now that I have talked with you."

They sat together in blissful ignorance of the passage of time, till some one shouted out that Frank Hill-house was coming with the watermelon. Then all the couples in sight or hearing ran to the spring, where Hillhouse could be seen plunging the big melon into the water. Hattie Alexander and Charlie Durant, who had been perched on a jutting bowlder high up on the hill behind Dolly and Alan, came half running, half sliding down, catching at the trees to keep from falling.

"Better come get your teeth in that melon," Hattie said, with a knowing smile at Dolly. They lived next door to each other and were quite intimate.

"Come on, Alan." Dolly rose. "Frank will never forgive me if I don't have some."

"I sha 'n' t have time, if I go to town to-night," replied Alan. "I have something to do at home first."

"Then I won't keep you," Dolly smiled, "for you must go and meet Rayburn Miller. I'm going to hope that he has had good luck in Atlanta."

The world had never seemed so full of joy and hope as Alan rode homeward. The sun was setting in glorious splendor beyond the towering mountains, above which the sky seemed an ocean of mother-of-pearl and liquid gold. Truly it was good to be alive. At the bars he met Abner Daniel with a fishing-cane in his hands, his bait-gourd under his arm.

"I know right whar you've been," he said, with a broad smile, as he threw down the bars for Alan to pass through. "I seed that gang drive by in all the'r flurry this mornin', the queen bee in the lead with that little makeshift of a man."

Alan dismounted to prevent his uncle from putting up the bars, and they walked homeward side by side.

"Yes, and I've had the time of my life," said the young man. "I talked to her for a solid hour."

"I could see that in yore face," said Abner, quietly. "You couldn't hide it, an' I 'll bet she didn't lose time in lettin' you know what she never could hide from me."

"We understand each other better now," admitted Alan.

"Well, I've certainly set my heart on the match—on gittin' her in our family," affirmed Abner. "Durn-ed ef—I declare, sometimes I'm afeerd I'm gone on 'er myse'f. Yes, I want you 'n' her to make it. I want to set an' smoke an' chaw on yore front porch, an' heer her back in the kitchen fryin' ham an' eggs, an'," the old man winked, "I don't know as I'd object to trottin' some 'n' on my knee, to sorter pass the time betwixt meals."

"Oh, come off, Uncle Ab!" said Alan, with a flush, "that's going too far."

The old man whisked his bait-gourd round under his other arm. His eyes twinkled, and he chuckled. "'Tain' t goin' as fur as havin' one on each knee an' both pine blank alike an' exactly the same age. I've knowed that to happen in my day an' time, when nobody wasn't even lookin' fer a' increase."

CHAPTER XVI

HATTIE ALEXANDER and Charlie Durant reached home before Dolly and Hillhouse, and as Dolly alighted from the buggy at the front gate and was going up the flower-bordered walk Hattie came to the side fence and called out:

"Oh, Dolly, come here quick; I've got some 'n' to tell you."

"Well, wait till I get my hat off," answered Dolly.

"No, I can't wait; come on, or you 'll wish you had."

"What is it, goosie?" Dolly smiled, as she tripped across the grass, her face flushed from her rapid drive.

"Doll, darling, I've got you in an *awful* scrape. I know you 'll never forgive me, but I couldn't help it. When Charlie left me at the gate mother come out and asked me all about the picnic, who was there an' who talked to who, and all about it. Among other things I told her about you and Alan getting together for such a nice, long talk, and—"

"Oh, I don't mind her," broke in Dolly, as she reached for the skirt of her gown to rescue it from the dew on the high grass.

"Wait, wait; I'm not through by a jugful," panted Hattie. "Just then your pa came along an' asked if you'd got home. I told him you hadn't, an' then he up and asked me if Alan Bishop was out there. I had to say yes, of course, for you know how strict mother is about telling a fib, and then what do you think he did? He come right out plain and asked if Alan talked to you by yourself. I didn't know what on earth to do. I reckon I actually turned white, and then mother chipped in and said: 'Tell the truth, daughter; a story never mends matters; besides, Colonel Barclay, you must be more reasonable; young folks will be young folks, and Alan Bishop would be my choice if I was picking out a husband for my girl.' And then you ought to have heard your pa snort; it was as loud as a horse kicking up his heels in the lot. He wheeled round an' made for the house like he was shot out of a gun."

"I reckon he 'll raise the very Old Harry," opined Dolly, grimly. "But I don't care; he's driven me about as far as he can."

"I wouldn't make him any madder," advised the innocent mischief-maker, with a doleful expression. "It's all my fault. I—"

"No, it wasn't," declared Dolly. "But he can't run over me with his unreasonable ideas about Alan Bishop."

With that she turned and went towards the house, her head down. On the veranda she met her mother, who was waiting for her with a pleasurable smile. "You've stirred up yore pa awful," she said, laughing impulsively, and then trying to veil it with a seriousness that sat awkwardly on her. "You'd better dodge him right now. Oh, he's hot! He was just saying this morning that he believed you and Frank were getting on fine, and now he says Frank is an idiot to take a girl to a picnic to meet his rival. How did it happen?"

"Just as I intended it should, mother," Dolly said. "I knew he was coming, and sent Frank off after a watermelon. He didn't have sense enough to see through my ruse. If I'd treated Alan that way he'd simply have looked straight through me as if I'd been a window-pane. Mother, I'm not going to put up with it. I tell you I won't. I know what there is in Alan Bishop better than father does, and I am not going to stand it."

"You ain't, heigh?" thundered Barclay across the hall, and he stalked out of the sitting-room, looking over his eye-glasses, a newspaper in his hand. "Now, my lady, let me say to you that Alan Bishop shall never darken my door, and if you meet him again anywhere you shall go away and stay."

"Father "—Dolly had never stood so tall in her high-heeled shoes nor so straight—"Father, you insulted Alan just now before Mrs. Alexander and Hattie, and I'm not going to have you do it any more. I love him, and I shall never love any other man, nor marry any other man. I know he loves me, and I'm going to stick to him."

"Then the quicker you get away from here the better," said the old man, beside himself with rage. "And when you go, don't you dare to come back again."

The Colonel stalked from the room. Dolly glanced at her mother, who had a pale smile of half-frightened enjoyment on her face.

"I think you said 'most too much," Mrs. Barclay said. "You'd better not drive him too far."

Dolly went up to her room, and when supper was called, half an hour later, she declined to come down. However, Mrs. Barclay sent up a tray of delicacies by Aunt Milly, the old colored woman, which came back untouched.

It was the custom of the family to retire rather early at that season of the year, and by half-past nine the house was dark and still. Mrs. Barclay dropped to sleep quickly, but waked about one o' clock, and lay unable to drift into unconsciousness again for the delightful pastime of thinking over her daughter's love affair. She began to wonder if Dolly, too, might not be awake, and the prospect of a midnight chat on that of all topics made her pulse beat quickly. Slipping noiselessly out of bed, so as not to wake her husband, who was snoring in his bed across the room, she glided upstairs. She had not been there a moment before the Colonel was waked by a low scream from her, and then he heard her bare feet thumping on the floor overhead as she crossed the hall into the other rooms. She screamed out again, and the Colonel sprang up, grasped his revolver, which always lay on the bureau, and ran into the hall. There he met his wife, half sliding down the stairs.

"Dolly's gone," she gasped. "Her bed hasn't been touched. Oh, Seth, do you reckon anything has happened to her?"

The old man stared in the dim light of the hall, and then turned towards the door which opened on the back veranda. He said not a word, but was breathing hard. The cabin of old Ned and his wife, Aunt Milly, was near by.

"Ned; oh, Ned!" called out the Colonel.

"Yes, marster!"

"Crawl out o' that bed and come heer!"

"Yes, marster; I'm a-comin'."

"Oh, Seth, do you reckon—do you—?"

"Dry up, will you?" thundered Barclay. "Are you comin', Ned?"

Uncle Ned's gray head was thrust out at the partly open door.

"You want me, marster?"

"Yes; what do you suppose I called you for if I didn't want you. Now I don't want any lies from you. You know you can't fool me. I want to know if you carried a note from this house to anybody since sundown."

"A note must have been sent," ventured Mrs. Barclay, in an undertone. "Dolly never would have gone to him. He must have been notified and come after her."

"Dry up, for God's sake!" yelled the Colonel over his shoulder to the spectre by his side. "Answer me, you black rascal."

"Marse Seth, young miss, she—"

"She sent a note to Alan Bishop, didn't she?" interpolated the Colonel.

"Marster, I didn't know it was any harm. I des 'lowed it was some prank o' young miss'. Oh, Lordy!"

"You might know you'd do suppen, you old sap-haid," broke in Aunt Milly from the darkness of the cabin. "I kin count on you ever' time."

"Get back in bed," ordered the Colonel, and he walked calmly into his room and lay down again. His wife followed him, standing in the middle of the room.

"Aren't you going to do anything?" she said. Her voice was charged with a blending of tears and a sort of feminine eagerness that is beyond the comprehension of man.

"Do anything? What do you think I ought to do? Raise an alarm, ring the church-bells, and call out the hook-and-ladder company? Huh! She's made her bed; let her lie on it."

"You are heartless—you have no feeling," cried his wife. The very core of her desire was to get him to talk about the matter. If he was not going to rouse the neighborhood, and thus furnish some one to talk to, he, at least, ought to be communicative.

"Well, you'd better go to bed," snarled her husband.

"No"—she scratched a match and lighted a candle—"I'm going up-stairs and see if she left a note. Now, you see, *I* had to think of that. The poor girl may have written something."

There did seem to be a vestige of reason in this, and the old man said nothing against it, throwing himself back on his pillow with a stifled groan.

After about half an hour Mrs. Barclay came back; she stood over him, holding the candle so that its best rays would fall on his face.

"She didn't write one word," was her announcement. "I reckon she knew we'd understand or find out from Uncle Ned. And just to think!"— Mrs. Barclay now sat down on a chair across the back of which lay the Colonel's trousers, holding the candle well to the right that she might still see the rigid torture of his face—"just to think, she's only taken the dress she had on at the picnic. It will be a poor wedding for her, when she's always said she wanted a lot of bridesmaids and ushers and decorations. Poor child! Maybe they had to drive into the country to get somebody to marry them. I know brother Lapsley wouldn't do it without letting us know. I reckon she 'll send the first thing in the morning for her trunk, if—" Mrs. Barclay gazed more steadily—"if she don't come herself."

"Well, she needn't come herself," grunted the reclining figure as it flounced under the sheets to turn its face to the wall.

"You wouldn't be that hard on our only child, just because she—"

"If you don't go to bed," the words rebounded from the white plastering an inch from the speaker's lips, "you 'n' me 'll have a row. I've said what I'd do, and I shall do it!"

"Well, I'm going out to speak to Aunt Milly a minute," said Mrs. Barclay, and, drawing on a thin graywrapper and sliding her bare feet into a pair of slippers, she shuffled out to the back porch.

"Come here, Aunt Milly," she called out, and she sat down on the highest step and waited till the fat old woman, enveloped in a coarse gray blanket, joined her.

"Aunt Milly, did you ever hear the like?" she said. "She 'ain't made off sho 'nough, have she, Miss Annie?"

"Yes, she's gone an' done it; her pa drove her just a little too far. I reckon she railly does love Alan Bishop, or thinks she does."

"I could take a stick an' baste the life out'n Ned," growled the black woman, leaning against the veranda post; she knew better than to sit down in the presence of her mistress, even if her mistress had invited her to talk.

"Oh, he didn't know any better," said Mrs. Barclay. "He always would trot his legs off for Dolly, and"—Mrs. Barclay's tone was tentative—"it wouldn't surprise me if Alan Bishop paid him to help to-night."

"No, he didn't help, Miss Annie. Ned's been in bed ever since he come back fum town des atter supper. He tol' me des now dat de young man was in a room at de hotel playin' cyards wid some more boys an' he got up an' writ Miss Dolly er note; but Ned went straight to bed when he got home."

"Then, Alan must have got her to meet him at the front gate, don't you reckon? He didn't drive up to the house either, for I think I would have heard the wheels. He must have left his turn-out at the corner."

"Are you a-goin' to set there all night?" thundered the Colonel from his bed. "How do you expect anybody to sleep with that low mumbling going on, like a couple of dogs under the house?"

Mrs. Barclay got up, with a soft, startled giggle.

"He can' t sleep because he's bothered," she said, in a confidential undertone. "We'd better go in. I don't want to nag him too far; it's going hard with Dolly as it is. I'm curious to see if he really will refuse to let her come back. Do you reckon he will, Milly?"

"I sw'ar I don't know, Miss Annie," replied the dark human shape from the depths of her blanket. "He sho is a caution, an' you kin see he's tormented. I 'll bet Ned won't have a whole skin in de mornin'."

The Colonel, despite his sullen effort to conceal the fact from his wide-awake wife, slept very little during the remainder of that night, and when he rose at the usual hour he went out to see his horse fed.

Mrs. Barclay was fluttering from the dining-room to the kitchen, gossiping with the cook, who had run out of anything to say on the subject and could only grunt, "Yes'um, and no'um," according to the reply she felt was expected. Aunt Milly was taking a plate of waffles into the dining-room when a little negro boy, about five years of age, the son of the cook at the Alexanders', crawled through a hole in the fence between the two houses and sauntered towards the kitchen. On the door-step he espied a black kitten that took his fancy and he caught it and began to stroke it with his little black hand.

"What you want *now?*" Aunt Milly hovered over him like an angry hen. "Want ter borrow suppen, I boun' you; yo'-alls folks is de beatenes' people ter borrow I ever lived alongst."

The boy seemed to have forgotten his errand in his admiration for the kitten.

"What you atter now?" snarled Aunt Milly, "eggs, flour, sugar, salt, pepper, flat-iron? Huh, we-all ain't keepin' er sto'."

The boy looked up suddenly and drew his ideas together with a jerk. "Miss Dolly, she say sen 'er Mother Hubbub wrappin' dress, hangin' on de foot er her bed-post."

"What?" gasped Aunt Milly, and, hearing the exclamation, Mrs. Barclay came to the door and paused to listen.

"Miss Dolly," repeated the boy, "she say sen 'er 'er wrappin' dress off'n de foot-post er 'er bed; en, en, she say keep 'er two waffles hot en, en dry — not sobby — en ter git 'er dat fresh cream fer 'er coffee in 'er lill pitcher whut she lef' in 'er ice-box."

"Dolly? Dolly?" cried Mrs. Barclay. "You are surely mistaken, Pete. Where did you see her?"

"Over 't we-all's house," said the boy, grabbing the kitten which had slid from his momentarily inattentive fingers.

"Over 't yo'-all's house!" cried Milly, almost in a tone of horror, "en, en is her husban' wid 'er?"

The boy grinned contemptuously.

"Huh, Miss Dolly ain't no married ooman—you know she ain't, huh! I seh, married! Look heer"—to the kitten—"don't you scratch me, boy!"

Mrs. Barclay bent over him greatly excited. "What was she doing over at your house, Pete?"

"Nothin' w'en I seed 'er 'cep'jest her en Miss Hattie lyin' in de bed laughin' en car'yin' on."

"Oh, Lordy!" Mrs. Barclay's eyes were riveted on Aunt Milly's beaming face, "do you reckon—?"

"She's slep 'over dar many times before now, Miss Annie," said Aunt Milly, and she burst into a round, ringing laugh, her fat body shaking like a mass of jelly. "She done it time en ergin—time en ergin."

"Well, ain't that a purty mess?" said Mrs. Barclay, almost in a tone of disappointment. "I'll get the wrapper, Pete, and you tell her to put it on and hurry over here as soon as she possibly can."

A few minutes later Dolly came from the Alexander's and met her mother at the gate. "Oh, Dolly," Mrs. Barclay cried, "you've got us in an awful mess. We missed you about midnight and we thought—your father made Ned acknowledge that he took a note to Alan Bishop from you, and we thought you had gone off to get married. Your father's in an awful temper, swearing you shall never—"

Dolly tossed her head angrily. "Well, you needn't say I got you into it; you did it yourselves and I don't care how much you suffer. I say! When I go to get married it will not be that way, you can depend on it. Now, I reckon, it will be all over town that—"

"No, it needn't get out of the family," Mrs. Barclay assured her, in a guilty tone of apology. "Your pa wouldn't let me raise any alarm. But you *did* send a note to Alan Bishop, Dolly."

"Yes, I knew he was in town, and would be here to-day, and I simply wrote him that father was angry at our seeing each other again and that I hoped he would avoid meeting him just now—that was all."

"Well, well, well." Mrs. Barclay hurried through the house and out to where Barclay stood at the lot fence watching Ned curry his horse.

"What do you reckon?" she gasped. "Dolly didn't go off at all; she just went to spend the night with Hattie Alexander."

His face changed its expression against his will; the blood flowed into the pallor and a satisfied gleam shot from his half-closed eyes. He turned from her, looking over the fence at the horse.

"You're leavin' a splotch on that right hind leg," he said. "Are you stone blind?"

"I was gittin' roun' to it, marster," said the negro, looking his surprise over such an unexpected reproof. "No; she just wrote Alan that you was displeased at them getting together yesterday and advised him to dodge you to-day while he is in town."

"Well, he'd better!" said the Colonel, gruffly, as they walked towards the house. "You tell her," he enjoined—"you tell her what I said when I thought she *was* gone. It will be a lesson to her. She can tell now how I'll do if she *does* go against me in this matter."

"I reckon you are glad she didn't run off," replied his wife thoughtfully. "The Lord only knows what you'd do about writing your letters without her help. I believe she knows more about your business right now than you do, and has a longer head. You'd' a' saved a thousand dollars by taking her advice the other day about that cotton sale."

CHAPTER XVII

ON his way to Rayburn Miller's office that morning Alan decided that he would not allude to the note he had received the previous evening from Dolly. He did not like the cynical mood into which such subjects seemed to draw his friend. He knew exactly what Miller would say, and felt that it would be too personal to be agreeable.

He found the lawyer standing in the door of his little office building waiting for him.

"I reckon my message surprised you," Miller said, tentatively, as he shook hands.

"It took me off my feet," smiled Alan. "You see, I never hoped to get you interested in that scheme, and when I heard you were actually going to Atlanta about it, I hardly knew what to make of it."

Miller turned into his office, kicked a chair towards Alan and dropped into his creaking rocker.

"It was not due to you that I did get interested," he said. "Do you know, I can't think of it without getting hot all over with shame. To tell you the truth, there is one thing I have always been vain about. I didn't honestly think there was a man in Georgia that could give me any tips about investments, but I had to take back water, and for a woman. Think of that—a woman knocked me off my perch as clean and easy as she could stick a hair-pin in a ball of hair. I'm not unfair; when anybody teaches me any tricks, I acknowledge the corn an' take off my hat. It was this way: I dropped in to see Miss Dolly the other evening. I accidentally disclosed two things in an offhand sort of way. I told her some of the views I gave you at the dance in regard to marriage and love and one thing and another, and then, in complimenting you most highly in other things, I confess I sort o' poked fun at your railroad idea."

"I thought you had," said Alan, good-naturedly; "but go on."

"Well, she first read me a lecture about bad, empty, shallow men, whose very souls were damned by their past careers, interfering with the pure impulses of younger men, and I 'll swear I felt like crawling in a hole and pulling the hole in after me. Well, I got through that, in a fashion, because she didn't want me to see her real heart, and that helped me. Then she took up the railroad scheme. You know I had heard that she advised her father in all his business matters, but, geewhilikins! I never dreamt she could give me points, but she did—she simply did. She looked me straight in the eye and stared at me like a national bank examiner as she asked me to explain why that particular road could not be built, and why it would not be a bonanza for the owners of the timber-land. I thought she was an easy fish at first, and I gave her plenty of line, but she kept peppering me with unanswerable questions till I lay down on the bank as weak as a rag. The first bliff she gave me was in wanting to know if there were not many branch roads that did not own their rolling stock. She said she knew one in the iron belt in Alabama that didn't own a car or an engine, and wouldn't have them as a free gift. She said if such a road were built as you plan these two main lines would simply fall over each other to send out cars to be loaded for shipment at competitive rates. By George! it was a corker. I found out the next day that she was right, and that doing away with the rolling stock, shops, and so forth, would cut down the cost of your road more than half."

"That's a fact," exclaimed Alan, "and I had not thought of it."

"She's a stronger woman than I ever imagined," said Miller. "By George! if she were not on your string, I'd make a dead set for her. A wife like that would make a man complete. She's in love with you—or thinks she is—but she hasn't that will o' the wisp glamour. She's business from her toes to her fingertips. By George! I believe she makes a business of her love affair; she seems to think she 'll settle it by a sum in algebra. But to get back to the railroad, for I've got lots to tell you. What do you reckon I found that day? You couldn't guess in a thousand years. It was a preliminary survey of a railroad once planned from Darley right through your father's purchase to Morganton, North Carolina. It was made just before the war, by old Colonel Wade, who, in his day, was one of the most noted surveyors in the State. This end of the line was all I cared about, and that was almost as level as a floor along the river and down the valley into the north end of town. It's a bonanza, my boy. Why that big bottle of timber-land has never been busted is a wonder to me. If as many Yankees had been nosing about here as there have been in other Southern sections it would have been snatched up long ago."

"I'm awfully glad to hear you say all this," said Alan, "for it is the only way out of our difficulty, and something has to be done."

"It may cost you a few years of the hardest work you ever bucked down to," said Miller, "and some sleepless nights, but I really believe you have fallen on to a better thing than any I ever struck. I could make it whiz. I've already done something that will astonish you. I happen to know slightly Tillman Wilson, the president of the Southern Land and Timber Company. Their offices are in Atlanta. I knew he was my man to tackle, so when I got to Atlanta yesterday I ran upon him just as if it were accidental. I invited him to lunch with me at the Capitol City Club—you know I'm a non-resident member. You see, I knew if I put myself in the light of a man with something to sell, he'd hurry away from me; but I didn't. As a pretext, I told him I had some clients up here who wanted to raise a considerable amount of money and that the security offered was fine timber-land. You see that caught him; he was on his own ground. I saw that he was interested, and I boomed the property to the skies. The more I talked the more he was interested, till it was bubbling out all over him. He's a New-Englander, who thinks a country lawyer without a Harvard education belongs to an effete civilization, and I let him think he was pumping me. I even left off my g's and ignored my r's. I let him think he had struck the softest thing of his life. Pretty soon he begun to want to know if you cared to sell, but I skirted that indifferently as if I had no interest whatever in it. I told him your father had bought the property to hold for an advance, that he had spent years of his life picking out the richest timber spots and buying them up. Then he came right out, as I hoped he would, and asked me the amount you wanted to borrow on the property. I had to speak quick, and remembering that you had said the old gentleman had put in about twenty thousand first and last, I put the amount at twenty-five thousand. I was taking a liberty, but I can easily get you out of it if you decide not to do it."

"Twenty-five thousand! On that land?" Alan cried. "It would tickle my father to death to sell it for that."

"I can arrange the papers so that you are not liable for any security outside of the land, and it would practically amount to a sale if you wished it, but you don't wish it. I finally told him that I had an idea that you would sell out for an even hundred thousand."

"A hundred thousand!" repeated Alan, with a cheery laugh. "Yes, we'd let go at that."

"Well, the figures didn't scarce him a bit, for he finally came right out and asked me if it was my opinion that in case his company made the loan, you would agree to give him the refusal of the land at one hundred thousand. I told him I didn't know, that I thought it possible, but that just then I had no interest in the matter beyond borrowing a little money on it. He asked me how long I was going to stay in Atlanta. I told him I was going to a bank and take the night train back. 'The banks will stick you for a high rate of interest,' he said, jealously. 'They don't do business for fun, while, really, our concern happens just now to have some idle capital on hand. Do you think you could beat five per cent.? I admitted that it was low enough, but I got up as if I was suddenly reminded that the banks close early in the afternoon. 'I think we can make the loan,' he said, 'but I must first see two or three of the directors. Can't you give me two hours?' I finally gave in and promised to meet him at the Kimball House at four. I went to a matinée, saw it half over, and went in at the ladies' entrance of the hotel. I saw him looking about for me and dodged him."

"Dodged him?" echoed Alan. "Why—"

Miller laughed. "You don't suppose I'd let a big fish like that see me flirting my hook and pole about in open sunlight, do you? I saw by his manner that he was anxious to meet me, and that was enough; besides, you can't close a deal like that in a minute, and there are many slips. I went back to the club and threw myself on a lounge and began to smoke and read an afternoon paper. Presently he came in a cab. I heard him asking for me in the hall and buried my head in the paper. He came in on me and I rose and looked stupid. I can do it when I try—if it *is* something God has failed at— and I began to apologize.

"He didn't seem to care. 'If it had been a deal of your own,' he said with a laugh, 'you'd have been more prompt,' and I managed to look guilty. Then he sat down.

"'Our directors are interested,' he said, confidentially. 'The truth is there is not another concern in America that can handle that property as cheaply as we can. We happen to have a railroad about that length up in East Tennessee that has played out, and you see we could move it to where it would do some good.'

"As soon as he told me that I knew he was our meat; besides, I saw trade in his eye as big as an arc-light. To make a long tale short, he is coming up here tonight, and if your father is willing to accept the loan, he can get the money, giving only the land as security—provided we don't slip up. Here's the only thing I'm afraid of. When Wilson gets here he may get to making inquiries around and drop on to the report that your father is disgusted with his investment, and smell a mouse and pull off. What I want to do is to get at him the first thing after breakfast in the morning, so you'd better bring your father and mother in early. If we once get Wilson's twenty-five thousand into it, we can eventually sell out. The main thing is the loan. Don't you think so?"

"I certainly do," said Alan. "Of course, a good many things might interfere; we'd have to get a right of way and a charter before the road could be built, and I reckon they won't buy till they are sure of those things."

"No it may take a long time and a lot of patience," said Miller. "But your father could afford to wait if he can get his money back by means of the loan. I tell you that's the main thing. If I had offered to sell Wilson the whole thing at twenty-five thousand he never would have come up here, but he is sure now that the property is just what he is looking for. Oh, we are not certain of him by a long jump! It all depends on whether he will insist on going over there or not. If he does, those moss-backs will bu'st the thing wide open. If he comes straight to my office in the morning the deal may be closed, but if he lies around the hotel talking, somebody will spoil our plans and Wilson will hang off to make his own terms later—if he makes any at all. It's ticklish, but we may win."

"It *is* a rather ticklish situation," admitted Alan, "but even if we do get the loan on the property, don't you think Wilson may delay matters and hope to scoop the property in for the debt?"

"He might," Miller smiled, "if he didn't want to move that railroad somewhere else, and, besides, your father can keep the money in suitable shape to pay off the note in any emergency and free himself."

"I don't know how to thank you, old man," answered Alan. "If you had been personally interested in this you could not have done more."

Miller threw himself back in his chair and smiled significantly. "Do I look like a man with nothing in it?" he asked.

"But you haven't anything in it," retorted Alan, wonderingly.

"That's all you know about it" Miller laughed.

"If the road is built I 'll make by it. This is another story. As soon as I saw you were right about putting a railroad into the mountains, I began to look around for some of that timber-land. I didn't have long to wait, for the only man that holds much of it besides Colonel Barclay—Peter Mosely, whom Perkins fooled just as he did your father—came in. He was laying for me, I saw it in his eye. The Lord had delivered him to me, and I was duly thankful. He was a morsel I liked to look at. He opened up himself, bless you! and bragged about his fine body of virgin timber. I looked bored, but let him run on till he was tired; then I said:

"'Well, Mosely, what do you intend to do with your white elephant? You know it's not just the sort Barnum is looking for.'

"He kind o' blinked at that, but he said, 'I've half a notion to sell. The truth is, I've got the finest investment open to me that I ever had. If I could afford to wait a few years I could coin money out of this property, but I believe in turning money quick.'

"'So do I,' said I, and watched him flirt about in the frying-pan. Then I said, 'What is the price you hold it at?'

"'I thought,' said he, 'that I ought to get as much as I paid.'

"'As much as you paid Abe Tompkins and Perkins?' I said, with a grin. 'Do you think you could possibly sell a piece of land for as much as those sharks? If you can, you'd better go in the real-estate business. You'd coin money. Why, they yanked two thousand out of you, didn't they?'

"'I don't really think Perkins had anything to do with it,' he said. 'That's just a report out about old man Bishop's deal. I bought my land on my own judgment.'

"'Well,' I said, 'how will fifteen hundred round wheels strike you?'

"'I believe I 'll take you up,' he said. 'I want to make that other investment.' So we closed and I went at once to have the deed recorded before he had a chance to change his mind. Now, you see, I'm interested in the thing, and I'm going to help you put it through. If your folks want the loan, bring them in in the morning, and if we can manage our Yankee just right, we 'll get the money."

CHAPTER XVIII

AFTER supper that evening the Bishops sat out on the veranda to get the cool air before retiring. There was only one light burning in the house, and that was the little, smoky lamp in the kitchen, where the cook was washing the dishes. Bishop sat near his wife, his coat off and vest unbuttoned, his chair tilted back against the weatherboarding. Abner Daniel, who had been trying ever since supper to cheer them up in regard to their financial misfortune, sat smoking in his favorite chair near the banisters, on top of which he now and then placed his stockinged feet.

"You needn't talk that away, brother Ab," sighed Mrs. Bishop. "Yo're jest doin' it out o' goodness o' heart. We might as well face the truth; we've got to step down from the position we now hold, an' present way o' livin'. And thar's Adele. Pore child! She said in 'er last letter that she'd cried 'er eyes out. She was bent on comin' home, but 'er uncle William won't let 'er. He said she'd not do any good."

"An' she wouldn't," put in Bishop, gruffly. "The sight o' you an' Alan before me all the time is enough to show me what a fool I've been."

"You are both crossin' bridges 'fore you git to 'em," said Abner. "A lots o' folks has come out'n scrapes wuss'n what you are in, ten to one. I 'ain't never mentioned it, but my land hain't got no mortgage on it, an' I could raise a few scads, to he'p keep up yore intrust an' taxes till you could see yore way ahead."

"Huh!" snorted his brother-in-law. "Do you reckon I'd let as old a man as you are, an' no blood kin, stake his little all to help me out of a hole that is gittin' deeper an' wider all the time—a hole I deliberately got myse'f into? Well, not much!"

"I wouldn't listen to that nuther," declared Mrs. Bishop, "but not many men would offer it."

They heard a horse trotting down the road and all bent their heads to listen. "It's Alan," said Abner. "I was thinkin' it was time he was showin' up."

Mrs. Bishop rose wearily to order the cook to get his supper ready, and returned to the veranda just as Alan Was coming from the stable. He sat down on the steps, lashing the legs of his dusty trousers with his riding-whip. It was plain that he had something of importance to say and they all waited in impatient silence.

"Father," he said, "I've had a talk with Rayburn Miller about your land; he and I have lately been working on a little idea of mine. You know there are people who will lend money on real-estate. How would it suit you to borrow twenty-five thousand dollars on that land, giving that alone as security."

There was a startled silence, and Bishop broke it in a tone of great irritation.

"Do you take me fer a plumb fool?" he asked. "When I want you an' Miller to dabble in my business I'll call on you. Twenty-five thousand, I say! If I could exchange every acre of it fer enough to lift the mortgage on this farm an' keep a roof over our heads I'd do it gladly. Pshaw!"

There was another silence, and then Alan began to explain. He almost seemed to his father and mother to be some stranger, as he sat there in the half dark ness, his eyes hidden by the brim of his soft hat, and told them how he had worried over their trouble till the idea of building a railroad had come to him. Then Miller had become interested, after discouraging him, and had gone to Atlanta to see Wilson, and it remained for the next day to decide what the outcome would be in regard to the big loan.

While he talked Mrs. Bishop sat like a figure cut from stone, and Bishop leaned forward, his elbows on his knees, his big face in his hands. It was as if a tornado of hope had blown over him, shaking him through and through.

"You been doin' this to he'p me out," he gasped, "an' I never so much as axed yore opinion one way or another."

"I'd rather see you make money out of that purchase than anything in the world," said his son, with feeling. "People have made fun of you in your old age, but if we can build the road and you can get your hundred thousand dollars some of these folks will laugh on the other side of their faces."

Bishop was so full of excitement and emotion that he dared not trust his voice to utterance. He leaned back against the wall and closed his eyes, pretending to be calm, though his alert wife saw that he was quivering in every limb.

"Oh, Alan," she cried, "don't you see how excited your pa is? You ought not to raise his hopes this way on such an uncertainty. As Mr. Miller said, there may be some slip and we'd be right back where we was, and feel wuss than ever."

Bishop rose from his chair and began to walk to and fro on the veranda. "It ain't possible," they heard him saying. "I won't git out as easy as that—I jest cayn't!"

"Perhaps it would be wrong to expect too much," said Alan, "but I was obliged to tell you what we are going in town for to-morrow."

Bishop wheeled and paused before them. "Ef Wilson puts up the money I'd have enough to lift the mortgage an' a clean twenty thousand besides to put in some good investment."

Aunt Maria, the colored cook, came out and timidly announced that Alan's supper was on the table, but no one heard her. She crossed the veranda and touched the young man on the shoulder.

"Supper's raidy, Marse Alan," she said, "en it's gittin' col' ergin."

He rose and followed her into the dining-room and sat down in his accustomed place at the long table. When he had eaten he went back to the group on the veranda.

"I think I 'll go up to bed," he told them. "My ride and running around at Darley has made me very tired. Father, get all your papers together and let's take an early start in the morning."

But despite his feeling of weariness, Alan found he could not sleep. The bright moonlight, streaming in at his window, seemed a disturbing element. About eleven o'clock he heard some one turning the windlass at the well, and later the clatter of falling utensils in the kitchen, and the dead thump of a heavy tread below. He knew then that his father was up, and, like himself, unable to sleep. Presently Mrs. Bishop slipped into his room.

"Are you awake, son?" She spoke in a whisper that she might not disturb him if he were asleep.

He laughed. "I haven't closed my eyes; it seems to me I have gone over my conversation with Miller a thousand times."

"I've give up tryin'," she told him, with a gratified little laugh. "I think I could, though, if your pa would 'a' kept still. He's in the kitchen now makin' him a cup o' strong coffee. He's been over them papers ever since you come up-stairs. Alan, I'm actually afeerd he couldn't stand it if that man didn't put up the money."

"It would go hard with him," said Alan. "Has Uncle Ab gone to sleep?"

"No; he's settin' in the door o' his room chawin' tobacco; he lays the blame on yore pa. I don't think I ever saw him so irritated before. But nobody ain't to blame but hisse'f. He's jest excited like the rest of us. I've seed 'im lie an' snore with a bigger noise goin' on around 'im 'an yore pa is a-makin'."

CHAPTER XIX

AS Henry, Aunt Maria's husband, who was the chief farm-hand, was busy patching fences the next morning, Bishop sent over for Pole Baker to drive the spring-wagon. Alan sat beside Pole, and Abner and Bishop and Mrs. Bishop occupied the rear seats.

Alan knew he could trust Pole, drunk or sober, and he confided his plans to the flattered fellow's ears. Pole seemed to weigh all the chances for and against success in his mind as he sat listening, a most grave and portentous expression on his massive face.

"My opinion is the feller 'll be thar as shore as preachin'," he said. "But whether you git his wad or not, that's another question. Miller's as sharp as a briar, an', as he says, if Wilson gits to talkin' about that land to any o' these hill-Billies they 'll bu'st the trade or die tryin'. Jest let 'em heer money's about to change hands an' it 'll make 'em so durn jealous they 'll swear a lie to keep it away from anybody they know. That's human natur'."

"I believe you are right," said Alan, pulling a long face; "and I'm afraid Wilson will want to make some inquiries before he closes."

"Like as not," opined the driver; "but what I'd do, ef I was a-runnin' it, would be to git some feller to strike up with 'im accidental-like, an' liter'ly fill 'im to the neck with good things about the property without him ever dreamin' he was bein' worked."

The two exchanged glances. Alan had never looked at the man so admiringly. At that moment he seemed a giant of shrewdness, as well as that of physical strength.

"I believe you are right, Pole," he said, thoughtfully.

"That's what I am, an', what's more, I'm the one that could do the fillin', without him ever knowin' I had a funnel in his mouth. If I can't do it, I 'll fill my hat with saft mud an' put it on."

Alan smiled warmly. "I 'll mention it to Miller," he said. "Yes, you could do it, Pole—if any man on earth could."

Driving up to Miller's office they found the door open, and the owner came out with a warm smile of greeting and aided Mrs. Bishop to alight.

"Well," he smiled, when they had taken seats in the office. "We have gained the first step towards victory. Wilson is at the hotel. I saw his name on the register this morning."

The elder Bishops drew a breath of relief. The old man grounded his heavy walking-stick suddenly, as if it had slipped through his inert fingers.

"I'm trustin' you boys to pull me through," he said, with a shaky laugh. "I hain't never treated Alan right, an' I'm heer to confess it. I 'lowed I was the only one in our layout with any business sense."

"So you are willing to accept the loan?" said Miller.

"Willin'? I reckon I am. I never slept one wink last night fer feer some 'n' 'll interfere with it."

Miller reflected a moment and then said: "I am afraid of only one thing, and that is this: Not one man in a million will make a trade of this size without corroborating the statements made by the people he is dealing with. Wilson is at breakfast by this time, and after he is through he may decide to nose around a little before coming to me. I'm afraid to go after him; he would think I was over-anxious. The trouble is that he may run upon somebody from out in the mountains—there are a lot in town already—and get to talking. Just one word about your biting off more than you can chaw, Mr. Bishop, would make 'im balk like a mean mule. He thinks I'm favoring him now, but let him get the notion that you haven't been holding that land for at least a hundred thousand an' the thing would bu'st like a bubble."

Alan mentioned Pole Baker's proposition. Miller thought it over for a moment, his brow wrinkled, and then he said: "Good!—a good idea, but you must call Pole in and let me give him a few pointers. By George! he could keep Wilson away from dangerous people anyway."

Alan went after Pole, and Miller took him into his consultation-room in the rear, where they remained for about fifteen minutes. When they came out Pole's face was very grave. "I won't forget a thing," he said to Miller. "I understand exactly what you want. When I git through with 'im he 'll want that land bad enough to pay anything fer it, an' he won't dream I'm in cahoot with you, nuther. I can manage that. I ain't no fool ef I do have fits."

"Do you remember my description of him?" asked Miller.

"You bet I do—thick-set, about fifty, bald, red-faced, sharp, black eyes, iron gray hair, an' mighty nigh always with a cigar in his mouth."

"That's right," laughed Miller, "now do your work, and we won't forget you. By all means keep him away from meddlesome people."

When Pole had left the office and Miller had resumed his revolving-chair Mrs. Bishop addressed him, looking straight into his eyes.

"I don't see," she said, in a timid, hesitating way, and yet with a note of firmness dominating her tone—"I don't see why we have to go through all this trickery to make the trade. Ef the land is good security fer the money we needn't be afeerd of what the man will find out. Ef it ain' t good security I don't want his money as fer as I'm concerned."

"I was jest thinkin' that, too," chimed in her husband, throwing a troubled glance all round. "I want money to help me out o' my scrape, but I don't want to trick no man, Yankee or what not, into toatin' my loads. As Betsy says, it seems to me if the land's wuth the money we needn't make such a great to-do. I'm afeerd I won't feel exactly right about it."

The young men exchanged alarmed glances.

"You don't understand," said Miller, lamely, but he seemed to be unprepared for views so heretical to financial dealings, and could not finish what he had started to say.

"Why," said Alan, testily, "the land is worth all Wilson can make out of it with the aid of his capital and the railroad he proposes to lay here. Father, you have spent several years looking up the best timbered properties, and getting good titles to it, and to a big lumber company a body of timber like you hold is no small tiling. We don't want to cheat him, but we do want to keep him from trying to cheat us by getting the upper hand. Rayburn thinks if he finds out we are hard up he 'll try to squeeze us to the lowest notch."

"Well," sighed Mrs. Bishop, "I'm shore I never had no idea we'd resort to gittin' Pole Baker to tole anybody around like a hog after a yeer o' corn. I 'lowed we was going to make a open-and-shut trade that we could be proud of, an' stop folk's mouths about Alfred's foolish dealin' s. But," she looked at Abner, who stood in the doorway leading to the consultation-room, "I 'll do whatever brother Ab thinks is right. I never knowed 'im to take undue advantage of anybody."

They all looked at Abner, who was smiling broadly.

"Well, I say git his money," he replied, with a short, impulsive laugh—"git his money, and then ef you find he's starvin', hand 'im back what you feel you don't need. I look on a thing like this sorter like I did on scramblin' fer the upper holt in war-times. I remember I shot straight at a feller that was climbin' up the enemy's breastworks on his all-fours. I said to myse'f, ef this ball strikes you right, old chap, 'fore you drap over the bank, yo're one less agin the Confederacy; ef it don't you kin pop away at me. I don't think I give 'im anything but a flesh-wound in the back—beca'se he jest sagged down a little an' crawled on—an' that's about the wust you could do fer Wilson. I believe he ort to hold the bag awhile. Alf's hung on to it till his fingers ache an' he's weak at the knees. I never did feel like thar was any harm in passin' a counterfeit bill that some other chap passed on me. Ef the government, with all its high-paid help, cayn't keep crooked shinplasters from slidin' under our noses, it ortn't to kick agin our lookin' out fer ourse'ves."

"You needn't lose any sleep about the Southern Land and Timber Company, Mrs. Bishop," said Miller. "They will take care of themselves—in fact, we 'll have to keep our eyes peeled to watch them even if we get this loan. Wilson didn't come up here for his health."

"Oh, mother's all right," said Alan, "and so is father, but they must not chip in with that sort of talk before Wilson."

"Oh no, you mustn't," said Miller. "In fact, I think you'd better let me and Alan do the talking. You see, if you sit perfectly quiet he 'll think you are reluctant about giving such big security for such a small amount of money, and he will trade faster."

"Oh, I'm perfectly willin' to keep quiet," agreed the old man, who now seemed better satisfied.

Pole Baker left the office with long, swinging strides. There was an entrance to the Johnston House through a long corridor opening on the street, and into this Pole slouched. The hotel office was empty save for the clerk who stood behind the counter, looking over the letters in the pigeon-holed key-rack on the wall. There was a big gong overhead which was rung by pulling a cord. It was used for announcing meals and calling the porter. A big china bowl on the counter was filled with wooden tooth-picks, and there was a show-case containing cigars. Pole glanced about cautiously without being noticed by the clerk, and then withdrew into the corridor, where he stood for several minutes, listening. Presently the dining-room door opened and Wilson strolled out and walked up to the counter.

"What sort of cigars have you got?" he said to the clerk.

"Nothing better than ten, three for a quarter," was the respectful reply, as the clerk recognized the man who had asked for the best room in the house.

Wilson thrust his fingers into his vest-pocket and drew out a cigar. "I guess I can make what I have last me," he said, transferring his glance to Pole Baker, who had shambled across the room and leaned heavily over the open register. "Want to buy any chickins—fine fryin' size?" he asked the clerk.

"Well, we are in the market," was the answer. "Where are they?"

"I didn't fetch 'em in to-day," said Pole, dryly. "I never do till I know what they are a-bringin'. You'd better make a bid on a dozen of 'em anyway. They are the finest ever raised on Upper Holly Creek, jest this side o' whar old man Bishop's lumber paradise begins."

Pole was looking out of the corner of his eye at the stranger, and saw his hand, which was in the act of striking a match, suddenly stay itself.

"We don't bid on produce till we see it," said the clerk.

"Well, I reckon no harm was done by my axin'," said Pole, who felt the eyes of the stranger on him.

"Do you live near here?" asked Wilson, with a smile half of apology at addressing a stranger, even of Pole's humble stamp.

"No." Pole laughed and waved his hand towards the mountains in the west, which were plainly discernible in the clear morning light. "No, I'm a mountain shanghai. I reckon it's fifteen mile on a bee-line to my shack."

"Didn't you say you lived near old Mr. Bishop's place?" asked Wilson, moving towards the open door which led to the veranda.

"I don't know which place o' his'n you mean," said Pole when they were alone outside and Wilson had lighted his cigar. "That old scamp owns the whole o' creation out our way. Well, I 'll take that back, fer he don't own any land that hain't loaded down with trees, but he's got territory enough. Some thinks he's goin' to secede from the United States an' elect himself President of his own country."

Wilson laughed, and then he said: "Have you got a few minutes to spare?"

"I reckon I have," said Pole, "ef you've got the mate to that cigar."

Wilson laughed again as he fished the desired article from his pocket and gave it and a match to Pole. Then he leaned against the heavy railing of the banisters. "I may as well tell you," he said, "I'm a dealer in lumber myself, and I'd like to know what kind of timber you have out there."

Pole pulled at the cigar, thrust it well into the corner of his mouth with the fire end smoking very near his left eye, and looked thoughtful. "To tell you the truth, my friend," he said, "I railly believe you'd be wastin' time to go over thar."

"Oh, you think so." It was a vocal start on the part of Wilson.

"Yes, sir; the truth is, old man Bishop has simply raked into his dern clutch ever' acre o' fine timber out that away. Now ef you went east, over t'other side o' the mountains, you mought pick out some good timber; but as I said, old man Bishop's got it all in a bag out our way. Saw-mill?"

"No, I don't run a saw-mill," said Wilson, with an avaricious sparkle in his eye. "I sometimes buy timbered lands for a speculation, that's all."

Pole laughed. "I didn't see how you could be a saw-mill man an' smoke cigars like this an' wear them clothes. I never knowed a saw-mill man to make any money."

"I suppose this Mr. Bishop is buying to sell again," said Wilson, tentatively. "People generally have some such idea when they put money into such property." Pole looked wise and thoughtful. "I don't know whether he is or not," he said. "But my opinion is that he 'll hold on to it till he's in the ground. He evidently thinks a good time's a-comin'! Thar was a feller out thar t'other day with money to throw at cats; he's been tryin' to honeyfuggle the old man into a trade, but I don't think he made a deal with 'im."

"Where was the man from?" Wilson spoke uneasily. "I don't railly know, but he ain't a-goin' to give up. He told Neil Fulmore at his store that he was goin' home to see his company an' write the old man a proposition that ud fetch 'im ef thar was any trade in 'im."

Wilson pulled out his watch.

"Do you happen to know where Mr. Rayburn Miller's law office is?" he asked.

"Yes; it's right round the corner. I know whar all the *white* men in this town do business, an' he's as white as they make 'em, an' as straight as a shingle."

"He's an acquaintance of mine," said Wilson. "I thought I'd run in and see him before I leave."

"It's right round the corner, an' down the fust side street, towards the court-house. I 'ain't got nothin' to do; I 'll p'int it out."

"Thank you," said Wilson, and they went out of the house and down the street together, Pole puffing vigorously at his cigar in the brisk breeze.

"Thar you are," said Pole, pointing to Miller's sign. "Good-day, sir; much obleeged fer this smoke," and with his head in the air Pole walked past the office without looking in.

"Good-morning," exclaimed Miller, as Wilson entered. "You are not an early riser like we are here in the country." He introduced Wilson all round, and then gave him a chair near his desk and facing him rather than the others.

"This is the gentleman who owns the property, I believe," said Wilson, suavely, as he indicated Bishop.

Miller nodded, and a look of cunning dawned in his clear eye.

"Yes. I have just been explaining to Mr. and Mrs. Bishop that the mere signing of a paper such as will be necessary to secure the loan will not bind them at all in the handling of their property. You know how cautious older people are nowadays in regard to legal matters. Now, Alan here, their son, understands the matter thoroughly, and his mind is not at all disturbed."

Wilson fell into the preliminary trap. "Oh no; it's not a binding thing at all," he said. "The payment of the money back to us releases you—that is, of course," Wilson recovered himself, "if we make the loan."

Several hearts in the room sank, but Miller's face did not alter in the slightest. "Oh, of course, if the loan is made," he said.

Wilson put his silk hat on the top of Miller's desk, and flicked the ashes from his cigar into a cuspidor. Then he looked at Mrs. Bishop suddenly— "Does the lady object to smoking?"

"Not at all," said the old lady—"not at all."

There was a pause as Wilson relighted his cigar and pulled at it in silence. A step sounded on the sidewalk and Trabue put his head in at the door. Miller could have sworn at him, but he smiled. "Good-morning, Squire," he said.

"I see you are busy," said the intruder, hastily.

"Just a little, Squire. I 'll see you in a few minutes."

"Oh, all right." The old lawyer moved on down the sidewalk, his hands in his pockets.

Miller brought up the subject again with easy adroitness. "I mentioned your proposition to my clients—the proposition that they allow you the refusal of the land at one hundred thousand, and they have finally come round to it. As I told them, they could not possibly market a thing like that as easily and for as good a price as a company regularly in the business. I may have been wrong in giving such advice, but it was the way I felt about it."

Without realizing it, Wilson tripped in another hole dug by Miller's inventive mind.

"They couldn't do half as well with it," the Boston man said. "In fact, no one could, as I told you, pay as much for the property as we can, considering the railroad we have to move somewhere, and our gigantic facilities for handling lumber in America and abroad. Still I think, and our directors think, a hundred thousand is a big price."

Miller laughed as if amused. "That's five dollars an acre, you know, but I'm not here to boom Mr. Bishop's timber-land. In fact, all this has grown out of my going down to Atlanta to borrow twenty-five thousand dollars on the property. I think I would have saved time if I hadn't run on you down there, Mr. Wilson."

Wilson frowned and looked at his cigar.

"We are willing," said he, "to make the loan at five per cent, per annum on two conditions."

"Well, out with them," laughed Miller. "What are they?"

"First," said Wilson, slowly and methodically, "we want the refusal of the property at one hundred thousand dollars."

A thrill of triumph passed over the silent group. Alan saw his father's face fill with sudden hope, and then it seemed to stand in abeyance as if doubt had already mastered it. Abner Daniel caught his beard in his stiff fingers and slowly slid them downward. Mrs. Bishop's bonnet hid her face, but her fingers were twitching excitedly as they toyed with the fringe of her shawl.

Miller's indifference was surprising. "For what length of time do you want the refusal of the property at that figure?" he asked, almost in a tone of contempt.

Wilson hung fire, his brow wrinkled thoughtfully.

"Till it is decided positively," he got out finally, "whether we can get a charter and a right of way to the property."

To those who were not following the details as closely as were Alan and Miller the reply of the latter fell discouragingly, even Abner Daniel glared in open horror of what he regarded as an unfavorable turn in the proceedings.

"That's entirely too indefinite to suit my clients," said the lawyer. "Do you suppose, Mr. Wilson, that they want to hang their property up on a hook like that? Why, if you didn't attend to pushing your road through—well, they would simply be in your hands, the Lord only knows how long."

"But we intend to do all we can to shove it through," said Wilson, with a flush.

"You know that is not a business-like proposition, Mr. Wilson," said Miller, with a bland smile. "Why, it amounts to an option without any limit at all."

"Oh, I don't know," said Wilson, lamely. "Mr. Bishop will be interested just as we are in getting a right of way through—in fact, it would insure us of his help. We can't buy a right of way; we can't afford it. The citizens through whose property the road runs must be persuaded to contribute the land for the purpose, and Mr. Bishop, of course, has influence up here with his neighbors."

"Still he would be very imprudent," said Miller, "to option his property without any limit. Now here's what we are willing to do. As long as you hold Mr. Bishop's note for twenty-five thousand dollars unpaid, you shall have the refusal of the land at one hundred thousand dollars. Now take my advice"—Miller was smiling broadly—"let it stand at that."

Wilson reflected for a moment, and then he said: "All right; let that go. The other condition is this—and it need be only a verbal promise—that nothing be said about my company's making this loan nor our securing the refusal of the property."

"That will suit us," said Miller. "Mr. Bishop' doesn't care to have the public know his business. Of course, the mortgage will have to be recorded at the court-house, but that need not attract attention. I don't blame Mr. Bishop," went on Miller, in a half-confidential tone. "These people are the worst gossips you ever saw. If you meet any of them they will tell you that Mr. Bishop has bu'sted himself wide open by buying so much timber-land, but this loan will make him as solid as the Bank of England. The people don't understand his dealings, and they are trying to take it out on him by blasting his reputation for being one of the solidest men in his county."

"Well, that's all, I believe," said Wilson, and Miller drew a blank sheet of legal-cap paper to him and began to write. Half an hour later the papers were signed and Miller carelessly handed Wilson's crisp pink check on a New York bank to Mr. Bishop.

"There you are, Mr. Bishop," he said, with a smile; "you didn't want any one else to have a finger in that big pie of yours over there, but you needed money, and I 'll tell you as a friend that a hundred thousand cash down will be about as well as you can do with that land. It takes money, and lots of it, to make money, and Mr. Wilson's company can move the thing faster than you can."

"That's a fact," said Wilson, in a tone that betrayed self-gratification. "Now we must all pull together for the railroad." He rose and turned to Miller. "Will you come with me to record the paper?"

"Certainly," said Miller, and they both left together.

The Bishop family were left alone, and the strain being lifted, they found themselves almost wholly exhausted.

"Is it all over?" gasped the old woman, standing up and grasping her son's arm.

"We've got his money," Alan told her, with a glad smile, "and a fair chance for more."

The pink check was fluttering in old Bishop's hand. Already the old self-willed look that brooked no interference with his personal affairs was returning to his wrinkled face.

"I 'll go over to Craig's bank an' deposit it," he said to Alan. "It 'll take a day or two to collect it, but he'd let me check on it right now fer any reasonable amount."

"I believe I'd ask him not to mention the deposit," suggested Alan.

"Huh! I reckon I've got sense enough to do that."

"I thought you intended to pay off the mortgage on our farm the fust thing," ventured Mrs. Bishop.

"We can' t do it till the note's due next January," said Bishop, shortly. "I agreed to keep the money a yeer, an' Martin Doe 'll make me hold to it. But what do you reckon I care as long as I've got some 'n' to meet it with?"

Mrs. Bishop's face fell. "I'd feel better about it if it was cleer," she faltered. "But the Lord knows we ort to feel thankful to come out as we have. If it hadn't been fer Alan—Mr. Miller said that Alan—"

"Ef you all hadn't made sech a eternal row," broke in Bishop, testily, "I'd 'a' had more timber-land than this. Colonel Barclay has as fine a strip as any I got, an' he's bantered me for a trade time an' agin."

Abner Daniel seldom sneered at anybody, no matter what the provocation was, but it seemed impossible for him to refrain from it now.

"You've been lookin' fer the last three months like a man that needed more land," he said. "Jest no furder back 'an last night you 'lowed ef you could git enough fer yore folly to raise the debt off'n yore farm you'd die happy, an' now yo' re a-frettin' beca'se you didn't buy up the sides o' the earth an' give nobody else a foothold. Le' me tell you the truth, even ef it *does* hurt a little. Ef Alan hadn't thought o' this heer railroad idea, you'd 'a' been the biggest human pancake that ever lay flat in its own grease."

"I hain't said nothin' to the contrary," admitted Bishop, who really took the reproof well. "Alan knows what I think about it."

Then Bishop and his wife went to Craig's bank, and a moment later Miller returned, rubbing his hands with satisfaction.

"We got through, and he's gone to catch his train," he said.

"It worked as smooth as goose-grease. I wonder what Pole Baker said to him, or if he saw him. I have an idea he did, from the way Wilson danced to our music."

"Heer's Pole now," said Abner, from the door. "Come in heer, you triflin' loafer, an' give an account o' yorese'f."

"I seed 'im makin' fer the train," laughed Pole, "an' so I sneaked in to see what you-uns done. He walked like he owned the town."

"It went through like lightning, without a hitch or a bobble," Abner told him. "We was jest a-won-derin' what you shot into 'im."

"I hardly know," Pole sniggered. "I got to talkin' to 'im an' it looked to me like I was chippin' off tan-bark with the sharpest tool I ever handled. Every lick seemed to draw blood, an' he stood an' tuck it without a start or a shiver. I said to myse'f: 'Pole Baker, yo're nothin' but a rag-tag, bob-tail mountain Hoosier, an' he's a slick duck from up North, with a gold watch-chain an' a silk beaver, but he's a lappin' up what you say like a hungry kitten does a pan o' milk. Go it, old boy, an' ef you win, you 'll he'p the finest man out o' trouble—I mean Alan Bishop, by gum—that ever lived.' It seemed to me I was filled with the fire of heaven. I could 'a' been at it yet—fer I'd jest started—but he drawed his watch on me, an' made a shoot fer this office, me with 'im, fer feer some yokel would strike up with 'im. I mighty nigh shoved 'im in at the door."

"You did noble," said Miller, while Pole and Alan were silently clasping hands. "Now I told you we wouldn't forget you. Go down to Wimbley's and tell him to give you the best suit of clothes he's got, and to charge them to me 'n' Alan."

Pole drew himself up to his full height, and stared at the lawyer with flashing eyes.

"Damn yore soul," he said; "don't you say a thing like that to me agin. I 'll have you know I've got feelin' s as well as you or anybody else. I'd cut off this right arm an' never wince to do Alan Bishop a favor, but I 'll be danged ef anybody kin look me over after I've done a *little* one an' pay me for it in store-clothes. I don't like that one bit, an' I ain't afeerd to say so."

"I didn't mean any offence, Pole," apologized Miller, most humbly.

"Well, you wouldn't 'a' said it to *some* men," growled Pole, "I know that. When I want pay fer a thing like that, I 'll jest go to that corner o' the street an' look down at that rock-pile, whar Alan found me one day an' paid me out jest to keep me from bein' the laughin'-stock o' this town."

Alan put his arm over his shoulder. "Rayburn didn't mean any harm," he said, gently. "You are both my friends, and we've had a big victory to-day; let's not have hard feelings."

Pole hung his head stubbornly and Miller extended his hand. Abner Daniel was an attentive listener, a half smile on his face.

"Say, Pole," he said, with a little laugh, "you run down to Wimbley's an' tell 'im not to wrop up that suit. I'm a-owin' him a bill, an' he kin jest credit the value of it on my account."

Pole laughed heartily and thrust his big hand into Miller's.

"Uncle Ab," he said, "you'd make a dog laugh."

"I believe yo' re right," said Abner, significantly, and then they all roared at Pole's expense.

The next day Alan received the following letter from Dolly Barclay:

"*DEAR ALAN,—Rayburn Miller told me in confidence of your wonderful success yesterday, and I simply cried with joy. I knew—I felt that you would win, and this is, as he says, a glorious beginning. I am so proud of you, and I am so full of hope to-day. All our troubles will come out right some day, and now that I know you love me I can wait. Rayburn would not have confided so much to me, but he said, while he would not let me tell father anything about the prospective railroad, he wanted me to prevent him from selling his tract of land near yours. You know my father consults me about all his business, and he will not dispose of that property without my knowing of it. Oh, wouldn't it be a fine joke on him to have him profit by your good judgment.*"

Alan was at the little post-office in Filmore's store when he received the letter, and he folded it and restored it to its envelope with a heart filled with love and tenderness. As he walked home through the woods, it seemed to him that everything in nature was ministering to his boundless happiness. He felt as light as air as he strode along. "God bless her dear, dear little soul!" he said, fervently.

CHAPTER XX

ABOUT a week after this transaction Rayburn Miller went to Atlanta on business for one of his clients, and while there he incidentally called at the offices of the Southern Land and Timber Company, hoping to meet Wilson and learn something about his immediate plans in regard to the new railroad. But he was informed that the president of the company had just gone to New York, and would not be back for a week.

Rayburn was waiting in the rotunda of the Kimball House for his train, which left at ten o' clock, when he ran across his friend, Captain Ralph Burton, of the Gate City Guards, a local military company.

"Glad to see you," said the young officer. "Did you run up for the ball?"

"What ball is that?" asked Miller. "I am at the first of it."

"Oh, we are giving one here in this house tonight," answered Burton, who was a handsome man of thirty-five, tall and erect, and appeared at his best in his close-fitting evening-suit and light overcoat. "Come up-stairs and I 'll introduce you to a lot of strangers."

"Can't," Rayburn told him. "I've got to leave at ten o' clock."

"Well, you've got a good hour yet," insisted the officer. "Come up on the next floor, where the orchestra is, anyway, and we can sit down and watch the crowd come in."

Miller complied, and they found seats on the spacious floor overlooking the thronged office. From where they sat they could look through several large drawing-rooms into the ballroom beyond. Already a considerable number of people had assembled, and many couples were walking about, even quite near to the two young men.

"By George!" suddenly exclaimed Miller, as a couple passed them, "who is that stunning-looking blonde; she walks like a queen."

"Where?" asked Burton, looking in the wrong direction.

"Why, there, with Charlie Penrose."

"Oh, that one," said Burton, trying to think, "I know as well as I know anything, but her name has slipped my memory. Why, she's visiting the Bishops on Peachtree Street—a Miss Bishop, that's it."

"Adele, little Adele? Impossible!" cried Rayburn, "and I've been thinking of her as a child all these years."

"So you know her?" said Captain Burton.

"Her brother is a chum of mine," explained Miller. "I haven't seen her since she went to Virginia to school, five years ago. I never would have recognized her in the world. My Lord! she's simply regal."

"I haven't had the pleasure of meeting her," said the Captain; "but I've heard lots about her from the boys who go to Bishop's. They say she's remarkably clever—recites, you know, and takes off the plantation negro to perfection. She's a great favorite with Major Middleton, who doesn't often take to the frying size. She has been a big drawing card out at Bishop's ever since she came. The boys say the house overflows every evening. Are you going to speak to her?"

"If I get a good chance," said Rayburn, his eyes on the couple as they disappeared in the ballroom. "I don't like to go in looking like this, but she'd want to hear from home."

"Oh, I see," said Burton. "Well, you'd better try it before the grand march sweeps everything before it."

As Miller entered the ballroom, Penrose was giving Adele a seat behind a cluster of palms, near the grand piano, around which the German orchestra was grouped. He went straight to her.

"You won't remember me, Miss Adele," he said, with a smile, "but I'm going to risk speaking to you, anyway."

She looked up from the bunch of flowers in her lap, and, in a startled, eager sort of way, began to study his face.

"No, I do not," she said, flushing a little, and yet smiling agreeably.

"Well, I call that a good joke," Penrose broke in, with a laugh, as he greeted Miller with a familiar slap on the shoulder. "Why, Rayburn, on my word, she hasn't talked of anybody else for the last week, and here she—"

"You are *not* Rayburn Miller!" Adele exclaimed, and she stood up to give him her hand. "Yes, I have been talking of you, and it seems to me I have a thousand things to say, and oh, so many thanks!"

There was something in this impulsive greeting that gave Miller a delectable thrill all over.

"You were such a little thing the last time I saw you," he said, almost tenderly. "I declare, you have changed—so, so remarkably."

She nodded to Penrose, who was excusing himself, and then she said to Miller, "Are you going to dance to-night?"

He explained that he was obliged to take the train which left in a few minutes.

He saw her face actually fall with disappointment. The very genuineness of the expression pleased him inexplicably. "Then I must hurry," she said. "Would you mind talking to me a little while?"

"Nothing could possibly please me so much," said he. "Suppose we stroll around?"

She took his arm and he led her back to the rotunda overlooking the office.

"So you are Rayburn Miller!" she said, looking at him wonderingly. "Do you know, I have pictured you in my mind many times since mother wrote me all about how you rescued us from ruin. Oh, Mr. Miller, I could not in a thousand years tell you how my heart filled with gratitude to you. My mother goes into the smallest details in her letters, and she described your every word and action during that transaction in your office. I could tell just where her eyes filled and her throat choked up by her quivering handwriting. I declare, I looked on you as a sort of king with unlimited power. If I were a man I'd rather use my brain to help suffering people than to be made President of the United States and be a mere figure-head. You must not think I am spoiled by all this glitter and parade down here. The truth is, I heartily despise it. I wanted to be at home so bad when I got that letter that I cried myself to sleep."

"You must not forget that your brother conceived the plan," Miller protested, "and that I only—"

"Oh yes; I know Alan thought of it," she interrupted, "but without your experience and firmness it would have remained in his dear old brain till the Lord knows when. The idea of their being in debt was slowly killing my father and mother, and you came to their relief just when they were unable to bear it any longer. I'm so glad you thought of borrowing that money."

Just then a young man, half a head shorter than Adele, came up hurriedly. "Oh, here you are," he exclaimed, in a gasp of relief. "I've been looking for you everywhere. This is mine, you know—the grand march. They are all ready."

Adele smiled pleasantly. "I hope you 'll excuse me from it, Mr. Tedcastle," she said. "I've just met a friend from home; I want to talk with him, and—"

"But, Miss Bishop, I—"

"I asked you to please excuse me, Mr. Tedcastle." Miller saw her face harden, as if from the sneer of contempt that passed over it. "I hope it will not be necessary for me to explain my reasons in detail until I have a little more time at my disposal."

"Oh, certainly not, Miss Bishop," said the young man, red with anger, as he bowed himself away.

"What's society coming to?" Adele asked Miller, with a nervous little laugh. "Does a lady have to get down on her knees and beg men, little jumping-jacks, like that one, to excuse her, and pet them into a good-humor when she has good reason to change her mind about an engagement? That's a sort of slavery I don't intend to enter."

"You served him right," said Miller, who had himself resented the young man's childish impetuosity, and felt like slapping him for his impertinence.

Adele shrugged her fine shoulders. "Let's not waste any more time talking about him," she said. "I was going to tell you how happy you made them all. When I read mother's description of their return home that night—how she went round looking at each object and touching it, that she might realize it was hers again; and how father sat up till past midnight talking incessantly about it; and all the droll things Uncle Abner said, I cried and laughed by turns. I longed to see you, to tell you how I felt about what you did, and yet, now that I'm with you, all I say seems utterly weak and—inadequate."

"It seems wonderfully nice to me," Miller declared. "I don't deserve anything, and yet—well, I like to hear you talk." He laughed. "Whether I deserve it or not, I could listen to you for a week on a stretch."

In truth, Rayburn Miller had never in all his varied social career become so suddenly and startlingly interested in any woman. It all seemed like a dream, and a most delicious one—the gay assemblage, the intermittent strains of the music, the touch of the stately creature on his arm, the perfume of her flowers, her hair, her eyes! He suddenly felt fearful of the passage of time, the leaving of his train, the approach of some one to claim her attention. He could not explain the spell she had thrown on him. Was it because she was his friend's sister, and so astoundingly pretty, frank, and sensible, or could it be that—?

His train of thought was broken by the approach of Miss Ida Bishop, Adele's cousin, a rather plain girl, who, with her scrawny neck and scant hair—which rebelled against being made much of—would have appeared to better advantage in a street costume.

"Oh, Adele," she cried, reproachfully, "what *do* you mean? Do you know you have mortally offended Mr. Tedcastle? He had the march with you."

"And I asked him as a favor to excuse me from it," said Adele, simply. "I had just met Mr. Miller, who is to leave on an early train, and I wanted to talk to him about home. Have you been introduced? My cousin, Miss Bishop, Mr. Rayburn Miller."

Miss Bishop bowed indifferently, and looked as if she still saw no justification in the slight under question.

"I'm awfully sorry," she said, reprovingly. "Mr. Tedcastle has been as nice to you as he could be, and this is the way you show appreciation for it. I don't blame him for being mad, do you, Mr. Miller?"

"I'm afraid I'd be a prejudiced witness," he smiled, "benefiting as I am by the gentleman' s discomfiture; but, really, I can' t think that any circumstances could justify a man in pressing a lady to fill an engagement when she chooses not to do so for any reason of hers."

"I knew you'd say that," said Adele. "If anybody has a right to be offended it is I, for the way he has acted without waiting for my full explanation."

"Oh, that is a high and mighty course that will do better for novels than real life," disagreed Miss Ida Bishop. "The young men are badly spoiled here, and if we want attention we've got to humor them."

"They shall not be spoiled by me," declared Adele. "Why," shrugging her shoulders, contemptuously, "if I had to run after them and bind up their bruises every time they fell down, I'd not appreciate their attentions. Besides, Mr. Tedcastle and his whole ilk actually put me to sleep. What do they talk about? Driving, pet dogs, flowers, candies, theatre-parties, and silly bosh, generally. Last Sunday Senator Hare dined at uncle's, and after dinner he and I were having really a wholesome sort of talk, and I was respecting myself—well, a little like I am now—when in traped 'Teddy' with his hangers-on. Of course, I had to introduce them to the Senator, and I felt like a fool, for he knew they were my 'company,' and it was impossible to keep them quiet. They went on with their baby talk, just as if Senator Hare were being given an intellectual treat. Of course, there are *some* grown-up men in Atlanta, but they are driven to the clubs by the swarms of little fellows. There comes Major Middleton, one of the old régime. He may ask me to dance with him. Now watch; if he does, I 'll answer him just as I did Mr. Tedcastle, and you shall see how differently he will treat it."

The Major, a handsome man of powerful physique and a great shock of curly, iron-gray hair, approached Adele, and with a low bow held out his hand.

"I'm after the next dance, my dear," he said. "You are one of the very few who ever dance with me, and I don't want to go home without it."

Adele smiled. "I'm very sorry, Major," she said; "but I hope you 'll excuse me this evening."

"Oh, that's all right, my dear *child*," he said. "No, don't explain. I know your reasons are all right. Go ahead and enjoy yourself in your own way."

"I won my bet," Adele laughed. "Major, I knew so well what you would say that I bet on it," and then she explained the situation.

"Tedcastle ought to be spanked," said the Major, in his high-keyed voice. "A girl who had not rather hear from home than spin around with him ought not to have a home. I'm going to mine rather early tonight. I came only to show the boys how to make my famous Kentucky punch."

When the Major and Miss Ida Bishop had gone and left them together, Adele looked over the railing at the big clock in the office. "We have only a few minutes longer—if you are to take that train," she said, regretfully.

"I never had as little interest in trains in my life," he said. And he meant it.

"Not in the trains on our new road?" she laughed.

"They are too far ahead to interfere with my comfort," he retorted. "This one is a steam nightmare."

"I presume you really could not miss it?" Her long-lashed eyes were down.

He hesitated; the simple thought suggested by her thrilled him as he had never been thrilled before.

"Because," she added, "it would be so nice to have you come out to-morrow afternoon to tea, about four."

He drew out his watch and looked at it waveringly.

"I could send a night message," he said, finally. "I really don't want to go. Miss Adele, I don't want to go at all."

"I don't want you to either," she said, softly. "It seems almost as if we are quite old friends. Isn't that strange?"

He restored his watch to his pocket. "I shall stay," he said, "and I shall call to-morrow afternoon."

Some one came for her a few minutes later, and he went down to the office and out into the street. He wanted to walk, to feel his body in action, keeping pace with his throbbing, bounding brain. His whole being was aflame with a fire which had never burned in him before.

"Alan's little sister!" he kept repeating to himself. "Little Adele—she's wonderful, wonderful! Perhaps she may be *the* woman. By George! she *is*— she *is!* A creature like that, with that soul full of appreciation for a man's best efforts, would lift a fellow to the highest rung on the ladder of human effort. Alan's little sister! And the idiot never told me, never intimated that she was—a goddess."

In his room at the hotel that night he slept little, his brain being so active with his new experience. He saw her the next afternoon alone, over a dainty tea-service of fragile china, in a Turkish corner in William Bishop's great, quiet, house, and then proposed driving her the next day to the Driving Club. He remained a week, seeing her, under some pretext or other, every day during that time. Sometimes it was to call with her on friends of hers. Once it was to attend a barbecue given by Captain Burton at a club-house in the country, and once he gave her and her cousin a luncheon at the Capitol City Club with a box at the matinée afterwards. He told himself that he had never lived before, and that, somehow, he was just beginning.

"No," he mused, as he sat in his train homeward bound. "I can't tell Alan. I simply couldn't do it, after all the rubbish I have crammed into him. Then she's his sister. I couldn't talk to him about her—not now, anyway."

CHAPTER XXI

IM glad you got back." Rayburn's sister, Mrs. Lampson, said to him at breakfast the morning following his return on the midnight train. "We are having a glorious meeting at our church."

"Oh, is that so?" said the young man, sipping his coffee. "Who is conducting it?"

"Brother Maynell," answered Mrs. Lampson, enthusiastically, a tinge of color in her wan, thin face. "He's a travelling evangelist, who has been conducting revivals all over the South. It is really remarkable the interest he has stirred up. We are holding prayer-meetings morning and afternoon, though only the ladies meet in the afternoon. I conducted the meeting yesterday."

"Oh no; did you, really? Why, sis—"

"Don't begin to poke fun at me," said Mrs. Lamp-son. "I know I didn't do as well as some of the others, but I did the best I could, because I felt it was my duty."

"I was not going to make fun," said Miller, soothingly; "but it seems mighty strange to think of you standing up before all the rest, and—"

"It was not such a very hard thing to do," said the lady, who was older than her brother by ten years. She had gray hairs at her temples, and looked generally as if she needed out-door exercise and some diversion to draw her out of herself.

Rayburn helped himself to the deliciously browned, fried chicken, in its bed of cream gravy, and a hot puffy biscuit.

"And how does Mr. Lapsley, the regular preacher, like this innovation?" he questioned. "I reckon you all pay the new man a fee for stirring things up?"

"Yes; we agreed to give him two hundred dollars, half of which goes to an orphan asylum he is building. Oh, I don't think brother Lapsley minds much, but of course it must affect him a little to see the great interest brother Maynell has roused, and I suppose some are mean enough to think he could have done the same, if he had tried."

"No, it's clearly a case of a new broom," smiled Rayburn, buttering his biscuit. "Old Lap might get up there and groan and whine for a week and not touch a mourner with a ten-foot pole. The other chap knows his business, and part of his business is not to stay long enough to wear out his pet phrases or exhaust his rockets. I'm sorry for Lapsley; he's paid a regular salary, and is not good for any other sort of work, and this shows him up unfairly. In the long run, I believe he 'll get as many into the church as the other man, and they will be more apt to stick. Sister, that's the trouble with these tin-pan revivals. The biggest converts backslide. I reckon you are working over old material now."

Mrs. Lampson frowned and her lip stiffened.

"I don't like your tone in speaking of such things," she said. "Indeed, Rayburn, I have been deeply mortified in the last week by some remarks that have been made about you. I didn't intend to mention them, but you make me do it."

"Oh, I knew they wouldn't let me rest," said Miller; "they never do in their annual shake-ups."

"Brother, you are looked on by nearly all religious workers in town as a dangerous young man—I mean dangerous to the boys who are just growing up, because they all regard you as a sort of standard to shape their conduct by. They see you going to balls and dances and playing cards, and they think it is smart and will not be interested in our meetings. They see that you live and seem to prosper under it, and they follow in your footsteps. I am afraid you don't realize the awful example you are setting. Brother Maynell has heard of you and asked me about you the other day. Some people think you have been in Atlanta all this time to avoid the meeting."

"I didn't know it was going on," said Miller, testily. "I assure you I never run from a thing like that. The best thing to do is to add fuel to the fire—it burns out quicker."

"Well, you will go out to meeting, won't you?" insisted the sweet-voiced woman. "You won't have them all thinking you have no respect for the religion of our father and mother—will you?"

Rayburn squirmed under this close fire.

"I shall go occasionally when there is *preaching*," he said, reluctantly. "I would be out of place at one of the—the knock-down and drag-out shouting-bees." Then, seeing her look of horror at the words which had unthoughtedly glided from his lips, he strove to make amends. "Oh, sister, do—*do* be reasonable, and look at it from my point of view. I don't believe that's the way to serve God or beautify the world. I believe in being happy in one's own way, just so that you don't tread on the rights of other people."

"But," said Mrs. Lampson, her eyes flashing, "you *are* treading on the rights of others. They are trying to save the souls of the rising generation in the community, and you and your social set use your influence in the other direction."

"But what about the rights of my social set, if you want to call it by that name?" Miller retorted, warmly. "We have the right to enjoy ourselves in our way, just as you have in yours. We don't interfere—we never ask you to close up shop so we can have a dance or a picnic, but you do. If we dare give a party while some revivalist is filling his pockets in town the revivalist jumps on us publicly and holds us up as examples of headlong plungers into fiery ruin. There is not a bit of justice or human liberty in that, and you 'll never reach a certain element till you quit such a course. Last year one of the preachers in this town declared in the pulpit that a girl could not be pure and dance a round dance. It raised the very devil in the hearts of the young men, who knew he was a dirty liar, and they got up as many dances out of spite as they possibly could. In fact, some of them came near knocking the preacher down on the street. I am a conservative sort of fellow, but I secretly wished that somebody would slug that man in the jaw."

"I'm really afraid you are worse than ever," sighed Mrs. Lampson. "I don't know what to do with you." She laughed good-naturedly as she rose and stood behind his chair, touching his head tenderly. "It really does make me rather mad," she confessed, "to hear them making you out such a bad stripe when I know what a wonderful man you really are for your age. I really believe some of them are jealous of your success and standing, but I do want you to be more religious." When Miller reached his office about ten o' clock and had opened the door he noticed that Craig's bank on the corner across the street was still closed. It was an unusual occurrence at that hour and it riveted Miller's attention. Few people were on the street, and none of them seemed to have noticed it. The church-bell in the next block was ringing for the revivalist's prayer-meeting, and Miller saw the merchants and lawyers hurrying by on their way to worship. Miller stood in his front door and bowed to them as they passed. Trabue hustled out of his office, pulling the door to with a jerk.

"Prayer-meeting?" he asked, glancing at Miller.

"No, not to-day," answered Miller; "got some writing to do."

"That preacher's a hummer," said the old lawyer. "I've never seen his equal. He'd 'a' made a bang-up criminal lawyer. Why, they say old Joe Murphy's converted—got out of his bed at midnight and went to Tim

Slocum's house to get 'im to pray for 'im. He's denied thar was a God all his life till now. I say a preacher's worth two hundred to a town if it can do that sort of work."

"He's certainly worth it to Slocum," said Miller, with a smile. "If I'd been denying there was a God as long as he has, I'd pay more than that to get rid of the habit. Slocum's able, and I think he ought to foot that preacher's bill."

"You are a tough customer, Miller," said Trabue, with a knowing laugh. "You'd better look out—May-nell's got an eye on you. He 'll call out yore name some o' these days, an' ask us to pray fer you."

"I was just wondering if there's anything wrong with Craig," said Miiler. "I see his door's not open."

"Oh, I reckon not," said the old lawyer. "He's been taking part in the meeting. He may have overslept."

There was a grocery-store near Miller's office, and the proprietor came out on the sidewalk and joined the two men. His name was Barnett. He was a powerful man, who stood six feet five in his boots; he wore no coat, and his suspenders were soiled and knotted.

"I see you-uns is watchin' Craig's door," he said. "I've had my eye on it ever since breakfast. I hardly know what to make of it. I went thar to buy some New York exchange to pay for a bill o' flour, but he wouldn't let me in. I know he's thar, for I seed 'im go in about an hour ago. I mighty nigh shook the door off'n the hinges. His clerk, that Western fellow, Win-ship, has gone off to visit his folks, an' I reckon maybe Craig's got all the book-keepin' to do."

"Well, he oughtn't to keep his doors closed at this time of day," remarked Miller. "A man who has other people's money in his charge can' t be too careful."

"He's got some o' mine," said the grocer, "and Mary Ann Tarpley, my wife's sister, put two hundred thar day before yesterday. Oh, I reckon nothin' s wrong, though I do remember I heerd somebody say Craig bought cotton futures an' sometimes got skeerd up a little about meetin' his obligations."

"I have never heard that," said Rayburn Miller, raising his brows.

"Well, I have, an' I've heerd the same o' Winship," said the grocer, "but I never let it go no furder. I ain't no hand to circulate ill reports agin a good member of the church."

Miller bit his lip and an unpleasant thrill passed over him as Trabue walked on. "Twenty-five thousand," he thought, "is no small amount. It would tempt five men out of ten if they were inclined to go wrong, and were in a tight."

The grocer was looking at him steadily.

"You bank thar, don't you?" he asked.

Miller nodded: "But I happen to have no money there right now. I made a deposit at the other bank yesterday."

"Suspicious, heigh? Now jest a little, wasn't you?" The grocer now spoke with undisguised uneasiness.

"Not at all," replied the lawyer. "I was doing some business for the other bank, and felt that I ought to favor them by my cash deposits."

"You don't think thar's anything the matter, do you?" asked the grocer, his face still hardening.

"I think Craig is acting queerly—very queerly for a banker," was Miller's slow reply. "He has always been most particular to open up early and—"

"Hello," cried out a cheery voice, that of the middle-aged proprietor of the Darley Flouring Mills, emerging from Barnett's store. "I see you fellows have your eye on Craig's front. If he was a drinking man we might suspicion he'd been on a tear last night, wouldn't we?"

"It looks damned shaky to me," retorted the grocer, growing more excited. "I'm goin' over there an' try that door again. A man 'at has my money can't attract the attention Craig has an' me say nothin'."

The miller pulled his little turf of gray beard and winked at Rayburn.

"You been scarin' Barnett," he said, with a tentative inflection. "He's easily rattled. By-the-way, now that I think of it, it does seem to me I heard some of the Methodists talkin' about reproving Craig an' Winship for speculatin' in grain and cotton. I know they've been dabblin' in it, for Craig always got my market reports. He's been dealin' with a bucket-shop in Atlanta."

"I'm going over there," said Miller, abruptly, and he hurried across in the wake of the big grocer. The miller followed him. On the other side of the street several people were curiously watching the bank door, and when Barnett went to it and grasped the handle and began to shake it vigorously they crossed over to him.

"What's wrong?" said a dealer in fruits, a short, thick-set man with a florid face; but Barnett's only reply was another furious shaking of the door.

"Why, man, what's got into you?" protested the fruit-dealer, in a rising tone of astonishment. "Do you intend to break that door down?"

"I will if that damned skunk don't open it an' give me my money," said Barnett, who was now red in the face and almost foaming at the mouth. "He's back in thar, an' he knows it's past openin' time. By gum! I know more 'n I'm goin' to tell right now."

This was followed by another rattling of the door, and the grocer's enormous weight, like a battering-ram, was thrown against the heavy walnut shutter.

"Open up, I say—open up in thar!" yelled the grocer, in a voice hoarse with passion and suspense.

A dozen men were now grouped around the doorway. Barnett released the handle and stood facing them.

"Somethin' s rotten in Denmark," he panted. "Believe me or not, fellows, I know a thing or two. This bank's in a bad fix."

A thrill of horror shot through Miller. The words had the ring of conviction. Alan Bishop's money was in bad hands if it was there at all. Suddenly he saw a white, trembling hand fumbling with the lower part of the close-drawn window-shade, as if some one were about to raise it; but the shade remained down, the interior still obscured. It struck Miller as being a sudden impulse, defeated by fear of violence. There was a pause. Then the storm broke again. About fifty men had assembled, all wild to know what was wrong. Miller elbowed his way to the door and stood on the step, slightly raised above the others, Barnett by his side. "Let me speak to him," he said, pacifically. Barnett yielded doggedly, and Rayburn put his lips to the crack between the two folding-doors.

"Mr. Craig!" he called out—"Mr. Craig!"

There was no reply, but Rayburn heard the rustling of paper on the inside near the crack against which his ear was pressed, and then the edge of a sheet of writing-paper was slowly shoved through. Rayburn grasped it, lifting it above a dozen outstretched hands. "Hold on!" he cried, authoritatively. "Til read it." The silence of the grave fell on the crowd as the young man began to read.

"Friends and citizens," the note ran, "Winship has absconded with every dollar in the vaults, except about two hundred dollars in my small safe. He has been gone two days, I thought on a visit to his kinfolks. I have just discovered the loss. I'm completely ruined, and am now trying to make out a report of my condition. Have mercy on an old man."

Rayburn's face was as white as that of a corpse. The paper dropped from his hand and he stepped down into the crowd. He was himself no loser, but the Bishops had lost their all. How could he break the news to them? Presently he began to hope faintly that old Bishop might, within the last week, have drawn out at least part of the money, but that hope was soon discarded, for he remembered that the old man was waiting to invest the greater part of the deposit in some Shoal Creek Cotton Mill stock which had been promised him in a few weeks. No, the hope was groundless. Alan, his father, Mrs. Bishop, and—Adele—Miller's heart sank down into the very ooze of despair. All that he had done for Adele's people, and which had roused her deepest, tenderest gratitude, was swept away. What would she think now?

His train of thought was rudely broken by an oath from Barnett, who, with the rage of a madman, suddenly threw his shoulder against the door. There was a crash, a groan of bursting timber and breaking bolts, and the door flew open. For one instant Miller saw the ghastly face and cowering form of the old banker behind the wire-grating, and then, with a scream of terror, Craig ran into a room in the rear, and thence made his escape at a door opening on the side street. The mob filled the bank, and did not discover Craig's escape for a minute; then, with a howl of rage, it surged back into the street. Craig was ahead of them, running towards the church, where prayer-meeting-was being held, the tails of his long frock-coat flying behind him, his worn silk hat in his convulsive grasp.

"Thar he goes!" yelled Barnett, and he led the mob after him, all running at the top of their speed without realizing why they were doing so. They gained on the fleeing banker, and Barnett could almost touch him when they reached the church. With a cry of fear, like that of a wild animal brought to bay, Craig sprang up the steps and ran into the church, crying and groaning for help.

A dozen men and women and children were kneeling at the altar to get the benefit of the prayers of the ministers and the congregation, but they stood up in alarm, some of them with wet faces.

The mob checked itself at the door, but the greater part of it crowded into the two aisles, a motley human mass, many of them without coats or hats. The travelling evangelist seemed shocked out of expression; but the pastor, Mr. Lapsley, who was an old Confederate soldier, and used to scenes of violence, stood calmly facing them.

"What's all this mean?" he asked.

"I came here for protection," whined Craig, "to my own church and people. This mob wants to kill me—tear me limb from limb."

"But what's wrong?" asked the preacher.

"Winship," panted Craig, his white head hanging down as he stood touching the altar railing—"Win-ship's absconded with all the money in my vault. I'm ruined. These people want me to give up what I haven't got. Oh, God knows, I would refund every cent if I had it!"

"You shall have our protection," said the minister, calmly. "They won't violate the sacredness of the house of God by raising a row. You are safe here, brother Craig. I'm sure all reasonable people will not blame you for the fault of another."

"I believe he's got my money," cried out Barnett, in a coarse, sullen voice, "and the money of some o' my women folks that's helpless, and he's got to turn it over. Oh, he's got money some'r's, I'll bet on that!"

"The law is your only recourse, Mr. Barnett," said the preacher, calmly. "Even now you are laying yourself liable to serious prosecution for threatening a man with bodily injury when you can't prove he's wilfully harmed you."

The words told on the mob, many of them being only small depositors, and Barnett found himself without open support. He was silent. Rayburn Miller, who had come up behind the mob and was now in the church, went to Craig's side. Many thought he was proffering his legal services.

"One word, Mr. Craig," he said, touching the quivering arm of the banker.

"Oh, you're no loser," said Craig, turning on him. "There was nothing to your credit."

"I know that," whispered Miller, "but as attorney for the Bishops, I have a right to ask if their money is safe." The eyes of the banker went to the ground.

"It's gone—every cent of it!" he said. "It was their money that tempted Winship. He'd never seen such a large pile at once."

"You don't mean—" But Miller felt the utter futility of the question on his tongue and turned away. Outside he met Jeff Dukes, one of the town marshals, who had been running, and was very red in the face and out of breath.

"Is that mob in thar?" he asked.

"Yes, and quiet now," said Miller. "Let them alone; the important thing is to put the police on Winship's track. Come back down-town."

"I'll have to git the particulars from Craig fust," said Dukes. "Are you loser?"

"No, but some of my clients are, and I'm ready to stand any expense to catch the thief."

"Well, I 'll see you in a minute, and we 'll heat all the wires out of town. I 'll see you in a minute."

Farther down the street Miller met Dolly Barclay. She had come straight from her home, in an opposite direction from the bank, and had evidently not heard the news.

"I'm on my way to prayer-meeting," she smiled. "I'm getting good to please the old folks, but—" She noticed his pale face. "What is the matter? Has anything—"

"Craig's bank has failed," Rayburn told her briefly. "He says Winship has absconded with all the cash in the vaults."

Dolly stared aghast. "And you—you—"

"I had no money there," broke in Miller. "I was fortunate enough to escape."

"But Alan—Mr. Bishop?" She was studying his face and pondering his unwonted excitement. "Had they money there?"

Miller did not answer, but she would not be put aside.

"Tell me," she urged—"tell me that."

"If I do, it's in absolute confidence," he said, with professional firmness. "No one must know—not a soul—that they were depositors, for much depends on it. If Wilson knew they were hard up he might drive them to the wall. They were not only depositors, but they lose every cent they have—twenty-five thousand dollars in a lump."

He saw her catch her breath, and her lips moved mutely, as if repeating the words he had just spoken. "Poor Alan!" he heard her say. "This is too, *too* much, after all he has gone through."

Miller touched his hat and started on, but she joined him, keeping by his side like a patient, pleading child. He marvelled over her strength and wonderful poise. "I am taking you out of your way, Miss Dolly," he said, gently, more gently than he had ever spoken to her before.

"I only want to know if Alan has heard. Do—do tell me that."

"No, he's at home. I shall ride out as soon as I get the matter in the hands of the police."

She put out her slender, shapely hand and touched his arm.

"Tell him," she said, in a low, uncertain voice, "that it has broken my heart. Tell him I love him more than I ever did, and that I shall stick to him always."

Miller turned and took off his hat, giving her his hand.

"And I believe you will do it," he said. "He's a lucky dog, even if he *has* just struck the ceiling. I know him, and your message will soften the blow. But it's awful, simply awful! I can't now see how they can possibly get from under it."

"Well, tell him," said Dolly, with a little, soundless sob in her throat— "tell him what I told you."

CHAPTER XXII

THAT afternoon the breeze swerved round from the south, bringing vague threats About three o' clock Alan, his his mother and father were in the front yard, looking at the house, with a view to making some alterations that had been talked of for several years past.

"I never had my way in anything before," Mrs. Bishop was running on, in the pleased voice of a happy child, "and I'm glad you are goin' to let me this once. I want the new room to jut out on this side from the parlor, and have a bay-window, and we must cut a wide foldin'-door between the two rooms. Then the old veranda comes down and the new one must have a double floor, like Colonel Sprague's on the river, except ours will have round, white columns instead o' square, if they do cost a trifle more."

"She knows what she wants," said Bishop, with one of his infrequent smiles, "and I reckon we'd save a little to let her boss the job, ef she don't hender the carpenters by too much talk. I don't want 'em to put in a stick o' lumber that ain't the best."

"I'm glad she's going to have her way," said Alan. "She's wanted a better house for twenty years, and she deserves it."

"I don't believe in sech fine feathers," said Bishop, argumentatively. "I'd a leetle ruther wait till we see whether Wilson's a-goin' to put that road through—then we *could* afford to put on a dab or two o' style. I don't know but I'd move down to Atlanta an' live alongside o' Bill, an' wear a claw-hammer coat an' a dicky cravat fer a change."

"Then you mought run fer the legislatur'," spoke up Abner Daniel, who had been an amused listener, "an' git up a law to pen up mad dogs at the dangerous part o' the yeer. Alf, I've always thought you'd be a' ornament to the giddy whirl down thar. William was ever' bit as green as you are when he fust struck the town. But he had the advantage o' growin' up an' sorter ripenin' with the place. It ud be hard on you at yore time o' life."

At this juncture Alan called their attention to a horseman far down the road. "It looks like Ray Miller's mare," he remarked. "This is one of his busy days; he can' t be coming to fish."

"Railroad news," suggested Abner. "It's a pity you hain't connected by telegraph."

They were all now sure that it was Miller, and with no little curiosity they moved nearer the gate.

"By gum! he's been givin' his mare the lash," said Abner. "She's fairly kivered with froth."

"Hello, young man," Alan called out, as Miller dismounted at a hitching-post just outside the fence and fastened his bridle-rein. "Glad to see you; come in."

Miller bowed and smiled as he opened the gate and came forward to shake hands.

"We are certainly glad you came, Mr. Miller," said Mrs. Bishop, with all her quaint cordiality. "Ever since that day in the office I've wanted a chance to show you how much we appreciate what you done fer us. Brother Ab will bear me out when I say we speak of it mighty nigh ever'day."

Miller wore an inexpressible look of embarrassment, which he tried to lose in the act of shaking hands all round the group, but his platitudes fell to the ground. Abner, the closest observer among them, already had his brows drawn together as he pondered Miller's unwonted lack of ease.

"Bring any fishing-tackle?" asked Alan.

"No, I didn't," said the lawyer, jerking himself to that subject awkwardly. "The truth is, I only ran out for a little ride. I've got to get back."

"Then it *is* business, as brother Ab said," put in Mrs. Bishop, tentatively.

Miller lowered his eyes to the ground and then raised them to Alan's face.

"Yes, it's railroad business," said Abner, his voice vibrant with suspense.

"And it's not favorable," said Alan, bravely. "I can see that by your looks."

Miller glanced at his mare, and lashed the leg of his top-boots with his riding-whip. "No, I have bad news, but it's not about the railroad. I could have written, but I thought I'd better come myself."

"Adele!" gasped Mrs. Bishop. "You have heard—"

"No, she's well," said Miller. "It's about the money you put in Craig's bank."

"What about that?" burst from old Bishop's startled lips.

"Craig claims Winship has absconded with all the cash. The bank has failed."

"Failed!" The word was a moan from Bishop, and for a moment no one spoke. A negro woman at the wash-place behind the house was using a batting-stick on some clothing, and the dull blows came to them distinctly.

"Is that so, Ray?" asked Alan, calm but pale to the lips.

"I'm sorry to say it is."

"Can anything at all be done?"

"I've done everything possible already. We have been telegraphing the Atlanta police all morning about tracing Winship, but they don't seem much interested. They think he's had too big a start on us. You see, he's been gone two days and nights. Craig says he thought he was on a visit to relatives till he discovered the loss last night."

"It simply spells ruin, old man," said Alan, grimly. "I can see that."

Miller said nothing for a moment—then:

"It's just as bad as it could be, my boy," he said. "I see no reason to raise false hopes. There is a strong feeling against Craig, and no little suspicion, owing to the report that he has been speculating heavily, but he has thrown himself on the protection of his church, and even some of his fellow-members, who lose considerably, are standing by him."

Here old Bishop, with compressed lips, turned and walked unsteadily into the house. With head hanging low and eyes flashing strangely, his wife followed him. At the steps she paused, her sense of hospitality transcending her despair. "You must stay to early supper, anyway, Mr. Miller," she said. "You could ride back in the cool o' the evening."

"Thank you, but I must hurry right back, Mrs. Bishop," Miller said.

"And Dolly—does she know?" asked Alan, when his mother had disappeared and Abner had walked to the hitching-post, and stood as if thoughtfully inspecting Miller's mare. Miller told him of their conversation that morning, and Alan' s face grew tender and more resigned.

"She's a brick!" said Miller. "She's a woman I now believe in thoroughly—she and one other."

"Then there is another?" asked Alan, almost cheerfully, as an effect of the good news that had accompanied the bad.

"Yes. I see things somewhat differently of late," admitted Miller, in an evasive, non-committal tone. "Dolly Barclay opened my eyes, and when they were open I saw—well, the good qualities of some one else. I may tell you about her some day, but I shall not now. Get your horse and come to town with me. We must be ready for any emergency."

Abner Daniel came towards them. "I don't want to harm nobody's character," he said; "but whar my own kin is concerned, I'm up an' wide awake. I don't know what you think, but I hain't got a speck o' faith in Craig hisse'f. He done me a low, sneakin' trick once that I ketched up with. He swore it was a mistake, but it wasn't. He's a bad egg—you mind what I say; he won't do."

"It may be as you say, Mr. Daniel," returned Miller, with a lawyer's reserve on a point unsubstantiated by evidence, "but even if he has the money hidden away, how are we to get it from him?"

"I'd find a way," retorted Daniel, hotly, "so I would."

"We 'll do all we can," said Miller.

Daniel strode into the house and Alan went after his horse. Miller stood at the gate, idly tapping his boot with his whip.

"Poor Mrs. Bishop!" he said, his eyes on the house; "how very much she resembled Adele just now, and she is bearing it just like the little girl would. I reckon they 'll write her the bad news. I wish I was there to—soften the blow. It will wring her heart."

CHAPTER XXIII

THAT evening after supper the family remained, till bedtime, in the big, bare-looking dining-room, the clean, polished floors of which gleamed in the light of a little fire in the big chimney. Bishop's chair was tilted back against the wall in a dark corner, and Mrs. Bishop sat knitting mechanically. Abner was reading—or trying to read—a weekly paper at the end of the dining-table, aided by a dimly burning glass-lamp. Aunt Maria had removed the dishes and, with no little splash and clatter, was washing them in the adjoining kitchen.

Suddenly Abner laid down his paper and began to try to console them for their loss. Mrs. Bishop listened patiently, but Bishop sat in the very coma of despair, unconscious of what was going on around him.

"Alf," Abner called out, sharply, "don't you remember what a close-fisted scamp I used to be about the time you an' Betsy fust hitched together?"

"No, I don't," said the man addressed, almost with a growl at being roused from what could not have been pleasant reflections.

"I remember folks said you was the stingiest one in our family," struck in Mrs. Bishop, plaintively. "Law me! I hain't thought of it from that day to this. It seems powerful funny now to think of you havin' sech a reputation, but I railly believe you had it once."

"An' I deserved it," Abner folded his paper, and rapped with it on the table. "You know, Betsy, our old daddy was as close as they make 'em; he had a rope tied to every copper he had, an' I growed up thinkin' it was the only safe course in life. I was too stingy to buy ginger-cake an' cider at camp-meetin' when I was dyin' fer it. I've walked round an' round a old nigger woman's stand twenty times with a dry throat an' my fingers on a slick dime, an' finally made tracks fer the nighest spring. I had my eyes opened to stinginess bein' ungodly by noticin' its effect on pa. He was a natural human bein' till a body tetched his pocket, an' then he was a rantin' devil. I got to thinkin' I'd be like 'im by inheritance ef I didn't call a halt, an' I begun tryin' in various ways to reform. I remember I lent money a little freer than I had, which wasn't sayin' much, fer thar was a time when I wouldn't 'a' sold a man a postage-stamp on a credit ef he'd 'a' left it stuck to the back o' my neck fer security.

"But I'll tell you how I made my fust great big slide towards reformation. It tuck my breath away, an' lots o' my money; but I did it with my eyes open. I was jest a-thinkin' a minute ago that maybe ef I told you-uns about how little it hurt me to give it up you mought sleep better to-night over yore own shortage. Alf, are you listenin'?"

"Yes, I heerd what you said," mumbled Bishop.

Abner cleared his throat, struck at a moth with his paper, and continued: "Betsy, you remember our cousin, Jimmy Bartow? You never knowed 'im well, beca'se you an' Alf was livin' on Holly Creek about that time, an' he was down in our neighborhood. He never was wuth shucks, but he twisted his mustache an' greased his hair an' got 'im a wife as easy as fallin' off a log. He got to clerkin' fer old Joe Mason in his store at the cross-roads, and the sight o' so much change passin' through his fingers sort o' turned his brain. He tuck to drinking an' tryin' to dress his wife fine, an' one thing or other, that made folks talk. He was our double fust cousin, you know, an' we tuck a big interest in 'im on that account. After a while old Joe begun to miss little dribs o' cash now an' then, an' begun to keep tab on Jimmy, an' 'fore the young scamp knowed it, he was ketched up with as plain as day.

"Old Joe made a calculation that Jimmy had done 'im, fust and last, to the tune of about five hundred dollars, an' told Jimmy to set down by the stove an' wait fer the sheriff.

"Jimmy knowed he could depend on the family pride, an' he sent fer all the kin fer miles around. It raised a awful rumpus, fer not one o' our stock an' generation had ever been jailed, an' the last one of us didn't want it to happen. I reckon we was afeerd ef it once broke out amongst us it mought become a epidemic. They galloped in on the'r hosses an' mules, an' huddled around Mason. They closed his doors, back an' front, an' patted 'im on the back, an' talked about the'r trade an' influence, an' begged 'im not to prefer charges; but old Joe stood as solid as a rock. He said a thief was a thief, ef you spelt it back'ards or for'ards, or ef he was akin to a king or a corn-fiel' nigger. He said it was, generally, the bigger the station the bigger the thief. Old Joe jest set at his stove an' chawed tobacco an' spit. Now an' then he'd stick his hands down in his pockets an' rip out a oath. Then Jimmy's young wife come with her little teensy baby, an' set down by Jimmy, skeerd mighty nigh out of 'er life. Looked like the baby was skeerd too, fer it never cried ur moved. Then the sheriff driv' up in his buggy an' come in clinkin' a pair o' handcuffs. He seed what they was all up to an' stood back to see who would win, Jimmy's kin or old Joe. All at once I tuck notice o' something that made me madder'n a wet hen. They all knowed I had money laid up, an' they begun to ax old Mason ef I'd put up the five hundred dollars would he call it off. I was actu'ly so mad I couldn't speak. Old Joe said he reckoned, seein' that they was all so turribly set back, that he'd do it ef I was willin'. The Old Nick got in me then as big as a side of a house, an' I give the layout about the toughest talk they ever had. It didn't faze 'em much, fer all they wanted was to git Jimmy free, an' so they tuck another tack. Ef they'd git up half amongst 'em all, would I throw in t'other half? That, ef anything, made me madder. I axed 'em what they tuck me fer—did I look like a durn fool? An' did they think beca'se they was sech fools I was one?

"Old Tommy Todd, Jimmy's own uncle, was thar, but he never had a word to say. He jest set an' smoked his pipe an' looked about, but he wouldn't open his mouth when they'd ax him a question. He was knowed to be sech a skinflint that nobody seemed to count on his help at all, an' he looked like he was duly thankful fer his reputation to hide behind in sech a pressure.

"Then they lit into me, an' showed me up in a light I'd never appeared in before. They said I was the only man thar without a family to support, an' the only one thar with ready cash in the bank, an' that ef I'd let my own double fust cousin be jailed, I was a disgrace to 'em all. They'd not nod to me in the big road, an' ud use the'r influence agin my stayin' in the church an' eventually gittin' into the kingdom o' Heaven. I turned from man to devil right thar. I got up on the head of a tater-barrel behind the counter, an' made the blamedest speech that ever rolled from a mouth inspired by iniquity. I picked 'em out one by one an' tore off their shirts, an' chawed the buttons. The only one I let escape was old Tommy; he never give me a chance to hit him. Then I finally come down to the prisoner at the bar an' I larruped him. Ever' time I'd give a yell, Jimmy ud duck his head, an' his wife ud huddle closer over the baby like she was afeerd splinters ud git in its eyes. I made fun of 'em till I jest had to quit. Then they turned the'r backs on me an' begun to figure on doin' without my aid. It was mortgage this, an' borrow this, an' sell this hoss or wagon or mule or cow, an' a turrible wrangle. I seed they was gittin' down to business an' left 'em.

"I noticed old Tommy make his escape, an' go out an' unhitch his hoss, but he didn't mount. Looked like he 'lowed he was at least entitled to carryin' the news home, whether he he'ped or not. I went to the spring at the foot o' the rise an' set down. I didn't feel right. In fact, I felt meaner than I ever had in all my life, an' couldn't 'a' told why. Somehow I felt all at once ef they did git Jimmy out o' hock an' presented 'im to his wife an' baby without me a-chippin' in, I'd never be able to look at 'em without remorse, an' I did think a lots o' Jimmy's wife an' baby. I set thar watchin' the store about as sorry as a proud sperit kin feel after a big rage. Fust I'd hope they'd git up the required amount, an' then I'd almost hope they wouldn't. Once I actually riz to go offer my share, but the feer that it ud be refused stopped me. On the whole, I think I was in the mud about as deep as Jimmy was in the mire, an' I hadn't tuck nobody's money nuther. All at once I begun to try to see some way out o' my predicament. They wouldn't let me chip in, but I wondered ef they'd let me pay it all. I believed they would, an' I was about to hurry in the store when I was balked by the thought that folks would say I was a born idiot to be payin' my lazy, triflin' kinfolks out o' the consequences o' the'r devilment; so I set down agin, an' had another wrastle. I seed old Tommy standin' by his hoss chawin' his ridin'-switch an' watchin' the door. All at once he looked mighty contemptible, an' it struck me that I wasn't actin' one bit better, so I ris an' plunged fer the door. Old Tommy ketched my arm as I was about to pass 'im an' said, 'What you goin' to do, Ab?' An' I said, 'Uncle Tommy, I'm a-goin' to pay that boy out ef they 'll let me.'

"'You don't say,' the old fellow grunted, lookin' mighty funny, an' he slid in the store after me. Somehow I wasn't afeerd o' nothin' with or without shape. I felt like I was walkin' on air in the brightest, saftest sunshine I ever felt. They was all huddled over Mason's desk still a-figurin' an' a-complainin' at the uneven division. Jimmy set thar with his head ducked an' his young wife was tryin' to fix some'n' about the baby. She looked like she'd been cryin.'I got up on my tater-barrel an' knocked on the wall with a axe-handle to attract the'r attention. Then I begun. I don't know what I said, or how it sounded, but I seed Jimmy raise his head an' look, an' his wife push back her poke-bonnet an' stare like I'd been raised from the grave. Along with my request to be allowed to foot the whole bill, I said I wanted to do it beca'se I believed I could show Jimmy an' his wife that I was doin' it out o' genuine regard fer 'em both, an' that I wanted 'em to take a hopeful new start an' not be depressed. Well, sir, it was like an avalanche. I never in all my life seed sech a knocked-out gang. Nobody wanted to talk. The sheriff looked like he was afeerd his handcuffs ud jingle, an' Jimmy bu'st out cryin'. His wife sobbed till you could 'a' heerd her to the spring. She sprung up an' fetched me her baby an' begged me to kiss it. With her big glad eyes, an' the tears in 'em, she looked nigher an angel than any human bein' I ever looked at. Jimmy went out the back way wipin' his eyes, an' I went to Mason's desk to write him a check fer the money. He come to my elbow an' looked troubled.

"'I said it was five hundred dollars,' said he, 'but I was sorter averagin' the loss. I ain't a-goin' to run no risks in a matter like this. I'd feel better to call it four hundred. You see, Jimmy's been a sort o' standby with me, an' has fetched me lots o' trade. Make it four hundred and I 'll keep 'im. I don't believe he 'll ever git wrong agin.'

"And Jimmy never did. He stayed thar for five yeer on a stretch, an' was the best clerk in the county. I was paid a thousandfold. I never met them two in my life that they didn't look jest like they thought I was all right, an' that made me feel like I was to some extent. Old Tommy, though, was the funniest thing about it. He bored me mighty nigh to death. He'd come to my cabin whar I was livin' at the time an' set by my fire an' smoke an' never say hardly a word. It looked like some 'n' was on his mind, an' he couldn't git it off. One night when he'd stayed longer 'n usual, I pinned 'im down an' axed 'im what was the matter. He got up quick an' said nothin' aileded 'im, but he stopped at the fence an' called me out. He was as white as a sheet an' quiverin' all over. Said he: 'I've got to have this over with, Ab. I may as well tell you an' be done with it. It's been botherin' the life out o' me, an' I 'll never git rid of it till it's done. I want to pay you half o' that money you spent on Jimmy. I had the cash that day, an' it 'ain't done me one bit o' good sence then. I 'll never sleep well till I go you halvers.'

"'I cayn't sell that to you, Uncle Tommy,' I said, laughin'. 'No, siree, you couldn't chip into that investment ef you doubled yore offer. I've found out what it is wuth. But,' said I, 'ef you've got two hundred that's burnin' a hole in yore pocket, ur conscience, an' want to yank it out, go give it to Jimmy's wife to he'p her educate that baby.'

"It struck 'im betwixt the eyes, but he didn't say yes or no. He slid away in the moonlight, all bent over an' quiet. I never seed 'im agin fer a month, an' then I called 'im out of a crowd o' fellers at the court-house an' axed 'im what he'd done. He looked bothered a little, but he gave me a straight look like he wasn't ready to sneak out o' anything.

"'I thought it over,' said he, 'but I railly don't see no reason why I ort to help Jimmy's child any more 'n a whole passle o' others that have as much claim on me by blood; but somehow I do feel like goin' cahoot with you in what's already been done, an' I'm still ready to jine you, ef you are willin'.'

"I didn't take his money, but it set me to thinkin'. When old Tommy died, ten years after that, they found he had six wool socks filled with gold an' silver coin under his house, an' nobody ever heerd o' his doin' any charity work. I wish now that I'd 'a' lifted that cash an' 'a' put it whar it would do good. If I had he'd 'a' had a taste o' some 'n' that never glorified his pallet."

When Abner concluded, Mrs. Bishop went to the fire and pushed the chunks together into a heap in the fireplace. Bishop moved in his chair, but he said nothing.

"I remember heerin' about that, brother Ab," Mrs. Bishop said, a reminiscent intonation in her voice. "Some folks wondered powerful over it. I don't believe money does a body much good jest to hold an' keep. As the Lord is my judge, I jest wanted that bank deposit fer Alan and Adele. I wanted it, an' I wanted it bad, but I cayn't believe it was a sin."

Something like a groan escaped Bishop's lips as he lowered the front posts of his chair to the floor.

"What's the use o' talkin' about it?" he said, impatiently. "What's the use o' anything?"

He rose and moved towards the door leading to his room.

"Alfred," Mrs. Bishop called to him, "are you goin' to bed without holdin' prayer?"

"I'm goin' to omit it to-night," he said. "I don't feel well, one bit. Besides, I reckon each pusson kin pray in private according to the way they feel."

Abner stood up, and removing the lamp-chimney he lighted a candle by the flame.

"I tried to put a moral lesson in what I said just now," he smiled, mechanically, "but I missed fire. Alf's sufferin' is jest unselfishness puore an' undefiled; he wants to set his children up in the world. This green globe is a sight better 'n some folks thinks it is. You kin find a little speck o' goody in mighty nigh ever' chestnut."

"That's so, brother Ab," said his sister; "but we are ruined now—ruined, ruined!"

"Ef you will look at it that way," admitted Abner, reaching for his candle; "but thar's a place ahead whar thar never was a bank, or a dollar, or a railroad, an' it ain't fur ahead, nuther. Some folks say it begins heer in this life."

CHAPTER XXIV

AS Abner Daniel leaned over the rail-fence in front of Pole Baker's log-cabin one balmy day, two weeks later, he saw evidences of the ex-moonshiner's thriftlessness combined with an inordinate love for his children. A little express-wagon, painted red, such as city children receive from their well-to-do parents on Christmas, was going to ruin under a cherry-tree which had been bent to the ground by a rope-swing fastened to one of its flexible boughs. The body of a mechanical speaking-doll lay near by, and the remains of a toy air-rifle. After a protracted spree Pole usually came home laden down with such peace-offerings to his family and conscience. His wife might go without a needed gown, and he a coat, but his children never without toys. Seeing Abner at the fence, Mrs. Baker came to the low door and stood bending her head to look out.

"I heerd at home," said Abner, "that Pole was over thar axin' fer me. I've been away to my peach-orchard on the hill."

"Yes, he's been over thar twice," said the woman. "He's back of the house some'r's settin' a trap fer the children to ketch some birds in. I 'll blow the horn. When I blow twice he knows he's wanted right off."

She took down a cow's-horn from a nail on the wall, and going to the door on the opposite side of the house she gave two long, ringing blasts, which set half a dozen dogs near by and some far off to barking mellowly. In a few minutes Pole appeared around the corner of the cabin.

"Hello, Uncle Ab," he said. "Won't you come in?"

"No, hain't time," smiled the old man. "I jest come over to see how much money you wanted to borrow."

"I don't want any o' yo'rn," said Pole, leaning over the fence, his unbuttoned shirt-sleeves allowing his brawny, bare arms to rest on the top rail. "I wanted to talk to you about Alan an' that bank bu'st-up."

"You've been to town, I heer," said Abner, deeply interested.

"Yes, an' I've been with Alan an' Miller fer the last week tryin' to do some 'n', but we couldn't. They've been sendin' telegrams by the basketful, an' Jeff Dukes has trotted his legs off back an' forth, but nothin' hain't been done."

"You say the' hain't?" Abner's voice quivered and fell.

"No; they both kept up the'r sperits purty well fer about ten days beca'se that dang Atlanta chief of police kept wirin' he was on a scent o' Winship; but day before yesterday they give in. We was a-settin' in Miller's office when the last message come from Atlanta. They said they'd been after the wrong man, an' that they'd give up. You ort to 'a' seed Alan's face. Miller tried to cheer 'im up, but it wasn't no go. Then who do you think come? Alan's sweetheart. She axed to see 'im, an' they talked awhile in the front room; then Miller come back an' said she'd axed to be introduced to me. Jest think of it! I went in and seed she'd been a-cryin'. She got up, by jinks! an' ketched my hand an' said she wanted to thank me beca'se I'd been sech a friend to Alan. Uncle Ab, I felt as mean as a egg-suckin' dog, beca'se thar was Alan flat o' his back, as the feller said, an' I hadn't turned a hand to he'p 'im. And thar she was, the gal he loves an' wants, an' his poverty standin' betwixt 'em. I couldn't say nothin', an' I reckon I looked more kinds of a damn fool than she ever seed on two legs."

"Well, what did you do?" asked Abner, too much moved by Pole's graphic picture to speak with his usual lightness.

"What did I do? I made my bow an' slid. I made a bee-line fer Murray's bar an' put two down as fast as they could shovel 'em out. Then I tuck another, an' quit countin'. I begun to think I owned the shebang, an' broke several billiard-cues an' throwed the chalk around. Then Dukes come an' said he'd give me a chance to escape trial fer misconduct, ef I'd straddle my hoss an' make fer home. I agreed, but thar was one thing I had to do fust. I had promised Alan not to drink any more, an' so I didn't want to sneak away to hide it. I went to Miller's house, whar he's stayin', an' called 'im out. I told 'im I'd jest come fer no other reason 'an to let 'im see me at my wust. I felt like it was the only manly way, after I'd broke faith with a friend as true as he is."

"Too bad!" sighed Abner. "I 'll bet it hurt Alan to see you in that fix."

"Well, he didn't complain," said Pole. "But he put his arm around me an' come as nigh cryin' as I ever seed a strong man. 'It's my fault, Pole,' ses he. 'I can see that.' Then him an' Miller both tried to git me to go up-stairs in that fine house an' go to bed an' sleep it off, but I wouldn't. I come on home an' got mad at Sally fer talkin' to me, an' come as nigh as peas hittin' 'er in the jaw. But that's over, Uncle Ab. What I'm in fer now is work. I ain't no fool. I'm on a still hunt, an' I jest want yore private opinion. I don't want you to commit yorese'f, unless you want to; but I'd go more on yore jedgment than any man' s in this county. I want to know ef you think old Craig is a honest man at heart. Now don't say you don't know, an' keep yore mouth shet; fer what I want to know, an' *all* I want to know, is how you feel about that one thing."

Abner hung his head down. His long thumb trembled as its nail went under a splinter on the rail and pried it off.

"I see what you are a-drivin' at," he said. "You jest want to feel shore o' yore ground." Abner began to chew the splinter and spit out the broken bits. He was silent, under Pole's anxious gaze, for a minute, and then he laughed dryly. "I reckon me 'n' you has about the same suspicions," he said. "That p'int's been worryin' me fer several days, an' I didn't let it end, thar nuther."

"Ah! you didn't?" exclaimed Baker. "You say you didn't, Uncle Ab?"

"No; I got so I couldn't lie down at night without the idea poppin' into my head that maybe Craig had made a tool of Winship fer some minor crime an' had hustled 'im out o' the country so he could gobble up what was in the bank an' pose as a injured man in the community."

"Same heer, pine blank!" said Pole, eagerly. "What did you do, Uncle Ab?"

"I went to Darley an' attended his church last Sunday," replied the old man, a tense expression in his eyes. "I got a seat in the amen-corner, whar I could see him, an' all through preachin' I watched 'im like a hawk. He didn't look to me like a man who had bu'sted on wind alone. He had a fat, oily, pink look, an' when they axed 'im to lead in prayer it looked to me like he was talkin' more to the people 'an he was to God. I didn't like his whine, an' what he said didn't seem to come from the cellar. But I seed that he was makin' converts to his side as fast as a dog kin trot. The Presbyterians an' Baptists has been accusin' the Methodists o' packin' more bad eggs 'an they have, an' it looks like Craig's crowd's a-goin' to swear he's fresh whether he is or not. After meetin' was over I walked ahead of him an' his fine lady, who has made the mistake o' tryin' to kiver the whole business up with silk an' feathers, an' waited fer 'em nigh the'r gate. I told 'im I wanted a word with 'im, an' they axed me in the parlor. I smelt dinner, but they didn't mention it. I wasn't goin' to eat thar nohow. Well, I set in an' jest told Craig what had been troublin' me. I said the loss o' my folk's money was as bad as death, an' that thar'd been so much talk agin him, an' suspicion, that I had jest come to headquarters. Ef he had any money laid away, I was thar to tell 'im it never would do 'im any good, an' ef he didn't, I wanted to beg his pardon fer my evil thoughts, an' try to git the matter off'n my mind."

"Good God! did you railly tell 'im that, Uncle Ab?"

"Yes, an' I had a deep-laid reason. I wanted to make 'im mad an' study 'im. He did git mad. He was as red as a dewberry, an' quivered from head to foot. Thar's two kinds o' mad—the justified an' the unjustified. Make a good man rail mad by accusin' 'im, an' he 'll justify hisse'f or bu'st; but ef you make a bad un mad by accusin' 'im, he 'll delight in showin' you he's done wrong—ef it hurts you *an' he's safe*. Thar's right whar I landed Craig. He had the look, as plain as day, o' sayin', 'Yes, dang you, I did it, an' you cayn't he'p yorese'f!' His wife had gone in the back part o' the house, an' after a while I heerd her new shoes a-creakin' at the door betwixt the two rooms. Now a pair o' shoes don't walk up to a door squeakin' like mice an' then stop all of a sudden without reason. I knowed she was a-listenin', an' I determined she should not heer me say she was purty. I told 'im louder 'an ever that folks was a-talkin', an' a-talkin', an' that fetched her. She flung open the door an' faced me as mad as a turtle on its back. She showed her hand, too, an' I knowed she was in cahoot with 'im. She cussed me black an' blue fer a uncouth, meddlin' devil, an' what not."

"By gum!" said Pole, his big eyes expanding. "But you didn't gain much by that, did you?"

"Jest satisfied myself that Alan's money—or some of it—wasn't out o' creation, that's all."

"I have my reasons fer believin' like you do," said Pole.

"You say you have."

Pole glanced furtively over his shoulder at his cabin to see that no one was within hearing, then said:

"You know Winship is old Fred Parson's nephew. Well, old Fred's always been a stanch friend to me. We moonshined it together two yeer, though he never knowed my chief hidin'-place. In fact, nobody knows about that spot, Uncle Ab, even now. Well, I had a talk with him an' axed his opinion about his nephew. He talks as straight as a shingle, an' he ain't no idiot. He says it's all bosh about Winship takin' away all that boodle."

"He does, does he?" Abner nodded, as if to himself.

"Yes, and he don't claim Winship ain't guilty, nuther; he jest holds that he was too small a dabbler in devilment. He thinks, as I do, that Craig run 'im off with threats of arrest an' picked that chance to bu'st. He thinks Winship's in a safe place an' never will be fetched back."

Abner drew himself up straight.

"Have you talked to Alan an' Miller on that line?"

"Tried to," grunted Pole, in high disgust, "but Miller says it's no good to think of accusin' Craig. He says we can' t prove a thing on 'im, unless we ketch Winship. He says that sort of a steal is the easiest thing on earth, an' that it's done every day. But that's beca'se he was fetched up in the law," Pole finished. "We-uns out heer in the mountains kin fish up other ways o' fetchin' a scamp to time without standin' 'im up before a thick-headed jury, or lettin' 'im out on bond till he dies o' old age. You've got sense enough to know that, Uncle Ab."

The slanting rays of the setting sun struck the old man in the face. There was a tinkle of cow-bells in the pasture below the cabin. The outlaw in Pole Baker was a thing Abner Daniel deplored; and yet, to-day it was a straw bobbing about on the troubled waters of the old man' s soul towards which, if he did not extend his hand, he looked interestedly. A grim expression stole into his face, drawing the merry lines down towards his chin.

"I wouldn't do nothin' foolhardy," he said.

Pole Baker grunted in sheer derision. "I've done fool things whar thar wasn't a thing to be made by 'em. By gum! I'd do ten dozen fer jest a bare chance o' shakin' that wad o' cash in Alan Bishop's face, an' so would you, dern yore hide—so would you, Uncle Ab Daniel!"

Abner blinked at the red sun.

"The boy's been bad treated," he said, evasively; "bad, bad, bad! It's squeezed life an' hope out o' him."

"Well, you are a church-member, an' so *fur* in good-standin'," said Pole, "an' I ain't agoin' to pull you into no devilment; but ef I see any way—I say *ef* I see any way, I 'll come an' tell you the news."

"I wouldn't do nothin' foolhardy," said Abner, and turned to go. He paused a few paces away and said, "I wouldn't do nothin' foolhardy, Pole." He motioned towards the cabin. "You've got them in thar to look after."

Pole let him walk on a few paces, then he climbed over the fence and caught him up. He drew the piece of quartz containing the tiny nugget of gold from his pocket, which he had shown Abner and Dole on a former occasion. "You see that, Uncle Ab," he said. "That dirty rock is like friendship in general, but that little yaller lump is like my friendship fer Alan Bishop. It's the puore thing, solid an' heavy, an' won't lose color. You don't know when that boy done his first favor to me. It was away back when we was boys together. A feller at Treadwell's mill one day, behind my back, called me a bad name—a name no man will take or can. He used my mother's name, God bless her! as puore an' holy a woman as ever lived, to git back at me. He hadn't no sooner spoke it than Alan was at his throat like a wild-cat.

The skunk was bigger 'n him, but Alan beat 'im till he was black all over. I never heerd about it till about two weeks after it happened an' the feller had moved out West. Alan wouldn't let nobody tell me. I axed 'im why he hadn't let me know. 'Beca'se,' ses he, 'you'd 'a' killed 'im an' 'a' got into trouble, an' he wasn't wuth it. 'That's what he said, Uncle Ab." Pole's big-jawed face was full of struggling emotion, his voice was husky, his eyes were filling. "That's why it's a-killin' me to see 'im robbed of all he's got—his pride, his ambition, an' the good woman that loves 'im. Huh! ef I jest *knowed* that pie-faced hypocrite had his money he wouldn't have it long."

"I wouldn't do nothin' foolhardy, Pole." Abner looked into the fellow's face, drew a long, trembling breath, and finished, "I wouldn't—but I 'll be dumed ef I know what I'd do!"

CHAPTER XXV

THE following morning Pole rose before daylight and rode to Darley. As he reached the place, the first rays of the sun were touching the slate-covered spire of the largest church in town.

He went to a public wagon-yard and hitched his horse to one of the long racks. A mountain family he knew slightly had camped in the yard, sleeping in their canvas-covered wagon, and were making coffee over a little fire. Pole wanted a cup of the beverage, but he passed on into a grocery-store across the street and bought a dime's worth of cheese and hard-tack crackers. This was his breakfast. He washed it down with a dipper of water from the street well, and sat around the store chatting with the clerk, who was sprinkling the floor, and sweeping and dusting the long room. The clerk was a red-headed young man with a short, bristling mustache, and a suit of clothes that was too large for him.

"Don't Mr. Craig stay around Fincher's warehouse a good deal?" Pole asked, as the clerk rested for a moment on his broom near him.

"Mighty nigh all day long," was the reply; "him an' Fincher's some kin, I think."

"On his wife's side," said Pole. "I want to see Mr. Craig. I wonder ef he 'll be down thar this mornin'."

"Purty apt," said the clerk. "Fincher's his best friend sence his bu'st-up, an' they are mighty thick. I reckon he gits the cold-shoulder at a lots o' places."

"You don't say!"

"An' of course he wants somewhar to go besides home. In passing I've seed 'im a-figurin' several times at Fincher's desk. They say he's got some notion o' workin' fer Fincher as his bookkeeper."

"Well, he 'll have to make a livin' some way," said Pole.

The clerk laughed significantly.

"Ef it ain't already made," said he, with a smile. Pole stood up. "I don't think that's right," he said, coldly. "Me nur you, nur nobody, hain't got no right to hint at what we don't know nothin' about. Mr. Craig may 'a' lost ever' cent he had."

"In a pig's valise!" sneered the red-headed man. "I'd bet my hat he's got money—an' plenty of it, huh!"

"Well, I don't know nothin' about it," said Pole, still coldly. "An' what's more, Dunn, I ain't a-goin' about smirchin' any helpless man's character, nuther. Ef I knowed he had made by the bu'st I'd talk different, but I don't know it!"

"Oh, I see which side you are on, Baker," laughed the clerk. "Folks are about equally divided. Half is fer 'im an' half agin. But mark my words, Craig will slide out o' this town some day, an' be heerd of after a while a-gittin' started agin some'r's else. That racket has been worked to death all over the country."

Pole carried the discussion no further. Half an hour passed. Customers were coming in from the wagon-yard and examining the wares on the counters and making slow purchases. The proprietor came in and let the clerk go to breakfast. Pole stood in the doorway, looking up the street in the direction of Craig's residence. Presently he saw the ex-banker coming from the post-office, reading his mail. Pole stepped back into the store and let him go by; then he went to the door again and saw Craig go into Fincher's warehouse at the end of the next block of straggling, wooden buildings. Pole sauntered down the sidewalk in that direction, passing the front door of the warehouse without looking in. The door at the side of the house had a long platform before it, and on it Fincher, the proprietor, was weighing bales of hay which were being unloaded from several wagons by the countrymen who were disposing of it.

"Hello, Mr. Fincher," Pole greeted him, familiarly. "Want any help unloadin'?"

"Hello, Baker," said Fincher, looking up from the blank-book in which he was recording the weights. "No, I reckon they can handle it all right." Fincher was a short, fat man, very bald, and with a round, laughing face. He had known Pole a long time and considered him a most amusing character. "How do you come on, Pole?"

"Oh, about as common. I jest thought them fellers looked sorter light-weight."

The men on the wagon laughed as they thumped a bale of hay on to the platform. "You'd better dry up," one of them said. "We'll git the mayor to put you to work agin."

"Well, he'll have to be quicker about it than he was the last time," said Pole, dryly.

Some one laughed lustily from behind a tall stack of wheat in bags in the warehouse. It was Lawyer Trabue. He came round and picked up Fincher's daily paper, as he did every morning, and sat down and began to read it.

"Now you are talkin'," he said. "Thar was more rest in that job, Pole, than any you ever undertook. They tell me you didn't crack a rock."

Fincher laughed as he closed his book and struck Baker with it playfully. "Pole was too tired to do that job," he said. "He was born that way."

"Say, Mr. Trabue," retaliated Pole, "did you ever heer how I got the best o' Mr. Fincher in a chicken trade?"

"I don't think I ever did, Pole," laughed the lawyer, expectantly. "How was it?"

"Oh, come off, don't go over that again," said Fincher, flushing.

"It was this away," said Pole, with a broad, wholesome grin. "My cousin, Bart Wilks, was runnin' the restaurant under the car-shed about two yeer ago. He was a new hand at the business, an' one day he had a awful rush. He got a telegram that a trainload o' passengers had missed connection at Chattanooga an' would have to eat with him. He was powerful rattled, runnin' round like a dog after its tail. He knowed he'd have to have a lot o' fryin' chickens, an' he couldn't leave the restaurant, so he axed me ef I'd take the money an' go out in town an' buy 'em fer 'im. I consented, an' struck Mr. Fincher, who was sellin' sech truck then. He 'lowed, you know, that I jest wanted one, or two at the outside, fer my own use, so when I seed a fine coop out in front an' axed the price of 'em he kinder drawed on his beerd till his mouth fell open, an' studied how he could make the most out o' me. After a while he said: 'Well, Pole, I 'll make 'em ten cents apiece ef I pick 'em, an' fifteen ef you pick 'em.' I sorter skeerd the chickens around an' seed thar was two or three tiny ones hidin' under the big ones, an' I seed what he was up to, but I was ready fer 'im. 'All right,' ses I, 'you pick 'em.' Thar was two or three loafers standin' round an' they all laughed at me when Mr. Fincher got down over the coop an' finally ketched one about the size of a robin an' hauled it out. 'Keep on a-pickin',' ses I, an' he made a grab fer one a little bigger an' handed it up to me. Then he stuck his hands down in his pockets, doin' his best to keep from laughin'. The gang yelled then, but I wasn't done. 'Keep on a-pickin',' ses I. An' he got down agin. An', sir, I got that coop at about four cents apiece less 'n he'd paid fer 'em. He tried to back, but the gang wouldn't let 'im. It was the cheapest lot o' chickens I ever seed. I turned the little ones out to fatten, an' made Wilks pay me the market-price all round fer the bunch."

"I 'll be bound you made some 'n' out of it," said Trabue. "Fincher, did you ever heer how that scamp tuck in every merchant on this street about two yeer ago?"

"Never heerd anything except his owin' 'em all," said Fincher, with a laugh.

"I could put 'im in the penitentiary fer it," affirmed the lawyer. "You know about that time thar was a powerful rivalry goin' on among the storekeepers. They was movin' heaven an' earth to sell the'r big stocks. Well, one of the spryest in the lot, Joe Gaylord, noticed that Pole was powerful popular with mountain-folks, an' he made 'im a proposition, bindin' 'im down to secrecy. He proposed to give Pole ten per cent, commission on all the goods he'd he'p sell by bringin' customers in the store. Pole hesitated, beca'se, he said, they might find it out, an' Joe finally agreed that all Pole would have to do was to fetch 'em in, give the wink, an' him an' his clerks would do the rest. It worked mighty slick fer a while, but Pole noticed that very often the folks he'd fetch in wouldn't be pleased with the goods an' prices an' ud go trade some'r's else. Then what do you think the scamp did? He went to every store in town an' made a secret contract to git ten per cent, on all sales, an' he had the softest snap you ever heerd of. He'd simply hang onto a gang from the country, whether he knowed 'em or not, an' foller 'em around till they bought; then he'd walk up an' rake in his part."

"I got left once," said Pole, laughing with the others. "One gang that I stuck to all day went over to Melton an' bought."

"Well, the merchants caught on after a while an' stopped him," said Trabue; "but he made good money while he was at it. They'd 'a' sent 'im up fer it, ef it hadn't been sech a good joke on 'em."

"I don't know about that," replied Pole, thoughtfully. "I was doin' all I agreed, an' ef they could afford to pay ten per cent, to anybody, they mought as well 'a' paid it to me. I drawed trade to the whole town. The cigars an' whiskey I give away amounted to a lots. I've set up many a night tellin' them moss-backs tales to make 'em laugh."

"Well, ef you ever git into any trouble let me know," said Trabue, as he rose to go. "I 'll defend you at half price; you'd be a sight o' help to a lawyer. I 'll be hanged if I ever seed a better case 'an you made out in the mayor's court, an' you hadn't a thing to back it up with, nuther."

The hay was unloaded and the wagons driven away. Fincher stood eying Pole with admiration. "It's a fact," he said. "You could 'a' made some 'n' out o' yorese'f, if you'd 'a' been educated, an' had a showin'." Pole jerked his thumb over his shoulder at Craig, who was standing in the front door, looking out into the street. "Everybody don't git a fair showin' in this world, Mr. Fincher," he said. "That man Craig hain't been treated right."

The jovial expression died out of the merchant's face, and he leaned against the door-jamb.

"You are right thar," he said—"dead right. He's been mighty unlucky and bad treated."

Pole grasped the brim of his massive hat, and drew it from his shaggy head. "It makes me so all-fired mad sometimes, Mr. Fincher, to heer folks a-runnin' that man down, that I want to fight. I ain't no religious man myse'f, but I respect one, an' I've always put him down in my book as a good man."

"So 've I," said the merchant, and he looked towards the subject of their conversation and called out: "Craig, oh, Craig, come back heer a minute."

Pole put on his hat and stared at the ground. He made a gesture as if of protest, but refrained from speaking.

"What's wanted?" Craig came down to them. He was smoking a cigar and wore a comfortable look, as if he had been fighting a hard but successful fight and now heard only random shots from a fleeing enemy.

"You ain't a candidate fer office," laughed Fincher, "but nearly all men like to know they've got friends. This chap heer's been standin' up fer you. He says it makes him mad to hear folks talk agin you."

"Oh, it's Baker!" exclaimed the ex-banker, shaking hands with Pole and beaming on him. "Well, I don't know a man I'd rather have for a friend," he said, smoothly.

Pole tossed his head, and looked straight into the speaker's eye. "I'm fer human justice, Mr. Craig," he said. "An' I don't think folks has treated you right. What man is thar that don't now an' then make mistakes, sir? You've always had means, an' I never was anything but a pore mountain-boy, but I've always looked on you as a good man, a law-abidin' man, an' I don't like to heer folks try to blame you fer what another man done. When you had plenty, I never come nigh you, beca'se I knowed you belonged to one life an' me another, but now you are flat o' yore back, sir, I'm yore friend."

Craig's face beamed; he pulled his beard; his eyes danced.

"I'm glad there are men in the world like you, Baker," he said. "I say I'm glad, and I mean it."

Fincher had begun to look over the figures in his book, and walked to the front.

"Oh, my friendship ain't wuth nothin'," said Pole. "I know that. I never was in the shape to he'p nobody, but I know when a man' s treated right or wrong."

"Well, if you ever need assistance, and I can help you, don't fail to call on me," Craig spoke with a tone of sincerity.

Pole took a deep breath and lowered his voice, glancing cautiously into the house, as if fearful of being overheard.

"Well, I *do* need advice, Mr. Craig," he said. "Not money, nor nothin' expensive, but I've laid awake night after night wishing 'at I could run on some man of experience that I could ax fer advice, an' that I could trust. Mr. Craig, I 'll be blamed ef I don't feel like tellin' you some 'n' that never has passed my lips."

Craig stared in interested astonishment. "Well, you can trust me, Baker," he said; "and if I can advise you, why, I 'll do it with pleasure."

There was a cotton compress near by, with its vast sheds and platforms, and Pole looked at it steadily. He thrust his hand into his pants pocket and kept it there for a full minute. Then he shook his head, drew out his hand, and said: "I reckon I won't bother you to-day, Mr. Craig. Some day I 'll come in town an' tell you, but—" Pole looked at the sun. "I reckon I'd better be goin'."

"Hold on," Craig caught Pole's arm. The exbanker was a natural man. Despite his recent troubles, he had his share of curiosity, and Pole's manner and words had roused it to unwonted activity. "Hold on," he said. "What's your hurry? I've got time to spare if you have."

Pole hung his head for a moment in silence, then he looked the old man in the face. "Mr. Craig," he began, in even a lower voice, "do you reckon thar's any gold in them mountains?" Pole nodded to the blue wave in the east.

Craig was standing near a bale of cotton and he sat down on it, first parting the tails of his long, black coat.

"I don't know; there might be," he said, deeply interested, and yet trying to appear indifferent. "There is plenty of it in the same range further down about Dalonega."

Pole had his hand in the right pocket of his rough jean trousers.

"Is thar anybody in this town that could tell a piece o' gold ef they seed it?" he asked.

"Oh, a good many, I reckon," said Craig, a steely beam of excitement in his unsteady eye. "I can, myself. I spent two years in the gold-mines of California when I was a young man."

"You don't say! I never knowed that." Pole had really heard of that fact, but his face was straight. He had managed to throw into it a most wonderful blending of fear and over-cautiousness.

"Oh yes; I've had a good deal of experience in such things."

"You don't say!" Pole was looking towards the compress again.

Craig laughed out suddenly, and put his hand on Pole's shoulder with a friendly, downward stroke.

"You can trust me, Baker," he said, persuasively, "and it may be that I could be of assistance to you."

There was something like an actual tremor of agitation in Pole's rough hand as he drew his little nugget from its resting-place at the bottom of his pocket. With a deep, indrawn breath, he handed it to Craig. "Is that thar little lump gold or not?" he asked.

Craig started visibly as his eyes fell on the piece of gold. But he took it indifferently, and examined it closely.

"Where did you run across that?" he asked.

"I want to know ef it's the puore thing," answered Pole.

Craig made another examination, obviously to decide on the method he would apply to a situation that claimed all his interest.

"I think it is," he said; "in fact, I know it is."

Pole took it eagerly, thrust it back into his pocket, and said:

"Mr. Craig, I know whar thar's a vein o' that stuff twenty yards thick, runnin' clean through a mountain."

"You do!" Craig actually paled under his suppressed excitement.

"Yes, sir; an' I kin buy it, lock, stock, and barrel, fer five hundred dollars—the feller that owns it ud jump at it like a duck on a June-bug. That's my secret, Mr. Craig. I hain't one dollar to my name, but from this day on I'm goin' to work hard an' save my money till I own that property. I'm a-goin' down to Atlanta next week, whar people don't know me, an' have a lump of it bigger 'n this examined, an' ef it's gold I 'll own the land sooner or later."

Craig glanced to the rear.

"Come back here," he said. Opening a door at the end of the warehouse, he led Pole into a more retired spot, where they would be free from possible interruption. Then, in a most persuasive voice, he continued: "Baker, you need a man of experience with you in this. Besides, if there is as much of—of that stuff as you say there is, you wouldn't be able to use all you could make out of it. Now, it might take you a long time to get up the money to buy the land, and there is no telling what might happen in the mean time. I'm in a close place, but I could raise five hundred dollars, or even a thousand. My friends still stick to me, you know. The truth is, Baker, I'd like the best in the world to be able to make money to pay back what some of my friends have lost through me."

Pole hung his head. He seemed to be speaking half to himself and on the verge of a smile when he replied: "I'd like to see you pay back some of 'em too, Mr. Craig."

Craig laid his hand gently on Pole's shoulder.

"How about lettin' me see the place, Baker?" he said.

Pole hesitated, and then he met the ex-banker's look with the expression of a man who has resigned himself to a generous impulse.

"Well, some day when you are a-passin' my way, stop in, an' I 'll—"

"How far is it?" broke in Craig, pulling his beard with unsteady fingers.

"A good fifteen miles from heer," said Pole.

Craig smiled. "Nothin' but an easy ride," he declared. "I've got a horse doin' nothing in the stable. What's to hinder us from going to-day—this morning—as soon as I can go by for my horse?"

"I don't keer," said Pole, resignedly. "But could you manage to go without anybody knowin' whar you was bound fer?"

"Easy enough," Craig laughed. He was really pleased with Pole's extreme cautiousness.

"Then you mought meet me out thar some'r's."

"A good idea—a good idea, Baker."

"Do you know whar the Ducktown road crosses Holly Creek, at the foot o' Old Pine Mountain?"

"As well as I know where my house is."

Pole looked at the sun, shading his eyes with his hand.

"Could you be thar by eleven o'clock?"

"Easy enough, Baker."

"Well, I 'll meet you—I'm a-goin' to trust you, Mr. Craig, an' when you see the vein, ef you think thar's enough money in it fer two—but we can see about that later."

"All right, Baker. I 'll be there. But say," as Pole was moving away, "you are a drinking man, and get a little off sometimes. You haven't said anything about this where anybody—"

Pole laughed reassuringly. "I never have been drunk enough to do that, Mr. Craig, an', what's more, I never will be."

CHAPTER XXVI

ABOUT noon that day, as Pole Baker sat on a fallen tree near the roadside in the loneliest spot of that rugged country, his horse grazing behind him, he saw Craig coming up the gradual incline from the creek. Pole stood up and caught the bridle-rein of his horse and muttered:

"Now, Pole Baker, durn yore hide, you've got brains—at least, some folks say you have—an' so has he. Ef you don't git the best of that scalawag yo' re done fer. You've put purty big things through; now put this un through or shet up."

"Well, heer you are," merrily cried out the ex-banker, as he came up. He was smiling expectantly. "Your secret's safe with me. I hain't met a soul that I know sence I left town."

"I'm glad you didn't, Mr. Craig," Pole said. "I don't want anybody a-meddlin' with my business." He pointed up the rather steep and rocky road that led gradually up the mountain. "We've got two or three mile furder to go. Have you had any dinner?"

"I put a cold biscuit and a slice of ham in my pocket," said Craig. "It 'll do me till supper."

Pole mounted and led the way up the unfrequented road.

"I may as well tell you, Mr. Craig, that I used to be a moonshiner in these mountains, an'—"

"Lord, I knew that, Baker. Who doesn't, I'd like to know?"

Pole's big-booted legs swung back and forth like pendulums from the flanks of his horse.

"I was a-goin' to tell you that I had a hide-out, whar I kept stuff stored, that wasn't knowed by one livin' man."

"Well, you must have had a slick place from all I've heerd," said Craig, still in his vast good-humor with himself and everybody else.

"The best natur' ever built," said Pole; "an' what's more, it was in thar that I found the gold. I reckon it ud 'a' been diskivered long ago, ef it had 'a' been above ground."

"Then it's in—a sort of cave?" ventured Craig.

"That's jest it; but I've got the mouth of it closed up so it ud fool even a bloodhound."

Half an hour later Pole drew rein in a most isolated spot, near a great yawning canon from which came a roaring sound of rushing water and clashing winds. The sky overhead was blue and cloudless; the air at that altitude was crisp and rarefied, and held the odor of spruce pine. With a laugh Pole dismounted. "What ef I was to tell you, Mr. Craig, that you was in ten yards o' my old den right now."

Craig looked about in surprise. "I'd think you was makin' fun o' me—tenderfootin', as we used to say out West."

"I'm givin' it to you straight," said Pole, pointing with his riding-switch. "Do you see that pile o' rocks?"

Craig nodded.

"Right under them two flat ones is the mouth o' my den," said Pole. "Now let's hitch to that hemlock, an' I 'll show you the whole thing."

When they had fastened their horses to swinging limbs in a dense thicket of laurel and rhododendron bushes, they went to the pile of rocks.

"I toted mighty nigh all of 'em from higher up," Pole explained. "Some o' the biggest I rolled down from that cliff above."

"I don't see how you are going to get into your hole in the ground," said Craig, with a laugh of pleasant anticipation.

Pole picked up a big, smooth stick of hickory, shaped like a crowbar, and thrust the end of it under the largest rock. "Huh! I 'll show you in a jiffy."

It was an enormous stone weighing over three hundred pounds; but with his strong lever and knotted muscles the ex-moonshiner managed to slide it slowly to the right, disclosing a black hole about two feet square in the ragged stone. From this protruded into the light the ends of a crude ladder leading down about twenty-five feet to the bottom of the cave.

"Ugh!" Craig shuddered, as he peered into the dank blackness. "You don't mean that we are to go down there?"

It was a crisis. Craig seemed to be swayed between two impulses—a desire to penetrate farther and an almost controlling premonition of coming danger. Pole met the situation with his usual originality and continued subtlety of procedure. With his big feet dangling in the hole he threw himself back and gave vent to a hearty, prolonged laugh that went ringing and echoing about among the cliffs and chasms.

"I 'lowed this ud make yore flesh crawl," he said. "Looks like the openin' to the bad place, don't it?"

"It certainly does," said Craig, somewhat reassured by Pole's levity.

"Why, it *ain' t* more 'n forty feet square," said Pole. "Wait till I run down an' make a light. I've got some fat pine torches down at the foot o' the ladder."

"Well, I believe I *will* let you go first," said Craig, with an uneasy little laugh.

Pole went down the ladder, recklessly thumping his heels on the rungs. He was lost to sight from above, but in a moment Craig heard him strike a match, and saw the red, growing flame of a sputtering torch from which twisted a rope of smoke. When it was well ablaze, Pole called up the ladder: "Come on, now, an' watch whar you put yore feet. This end o' the ladder is solid as the rock o' Gibralty."

The square of daylight above was cut off, and in a moment the ex-banker stood beside his guide.

"Now come down this way," said Pole, and with the torch held high he led the way into a part of the chamber where the rock overhead sloped, down lower. Here lay some old whiskey-barrels, two or three lager-beer kegs, and the iron hoops of several barrels that had been burned. There were several one-gallon jugs with corn-cob stoppers. Pole swept his hand over them with a laugh. "If you was a drinkin' man, I could treat you to a thimbleful or two left in them jugs," he said, almost apologetically.

"But I don't drink, Baker," Craig said. His premonition of danger seemed to have returned to him, and to be driven in by the dank coolness of the cavern, the evidence of past outlawry around him.

Pole heaped his pieces of pine against a rock, and added to them the chunks of some barrel-staves, which set up a lively popping sound like a tiny fusillade of artillery.

"You see that rock behind you, Mr. Craig?" asked Pole. "Well, set down on it. Before we go any furder, me'n you've got to have a understanding."

The old man stared hesitatingly for an instant, and then, after carefully feeling of the stone, he complied.

"I thought we already—but, of course," he said, haltingly, "I'm ready to agree to anything that 'll make you feel safe."

"I kinder 'lowed you would," and to Craig's overwhelming astonishment Pole drew a revolver from his hip-pocket and looked at it, twirling the cylinder with a deft thumb.

"You mean, Baker—" But Craig's words remained unborn in his bewildered brain. The rigor of death itself seemed to have beset his tongue. A cold sweat broke out on him.

"I mean that I've tuck the trouble to fetch you heer fer a purpose, Mr. Craig, an' thar ain't any use in beatin' about the bush to git at it."

Craig made another effort at utterance, but failed. Pole could hear his rapid breathing and see the terrified gleaming of his wide-open eyes.

"You've had a lots o' dealin' s, Mr. Craig," said Pole. "You've made yore mistakes an' had yore good luck, but you never did a bigger fool thing 'an you did when you listened to my tale about that lump o' gold."

"You've trapped me!" burst from Craig's quivering lips.

"That's about the size of it."

"But—why?" The words formed the beginning and the end of a gasp.

Pole towered over him, the revolver in his tense hand.

"Mr. Craig, thar is one man in this world that I'd die fer twenty times over. I love 'im more than a brother. That man you've robbed of every dollar an' hope on earth. I've fetched you heer to die a lingerin' death, ef— ef, I say, ef—you don't refund his money. That man is Alan Bishop, an' the amount is twenty-five thousand dollars to a cent."

"But I haven't any money," moaned the crouching figure; "not a dollar that I kin lay my hands on."

"Then you are in a damn bad fix," said Pole. "Unless I git that amount o' money from you you 'll never smell a breath o' fresh air or see natural daylight."

"You mean to kill a helpless man?" The words were like a prayer.

"I'd bottle you up heer to die," said Pole Baker, firmly. "You've met me in this lonely spot, an' no man could lay yore end to me. In fact, all that know you would swear you'd run off from the folks you've defrauded. You see nothin' but that money o' Alan Bishop's kin possibly save you. You know that well enough, an' thar ain't a bit o' use palaverin' about it. I've fetched a pen an' ink an' paper, an' you've got to write me an order fer the money. If I have to go as fur off as Atlanta, I 'll take the fust train an' go after it. If I git the money, you git out, ef I don't you won't see me agin, nur nobody else till you face yore Maker."

Craig bent over his knees and groaned.

"You think I *have* money," he said, straightening up. "Oh, my God!"

"I *know* it," said Pole. "I don't think anything about it—I *know* it."

He took out the pen and ink from his pants pocket and unfolded a sheet of paper. "Git to work," he said. "You needn't try to turn me, you damned old hog!"

Craig raised a pair of wide-open, helpless eyes to the rigid face above him.

"Oh, my God!" he said, again.

"You let God alone an' git down to business," said Pole, taking a fresh hold on the handle of his weapon. "I'm not goin' to waste time with you. Either you git me Alan Bishop's money or you 'll die. Hurry up!"

"Will you keep faith with me—if—if—"

"Yes, durn you, why wouldn't I?" A gleam of triumph flashed in the outlaw's eyes. Up to this moment he had been groping in experimental darkness. He now saw his way clearly and his voice rang with dawning triumph.

The ex-banker had taken the pen and Pole spread out the sheet of paper on his knee.

"What assurance have I?" stammered Craig, his face like a death-mask against the rock behind him. "You see, after you got the money, you might think it safer to leave me here, thinking that I would prosecute you. I wouldn't, as God is my judge, but you might be afraid—"

"I'm not afraid o' nothin'," said Pole. "Old man, you couldn't handle me without puttin' yorese'f in jail fer the rest o' yore life. That order's a-goin' to be proof that you have money when you've swore publicly that you didn't. No; when I'm paid back Alan Bishop's money I 'll let you go. I don't want to kill a man fer jest tryin' to steal an' not makin' the riffle."

The logic struck home. The warmth of hope diffused itself over the gaunt form. "Then I 'll write a note to my wife," he said.

Pole reached for one of the torches and held it near the paper.

"Well, I'm glad I won't have to go furder'n Darley," he said. "It 'll be better fer both of us. By ridin' peert I can let you out before sundown. You may git a late supper at Darley, but it's a sight better'n gittin' none heer an' no bed to speak of."

"I'm putting my life in your hands, Baker," said Craig, and with an unsteady hand he began to write.

"Hold on thar," said Pole. "You 'll know the best way to write to her, but when the money's mentioned I want you to say the twenty-five thousand dollars deposited in the bank by the Bishops. You see I'm not goin' to tote no order fer money I hain't no right to. An' I 'll tell you another thing, old man, you needn't throw out no hint to her to have me arrested. As God is my final judge, ef I'm tuck up fer this, they 'll never make me tell whar you are. I'd wait until you'd pegged out, anyway."

"I'm not setting any trap for you, Baker," whined Craig. "You've got the longest head of any man I ever knew. You've got me in your power, and all I can ask of you is my life. I've got Bishop's money hidden in my house. I am willing to restore it, if you will release me. I can write my wife a note that will cause her to give it to you. Isn't that fair?"

"That's all I want," said Pole; "an' I 'll say this to you, I 'll agree to use my influence with Alan Bishop not to handle you by law; but the best thing fer you an' yore family to do is to shake the dirt of Darley off'n yore feet an' seek fresh pastures. These 'round heer ain't as green, in one way, as some I've seed."

Craig wrote the note and handed it up to Baker. Pole read it slowly, and then said: "You mought 'a' axed 'er to excuse bad writin' an' spellin', an' hopin' these few lines will find you enjoyin' the same blessin' s; but ef it gits the boodle that's all I want. Now you keep yore shirt on, an' don't git skeerd o' the darkness. It will be as black as pitch, an' you kin heer yore eyelids creak after I shet the front door, but I 'll be back—ef I find yore old lady hain't run off with a handsomer man an' tuck the swag with 'er. I'm glad you cautioned 'er agin axin' me questions."

Pole backed to the foot of the ladder, followed by Craig.

"Don't leave me here, Baker," he said, imploringly. "Don't, for God's sake! I swear I 'll go with you and get you the money."

"I can't do that, Mr. Craig; but I 'll be back as shore as fate, ef I get that cash," promised Pole. "It all depends on that. I 'll keep my word, if you do yore'n."

"I am going to trust you," said the old man, with the pleading intonation of a cowed and frightened child.

After he had gotten out, Pole thrust his head into the opening again. "It 'll be like you to come up heer an' try to move this rock," he called out, "but you mought as well not try it, fer I'm goin' to add about a dump-cart load o' rocks to it to keep the wolves from diggin' you out."

CHAPTER XXVII

RAYBURN MILLER and Alan spent that day on the river trying to catch fish, but with no luck at all, returning empty-handed to the farm-house for a late dinner. They passed the afternoon at target-shooting on the lawn with rifles and revolvers, ending the day by a reckless ride on their horses across the fields, over fences and ditches, after the manner of fox-hunting, a sport not often indulged in in that part of the country.

In the evening as they sat in the big sitting-room, smoking after-supper cigars, accompanied by Abner Daniel, with his long, cane-stemmed pipe, Mrs. Bishop came into the room, in her quiet way, smoothing her apron with her delicate hands.

"Pole Baker's rid up an' hitched at the front gate," she said. "Did you send 'im to town fer anything, Alan?"

"No, mother," replied her son. "I reckon he's come to get more meat. Is father out there?"

"I think he's some'r's about the stable," said Mrs. Bishop.

Miller laughed. "I guess Pole isn't the best pay in the world, is he?"

"Father never weighs or keeps account of anything he gets," said Alan. "They both make a guess at it, when cotton is sold. Father calls it 'lumping' the thing, and usually Pole gets the lump. But he's all right, and I wish we could do more for him. Father was really thinking about helping him in some substantial way when the crash came—"

"Thar!" broke in Daniel, with a gurgling laugh, "I've won my bet. I bet to myse'f jest now that ten minutes wouldn't pass 'fore Craig an' his bu'st-up would be mentioned."

"We have been at it, off and on, all day," said Miller, with a low laugh. "The truth is, it makes me madder than anything I ever encountered."

"Do you know why?" asked Abner, seriously, just as Pole Baker came through the dining-room and leaned against the door-jamb facing them. "It's beca'se"—nodding a greeting to Pole along with the others—"it's beca'se you know in reason that he's got that money."

"Oh, I wouldn't say *that*," protested Miller, in the tone of a man of broad experience in worldly affairs. "I wouldn't say that."

"Well, I would, an' do," said Abner, in the full tone of decision. "I *know* he's got it!"

"Well, yo' re wrong thar, Uncle Ab," said Pole, striding forward and sinking into a chair. "You've got as good jedgment as any man I ever run across. I thought like you do once. I'd 'a' tuck my oath that he had it about two hours by sun this evenin', but I kin swear he hain't a cent of it now."

"Do you mean that, Pole?" Abner stared across the wide hearth at him fixedly.

"He hain't got it, Uncle Ab." Pole was beginning to smile mysteriously. "He *did* have it, but he hain't got it now. I got it from 'im, blast his ugly pictur'!"

"*You* got it?" gasped Daniel. "*You?*"

"Yes. I made up my mind he had it, an' it deviled me so much that I determined to have it by hook or crook, ef it killed me, or put me in hock the rest o' my life." Pole rose and took a packet wrapped in brown paper from under his rough coat and laid it on the table near Alan. "God bless you, old boy," he said, "thar's yore money! It's all thar. I counted it. It's in fifties an' hundreds."

Breathlessly, and with expanded eyes, Alan broke the string about the packet and opened it.

"Great God!" he muttered.

Miller sprang up and looked at the stack of bills, but said nothing. Abner, leaning forward, uttered a little, low laugh.

"You—you didn't kill 'im, did you, Pole, old boy—you didn't, did you?" he asked.

"Didn't harm a hair of his head," said Pole. "All I wanted was Alan' s money, an' thar it is!"

"Well," grunted Daniel, "I'm glad you spared his life. And I thank God you got the money."

Miller was now hurriedly running over the bills.

"You say you counted it, Baker?" he said, pale with pleased excitement.

"Three times; fust when it was turned over to me, an' twice on the way out heer from town."

Mrs. Bishop had not spoken until now, standing in the shadows of the others as if bewildered by what seemed a mocking impossibility.

"Is it our money—is it our'n?" she finally found voice to say. "Oh, is it, Pole?"

"Yes, 'm," replied Pole. "It's yo'rn." He produced a crumpled piece of paper and handed it to Miller. "Heer's Craig's order on his wife fer it, an' in it he acknowledges it's the cash deposited by Mr. Bishop. He won't give me no trouble. I've got 'im fixed. He 'll leave Darley in the mornin'. He's afeerd this 'll git out an' he 'll be lynched."

Alan was profoundly moved. He transferred his gaze from the money to Pole's face, and leaned towards him.

"You did it out of friendship for me," he said, his voice shaking.

"That's what I did it fer, Alan, an' I wish I could do it over agin. When I laid hold o' that wad an' knowed it was the thing you wanted more'n anything else, I felt like flyin'."

"Tell us all about it, Baker," said Miller, wrapping up the stack of bills.

"All right," said Pole, but Mrs. Bishop interrupted him.

"Wait fer Alfred," she said, her voice rising and cracking in delight. "Wait; I 'll run find 'im."

She went out through the dining-room towards the stables, calling her husband at every step. "Alfred, oh, Alfred!"

"Heer!" she heard him call out from one of the stables.

She leaned over the fence opposite the closed door, behind which she had heard his voice.

"Oh, Alfred!" she called, "come out, quick! I've got news fer you—big, big news!"

She heard him grumbling as he emptied some ears of corn into the trough of the stall containing Alan' s favorite horse, and then with a growl he emerged into the starlight.

"That fool nigger only give Alan's hoss six ears o' corn," he fumed. "I know, beca'se I counted the cobs; the hoss had licked the trough clean, an' gnawed the ends o' the cobs. The idea o' starvin' my stock right before my—"

"Oh, Alfred, what *do* you think has happened?" his wife broke in. "We've got the bank money back! Pole Baker managed somehow to get it. He's goin' to tell about it now. Come on in!"

Bishop closed the door behind him; he fumbled with the chain and padlock for an instant, then he moved towards her, his lip hanging, his eyes protruding.

"I 'll believe my part o' that when—"

"But," she cried, opening the gate for him to pass through, "the money's thar in the house on the table; it's been counted. I say it's thar! Don't you believe it?"

The old man moved through the gate mechanically. He paused to fasten it with the iron ring over the two posts. But after that he seemed to lose the power of locomotion. He stood facing her, his features working.

"I 'll believe my part o' that cat-an'-bull story when I see—"

"Well, come in the house, then," she cried. "You kin lay yore hands on it an' count it. It's a awful big pile, an' nothin' less than fifty-dollar bills."

Grasping his arm, she half dragged, half led him into the house. Entering the sitting-room, he strode to the table and, without a word, picked up the package and opened it. He made an effort to count the money, but his fingers seemed to have lost their cunning, and he gave it up.

"It's all there," Miller assured him, "and it's your money. You needn't bother about that."

Bishop sat down in his place in the chimney corner, the packet on his knees, while Pole Baker, modestly, and not without touches of humor, recounted his experiences.

"The toughest job I had was managin' the woman," Pole laughed. "You kin always count on a woman to be contrary. I believe ef you was tryin' to git some women out of a burnin' house they'd want to have the'r way about it. She read the order an' got white about the gills an' screamed, low, so nobody wouldn't heer 'er, an' then wanted to ax questions. That's the female of it. She knowed in reason that Craig was dead fixed an' couldn't git out until she complied with the instructions, but she wanted to know all about it. I reckon she thought he wouldn't give full particulars—an' he won't, nuther. She wouldn't budge to git the money, an' time was a-passin'. I finally had a thought that fetched 'er. I told 'er Craig was confined in a place along with a barrel o' gunpowder; that a slow fuse was burnin' towards 'im, an' that he'd go sky-high at about sundown ef I didn't git thar an' kick out the fire. Then I told 'er she'd be arrested fer holdin' the money, an' that got 'er in a trot. She fetched it out purty quick, a-cryin' an' abusin' me by turns. As soon as the money left 'er hands though, she begun to beg me to ride fast. I wanted to come heer fust; but I felt sorter sorry fer Craig, an' went an' let 'im out. He was the gladdest man to see me you ever looked at. He thought I was goin' to leave 'im thar. He looked like he wanted to hug me. He says Winship wasn't much to blame. They both got in deep water speculatin', an' Craig was tempted to cabbage on the twenty-five thousand dollars."

When Pole had concluded, the group sat in silence for a long time. It looked as if Bishop wanted to openly thank Pole for what he had done, but he had never done such a thing in the presence of others, and he could not pull himself to it. He sat crouched up in his tilted chair as if burning up with the joy of his release.

The silence was broken by Abner Daniel, as he filled his pipe anew and stood over the fireplace.

"They say money's a cuss an' the root of all evil," he said, dryly. "But in this case it's give Pole Baker thar a chance to show what's in 'im. I'd 'a' give the last cent I have to 'a' done what he did to-day. I grant you he used deception, but it was the fust-water sort that that Bible king resorted to when he made out he was goin' to divide that baby by cuttin' it in halves. He fetched out the good an' squelched the bad." Abner glanced at Pole, and gave one of his impulsive inward laughs. "My boy, when I reach t'other shore I expect to see whole strings o' sech law-breakers as you a-playin' leap-frog on the golden sands. You don't sing an' pray a whole lot, nur keep yore religion in sight, but when thar's work to be done you shuck off yore shirt an' do it like a wild-cat a-scratchin'."

No one spoke after this outburst for several minutes, though the glances cast in his direction showed the embarrassed ex-moonshiner that one and all had sanctioned Abner Daniel's opinion.

Bishop leaned forward and looked at the clock, and seeing that it was nine, he put the money in a bureau-drawer and turned the key. Then he took down the big family Bible from its shelf and sat down near the lamp. They all knew what the action portended.

"That's another thing," smiled Abner Daniel, while his brother-in-law was searching for his place in the big Book. "Money may be a bad thing, a cuss an' a evil, an' what not, but Alf 'ain't felt like holdin' prayer sence the bad news come; an' now that he's got the scads once more the fust thing is an appeal to the Throne. Yes, it may be a bad thing, but sometimes it sets folks to singin' an' shoutin'. Ef I was a-runnin' of the universe, I believe I'd do a lots o' distributin' in low places. I'd scrape off a good many tops an' level up more. Accordin' to some, the Lord's busy watchin' birds fall to the ground. I reckon our hard times is due to them pesky English sparrows that's overrun ever'thing."

"You'd better dry up, Uncle Ab," said Pole Baker. "That's the kind o' talk that made brother Dole jump on you."

"Huh! That's a fact," said Daniel; "but this is in the family."

Then Bishop began to read in his even, declamatory voice, and all the others looked steadily at the fire in the chimney, their faces lighted up by the flickering flames.

When they had risen from their knees after prayer, Pole looked at Abner with eyes from which shot beams of amusement. He seemed to enjoy nothing so much as hearing Abner's religious opinions.

"You say this thing has set Mr. Bishop to prayin', Uncle Ab?" he asked.

"That's what," smiled Abner, who had never admired Baker so much before. "Ef I stay heer, an' they ever git that railroad through, I'm goin' to have me a pair o' knee-pads made."

CHAPTER XXVIII

ABOUT a week after the events recorded in the preceding chapter, old man Bishop, just at dusk one evening, rode up to Pole Baker's humble domicile.

Pole was in the front yard making a fire of sticks, twigs, and chips.

"What's that fer?" the old man questioned, as he dismounted and hitched his horse to the worm fence.

"To drive off mosquitoes," said Pole, wiping his eyes, which were red from the effects of the smoke. "I 'll never pass another night like the last un ef I kin he'p it. I 'lowed my hide was thick, but they bored fer oil all over me from dark till sun-up. I never 've tried smoke, but Hank Watts says it's ahead o' pennyr'yal."

"Shucks!" grunted the planter, "you ain't workin' it right. A few rags burnin' in a pan nigh yore bed may drive 'em out, but a smoke out heer in the yard 'll jest drive 'em in."

"What?" said Pole, in high disgust. "Do you expect me to sleep sech hot weather as this is with a fire nigh my bed? The durn things may eat me raw, but I 'll be blamed ef I barbecue myse'f to please 'em."

Mrs. Baker appeared in the cabin-door, holding two of the youngest children by their hands. "He won't take my advice, Mr. Bishop," she said. "I jest rub a little lamp-oil on my face an' hands an' they don't tetch me." Pole grunted and looked with laughing eyes at the old man.

"She axed me t'other night why I'd quit kissin' 'er," he said. "An' I told 'er I didn't keer any more fer kerosene than the mosquitoes did."

Mrs. Baker laughed pleasantly, as she brought out a chair for Bishop and invited him to sit down. He complied, twirling his riding-switch in his hand. From his position, almost on a level with the floor, he could see the interior of one of the rooms. It was almost bare of furniture. Two opposite corners were occupied by crude bedsteads; in the centre of the room was a cradle made from a soap-box on rockers sawn from rough poplar boards. It had the appearance of having been in use through several generations. Near it stood a spinning-wheel and a three-legged stool. The sharp steel spindle gleamed in the firelight from the big log and mud chimney.

"What's the news from town, Mr. Bishop?" Pole asked, awkwardly, for it struck him that Bishop had called to talk with him about some business and was reluctant to introduce it.

"Nothin' that interests any of us, I reckon, Pole," said the old man, "except I made that investment in Shoal Cotton Factory stock."

"That's good," said Pole, in the tone of anybody but a man who had never invested a dollar in anything. "It's all hunkey, an' my opinion is that it 'll never be wuth less."

"I did heer, too," added Bishop, "that it was reported that Craig had set up a little grocery store out in Texas, nigh the Indian Territory. Some thinks that Winship 'll turn up thar an' jine 'im, but a body never knows what to believe these days."

"That shore is a fact," opined Pole. "Sally, that corn-bread's a-burnin'; ef you'd use less lamp-oil you'd smell better."

Mrs. Baker darted to the fireplace, raked the live coals from beneath the cast-iron oven, and jerked off the lid in a cloud of steam and smoke. She turned over the pone with the aid of a case-knife, and then came back to the door.

"Fer the last month I've had my eye on the Bascome farm," Bishop was saying. "Thar's a hundred acres even, some good bottom land and upland, an' in the neighborhood o' thirty acres o' good wood. Then thar's a five-room house, well made an' tight, an' a barn, cow-house, an' stable."

"Lord! I know the place like a book," said Pole; "an' it's a dandy investment, Mr. Bishop. They say he offered it fer fifteen hundred. It's wuth two thousand. You won't drap any money by buyin' that property, Mr. Bishop. I'd hate to contract to build jest the house an' well an' out-houses fer a thousand."

"I bought it," Bishop told him. "He let me have it fer a good deal less 'n fifteen hundred, cash down."

"Well, you made a dandy trade, Mr. Bishop. Ah, that's what ready money will do. When you got the cash things seem to come at bottom figures."

Old Bishop drew a folded paper from his pocket and slapped it on his knee. "Yes, I closed the deal this evenin', an' I was jest a-thinkin' that as you hain't rented fer next yeer—I mean—" Bishop was ordinarily direct of speech, but somehow his words became tangled, and he delivered himself awkwardly on this occasion. "You see, Alan thinks that you 'n Sally ort to live in a better house than jest this heer log-cabin, an'—"

The wan face of the tired woman was aglow with expectation. She sank down on the doorstep, and sat still and mute, her hands clasping each other in her lap. She had always disliked that cabin and its sordid surroundings, and there was something in Bishop's talk that made her think he was about to propose renting the new farm, house and all, to her husband. Her mouth fell open; she scarcely allowed herself to breathe. Then, as Bishop paused, her husband's voice struck dumb dismay to her heart. It was as if she were falling from glowing hope back to tasted despair.

"Thar's more land in that farm an' I could do jestice to, Mr. Bishop; but ef thar's a good cabin on it an' you see fit to cut off enough fer me'n one hoss I'd jest as soon tend that as this heer. I want to do what you an' Alan think is best all'round."

"Oh, Pole, Pole!" The woman was crying it to herself, her face lowered to her hands that the two men might not see the agony written in her eyes. A house like that to live in, with all those rooms and fireplaces, and windows with panes of glass in them! She fancied she saw her children playing on the tight, smooth floors and on the honeysuckled porch. For one minute these things had been hers, to be snatched away by the callous indifference of her husband, who, alas! had never cared a straw for appearances.

"Oh, I wasn't thinking about *rentin'* it to you," said Bishop, and the woman's dream was over. She raised her head, awake again. "You see," went on Bishop, still struggling for proper expression, "Alan thinks—well, he thinks you are sech a born fool about not acceptin' help from them that feels nigh to you, an' I may as well say grateful, exceedingly grateful, fer what you've done, things that no other livin' man could 'a' done. Alan thinks you ort to have the farm fer yore own property, an' so the deeds has been made out to—"

Pole drew himself up to his full height. His big face was flushed, half with anger, half with a strong emotion of a tenderer kind. He stood towering over the old man like a giant swayed by the warring winds of good and evil, "I won't heer a word more of that, Mr. Bishop," he said, with a quivering lip; "not a word more. By golly! I mean what I say. I don't want to heer another word of it. This heer place is good enough fer me an' my family. It's done eight yeer, an' it kin do another eight."

"Oh, Pole, Pole, *Pole!*" The woman's cry was now audible. It came straight from her pent-up, starving soul and went right to Bishop's heart

"You want the place, don't you, Sally?" he said, calling her by her given name for the first time, as if he had just discovered their kinship. He could not have used a tenderer tone to child of his own.

"Mind, mind what you say, Sally!" ordered Pole, from the depths of his fighting emotions. "Mind what you say!"

The woman looked at Bishop. Her glance was on fire.

"Yes, I want it—I *want* it!" she cried. "I ain't goin' to lie. I want it more right now than I do the kingdom of heaven. I want it ef we have a right to it. Oh, I don't know." She dropped her head in her lap and began to sob.

Bishop stood up. He moved towards her in a jerky fashion and laid his hand on the pitifully tight knot of hair at the back of her head.

"Well, it's yores," he said. "Alan thought Pole would raise a kick agin it, an' me'n him had it made out in yore name, so he couldn't tetch it. It's yores, Sally Ann Baker. That's the way it reads."

The woman's sobs increased, but they were sobs of unbridled joy. With her apron to her eyes she rose and hurried into the house.

The eyes of the two men met. Bishop spoke first:

"You've got to give in, Pole," he said. "You'd not be a man to stand betwixt yore wife an' a thing she wants as bad as she does that place, an', by all that's good an' holy, you sha 'n' t."

"What's the use o' me tryin' to git even with Alan," Pole exclaimed, "ef he's eternally a-goin' to git up some 'n'? I've been tickled to death ever since I cornered old Craig till now, but you an' him has sp'iled it all by this heer trick. It ain't fair to me."

"Well, it's done," smiled the old man, as he went to his horse; "an' ef you don't live thar with Sally, I 'll make 'er git a divorce."

Bishop had reached a little pig-pen in a fence-corner farther along, on his way home, when Mrs. Baker suddenly emerged from a patch of high corn in front of him.

"Is he a-goin' to take it, Mr. Bishop?" she asked, panting from her hurried walk through the corn that hid her from the view of the cabin.

"Yes," Bishop told her; "I'm a-goin' to send two wagons over in the morning to move yore things. I wish it was ten times as good a place as it is, but it will insure you an' the children a living an' a comfortable home."

After the manner of many of her kind, the woman uttered no words of thanks, but simply turned back into the corn, and, occupied with her own vision of prosperity and choking with gratitude, she hurried back to the cabin.

CHAPTER XXIX

THE summer ended, the autumn passed, 'and Christmas approached. Nothing of much importance had taken place among the characters of this little history. The Southern Land and Timber Company, and Wilson in particular, had disappointed Miller and Alan by their reticence in regard to the progress of the railroad scheme. At every meeting with Wilson they found him either really or pretendedly indifferent about the matter. His concern, he told them, was busy in other quarters, and that he really did not know what they would finally do about it.

"He can' t pull the wool over my eyes," Miller told his friend, after one of these interviews. "He simply thinks he can freeze you out by holding off till you have to raise money."

"He may have inquired into my father's financial condition," suggested Alan, with a long face.

"Most likely," replied the lawyer.

"And discovered exactly where we stand."

"Perhaps, but we must not believe that till we know it. I'm going to try to checkmate him. I don't know how, but I 'll think of something. He feels that he has the upper hand now, but I 'll interest him some of these days."

Alan's love affair had also been dragging. He had had numerous assurances of Dolly's constancy, but since learning how her father had acted the night he supposed she had eloped with Alan, her eyes had been opened to the seriousness of offending Colonel Barclay. She now knew that her marriage against his will would cause her immediate disinheritance, and she was too sensible a girl to want to go to Alan without a dollar and with the doors of her home closed against her. Besides, she believed in Alan' s future. She, somehow, had more faith in the railroad than any other interested person. She knew, too, that she was now more closely watched than formerly. She had, with firm finality, refused Frank Hillhouse's offer of marriage, and that had not helped her case in the eyes of her exasperated parent. Her mother occupied neutral ground; she had a vague liking for Alan Bishop, and, if the whole truth must be told, was heartily enjoying the situation. She was enjoying it so subtly and so heartily, in her own bloodless way, that she was at times almost afraid of its ending suddenly.

On Christmas Eve Adele was expected home from Atlanta, and Alan had come in town to meet her. As it happened, an accident delayed her train so that it would not reach Darley till ten o' clock at night instead of six in the evening, so there was nothing for her brother to do but arrange for their staying that night at the Johnston House. Somewhat to Alan' s surprise, who had never discovered the close friendship and constant correspondence existing between Miller and his sister, the former announced that he was going to spend the night at the hotel and drive out to the farm with them the next morning. Of course, it was agreeable, Alan reflected, but it was a strange thing for Miller to propose.

From the long veranda of the hotel after supper that evening the two friends witnessed the crude display of holiday fireworks in the street below. Half a dozen big bonfires made of dry-goods boxes, kerosene and tar barrels, and refuse of all kinds were blazing along the main street. Directly opposite the hotel the only confectionery and toy store in the place was crowded to overflowing by eager customers, and in front of it the purchasers of fireworks were letting them off for the benefit of the bystanders. Fire-crackers were exploded by the package, and every now and then a clerk in some store would come to the front door and fire off a gun or a revolver.

All this noise and illumination was at its height when Adele's train drew up in the car-shed. The bonfires near at hand made it as light as day, and she had no trouble recognizing the two friends.

"Oh, what an awful racket!" she exclaimed, as she released herself from Alan' s embrace and gave her hand to Miller.

"It's in your honor," Miller laughed, as, to Alan' s vast astonishment, he held on to her hand longer than seemed right. "We ought to have had the brass band out."

"Oh, I'm so glad to get home," said Adele, laying her hand on Miller's extended arm. Then she released it to give Alan her trunk-checks. "Get them, brother," she said. "Mr. Miller will take care of me. I suppose you are not going to drive home to-night."

"Not if you are tired," said Miller, in a tone Alan had never heard his friend use to any woman, nor had he ever seen such an expression on Miller's face as lay there while the lawyer's eyes were feasting themselves on the girl's beauty.

Alan hurried away after the trunks and a porter. He was almost blind with a rage that was new to him. Was Miller deliberately beginning a flirtation with Adele at a moment's notice? And had she been so spoiled by the "fast set" of Atlanta during her stay there that she would allow it—even if Miller was a friend of the family? He found a negro porter near the heap of luggage that had been hurled from the baggage-car, and ordered his sister's trunks taken to the hotel. Then he followed the couple moodily up to the hotel parlor. He was destined to undergo another shock, for, on entering that room, he surprised Miller and Adele on a sofa behind the big square piano with their heads suspiciously near together, and so deeply were they engaged in conversation that, although he drew up a chair near them, they paid no heed to him further than to recognize his appearance with a lifting of their eyes. They were talking of social affairs in Atlanta and people whose names were unfamiliar to Alan. He rose and stood before the fireplace, but they did not notice his change of position. Truly it was maddening. He told himself that Adele's pretty face and far too easy manner had attracted Miller's attention temporarily, and the fellow was daring to enter one of his flirtations right before his eyes. Alan would give him a piece of his mind at the first opportunity, even if he was under obligations to him. Indeed, Miller had greatly disappointed him, and so had Adele. He had always thought she, like Dolly Barclay, was different from other girls; but no, she was like them all. Miller's attention had simply turned her head. Well, as soon as he had a chance he would tell her a few things about Miller and his views of women. That would put her on her guard, but it would not draw out the poisoned sting left by Miller's presumption, or indelicacy, or whatever it was. Alan rose and stood at the fire unnoticed for several minutes, and then he showed that he was at least a good chaperon, for he reached out and drew on the old-fashioned bell-pull in the chimney-corner. The porter appeared, and Alan asked: "Is my sister's room ready?"

"Yes, it's good and warm now, suh," said the negro. "I started the fire an hour ago."

Miller and Adele had paused to listen.

"Oh, you are going to hurry me off to bed," the girl said, with an audible sigh.

"You must be tired after that ride," said Alan, coldly.

"That's a fact, you must be," echoed Miller. "Well, if you have to go, you can finish telling me in the morning. You know I'm going to spend the night here, where I have a regular room, and I 'll see you at breakfast."

"Oh, I'm so glad," said Adele. "Yes, I can finish telling you in the morning." Then she seemed to notice her brother's long face, and she laughed out teasingly: "I 'll bet he and Dolly are no nearer together than ever."

"You are right," Miller joined in her mood; "the Colonel still has his dogs ready for Alan, but they 'll make it up some day, I hope. Dolly is *next* to the smartest girl I know."

"Oh, you *are* a flatterer," laughed Adele, and she gave Miller her hand. "Don't forget to be up for early breakfast. We must start soon in the morning. I'm dying to see the home folks."

Alan was glad that Miller had a room of his own, for he was not in a mood to converse with him; and when Adele had retired he refused Miller's proffered cigar and went to his own room.

Miller grunted as Alan turned away. "He's had bad news of some sort," he thought, "and it's about Dolly Barclay. I wonder, after all, if she would stick to a poor man. I begin to think some women would. Adele is of that stripe—yes, she is, and isn't she stunning-looking? She's a gem of the first water, straight as a die, full of pluck and—she's all right—all right!"

He went out on the veranda to smoke and enjoy repeating these things over to himself. The bonfires in the street were dying down to red embers, around which stood a few stragglers; but there was a blaze of new light over the young man' s head. Along his horizon had dawned a glorious reason for his existence; a reason that discounted every reason he had ever entertained. "Adele, Adele," he said to himself, and then his cigar went out. Perhaps, his thoughts ran on in their mad race with happiness—perhaps, with her fair head on her pillow, she was thinking of him as he was of her.

Around the corner came a crowd of young men singing negro songs. They passed under the veranda, and Miller recognized Frank Hillhouse's voice. "That you, Frank?" Miller called out, leaning over the railing.

"Yes—that you, Ray?" Hillhouse stepped out into view. "Come on; we are going to turn the town over. Every sign comes down, according to custom, you know. Old Thad Moore is drunk in the calaboose. They put him in late this evening. We are going to mask and let him out. It's a dandy racket; we are going to make him think we are White Caps, and then set him down in the bosom of his family. Come on."

"I can't to-night," declined Miller, with a laugh. "I'm dead tired."

"Well, if you hear all the church bells ringing, you needn't think it's fire, and jump out of your skin. We ain't going to sleep to-night, and we don't intend to let anybody else do it."

"Well, go it while you are young," Miller retorted, with a laugh, and Hillhouse joined his companions in mischief and they passed on singing merrily.

Miller threw his cigar away and went to his room. He was ecstatically happy. The mere thought that Adele Bishop was under the same roof with him, and on the morrow was going to people who liked him, and leaned on his advice and experience, gave him a sweet content that thrilled him from head to foot.

"Perhaps I ought to tell Alan," he mused, "but he 'll find it out soon enough; and, hang it all, I can' t tell him how I feel about his own sister, after all the rot I've stuffed into him."

CHAPTER XXX

THE next morning, as soon as he was up, Alan went to his sister's room. He found her dressed and ready for him. She was seated before a cheerful grate-fire, looking over a magazine she had brought to pass the time on the train.

"Come in," she said, pleasantly enough, he reflected, now that Miller was not present to absorb her attention. "I expected you to get up a little earlier. Those guns down at the bar-room just about daybreak waked me, and I couldn't go to sleep again. There is no use denying it, Al, we have a barbarous way of amusing ourselves up here in North Georgia."

He went in and stood with his back to the fire, still unable to rid his brow of the frown it had worn the night before.

"Oh, I reckon you've got too citified for us," he said, "along with other accomplishments that fast set down there has taught you."

Adele laid her book open on her lap.

"Look here, Alan," she said, quite gravely. "What's the matter with you?"

"Nothing, that I know of," he said, without meeting her direct gaze.

"Well, there is," she said, as the outcome of her slow inspection of his clouded features.

He shrugged his shoulders and gave her his eyes steadily.

"I don't like the way you and Miller are carrying on." He hurled the words at her sullenly. "You see, I know him through and through."

"Well, that's all right," she replied, not flinching from his indignant stare; "but what's that got to do with my conduct and his?"

"You allow him to be too familiar with you," Alan retorted. "He's not the kind of a man for you to—to act that way with. He has flirted with a dozen women and thrown them over; he doesn't believe in the honest love of a man for a woman, or the love of a woman for a man."

"Ah, I am at the first of this!" Adele, instead of being put down by his stormy words, was smiling inwardly. Her lips were rigid, but Alan saw the light of keen amusement in her eyes. "Is he *really* so dangerous? That makes him doubly interesting. Most girls love to handle masculine gunpowder. Do you know, if I was Dolly Barclay, for instance, an affair with you would not be much fun, because I'd be so sure of you. The dead level of your past would alarm me."

"Thank Heaven, all women are not alike!" was the bolt he hurled at her. "If you knew as much about Ray Miller as I do, you'd act in a more dignified way on a first acquaintance with him."

"On a first—oh, I see what you mean!" Adele put her handkerchief to her face and treated herself to a merry laugh that exasperated him beyond endurance. Then she stood up, smoothing her smile away. "Let's go to breakfast. I'm as hungry as a bear. I told Rayburn—I mean your dangerous friend, Mr. Miller—that we'd meet him in the dining-room. He says he's crazy for a cup of coffee with whipped cream in it. I ordered it just now."

"The dev—" Alan bit the word in two and strode from the room, she following. The first person they saw in the big dining-room was Miller, standing at the stove in the centre of the room warming himself. He scarcely looked at Alan in his eagerness to have a chair placed for Adele at a little table reserved for three in a corner of the room, which was presided over by a slick-looking mulatto waiter, whose father had belonged to Miller's family.

"I've been up an hour," he said to her. "I took a stroll down the street to see what damage the gang did last night. Every sign is down or hung where it doesn't belong. To tease the owner, an old negro drayman, whom everybody jokes with, they took his wagon to pieces and put it together again on the roof of Harmon's drug-store. How they got it there is a puzzle that will go down in local history like the building of the Pyramids."

"Whiskey did it," laughed Adele; "that will be the final explanation."

"I think you are right," agreed Miller.

Alan bolted his food in grum silence, unnoticed by the others. Adele's very grace at the table, as she prepared Miller's coffee, and her apt repartee added to his discomfiture. He excused himself from the table before they had finished, mumbling something about seeing if the horses were ready, and went into the office. The last blow to his temper was dealt by Adele as she came from the dining-room.

"Mr. Miller wants to drive me out in his buggy to show me his horses," she said, half smiling. "You won't mind, will you? You see, he 'll want his team out there to get back in, and—"

"Oh, I don't mind," he told her. "I see you are bent on making a goose of yourself. After what I've told you about Miller, if you still—"

But she closed his mouth with her hand.

"Leave him to me, brother," she said, as she turned away. "I'm old enough to take care of myself, and—and—well, I know men better than you do."

When Alan reached home he found that Miller and Adele had been there half an hour. His mother met him at the door with a mysterious smile on her sweet old face, as she nodded at the closed door of the parlor.

"Don't go in there now," she whispered. "Adele and Mr. Miller have been there ever since they come. I railly believe they are in love with each other. I never saw young folks act more like it. When I met 'em it looked jest like he wanted to kiss me, he was so happy. Now wouldn't it be fine if they was to get married? He's the nicest man in the State, and the best catch."

"Oh, mother," said Alan, "you don't understand. Rayburn Miller is—"

"Well, Adele will know how to manage him," broke in the old lady, too full of her view of the romance to harken to his; "she ain't no fool, son. She 'll twist him around her finger if she wants to. She's pretty, an' stylish, an' as sharp as a brier. Ah, he's jest seen it all and wants her; you can't fool me! I know how people act when they are in love. I've seen hundreds, and I never saw a worse case on both sides than this is."

Going around to the stables to see that his horses were properly attended to, Alan met his uncle leaning over the rail-fence looking admiringly at a young colt that was prancing around the lot.

"Christmas gift," said the old man, suddenly. "I ketched you that time shore pop."

"Yes, you got ahead of me," Alan admitted.

The old man came nearer to him, nodding his head towards the house. "Heerd the news?" he asked, with a broad grin of delight.

"What news is that?" Alan asked, dubiously. "Young Miss," a name given Adele by the negroes, and sometimes used jestingly by the family— "Young Miss has knocked the props clean from under Miller." Alan frowned and hung his head for a moment; then he said:

"Uncle Ab, do you remember what I told you about Miller's opinion of love and women in general?"

The old man saw his drift and burst into a full, round laugh.

"I know you told me what he said about love an' women in general, but I don't know as you said what he thought about women in *particular*. This heer's a particular case. I tell you she's fixed 'im. Yore little sis has done the most complete job out o' tough material I ever inspected. He's a gone coon; he 'll never make another brag; he's tied hand an' foot."

Alan looked straight into his uncle's eyes. A light was breaking on him. "Uncle Ab," he said, "do you think he is—really in love with her?"

"Ef he ain't, an' don't ax yore pa an' ma fer 'er before a month's gone, I 'll deed you my farm. Now, look heer. A feller knows his own sister less'n he does anybody else; that's beca'se you never have thought of Adele follerin' in the trail of womankind. You'd hate fer a brother o' that town gal to be raisin' sand about you, wouldn't you? Well, you go right on an' let them two kill the'r own rats."

Alan and his uncle were returning to the house when Pole Baker dismounted at the front gate and came into the yard.

Since becoming a landed proprietor his appearance had altered for the better most materially. He wore a neat, well-fitting suit of clothes and a new hat, but of the same broad dimensions as the old. Its brim was pinned up on the right side by a little brass ornament.

"I seed Mr. Miller drive past my house awhile ago with Miss Adele," he said, "an' I come right over. I want to see all of you together."

Just then Miller came out of the parlor and descended the steps to join them.

"Christmas gift, Mr. Miller!" cried Pole. "I ketched you that time."

"And if I paid up, you'd cuss me out," retorted the lawyer, with a laugh. "I haven't forgotten the row you raised about that suit of clothes. Well, what's the news? How's your family?"

"About as common, Mr. Miller," said Pole. "My wife's gittin' younger an' younger ever'day. Sence she moved in 'er new house, an' got to whitewashin' fences an' makin' flower-beds, an' one thing another, she looks like a new person. I'd 'a' bought 'er a house long ago ef I'd 'a' knowed she wanted it that bad. Oh, we put on the lugs now! We wipe with napkins after eatin', an' my littlest un sets in a high-chair an' says 'Please pass the gravy,' like he'd been off to school. Sally says she's a-goin' to send 'em, an' I don't keer ef she does; they 'll stand head, ef they go; the'r noggin' s look like squashes, but they're full o' seeds, an' don't you ferget it."

"That they are!" intoned Abner Daniel.

"I've drapped onto a little news," said Pole. "You know what a old moonshiner cayn't pick up in these mountains from old pards ain't wuth lookin' fer."

"Railroad?" asked Miller, interestedly.

"That's fer you-uns to make out," said Baker. "Now, I ain't a-goin' to give away my authority, but I rid twenty miles yesterday to substantiate what I heerd, an' know it's nothin' but the truth. You all know old Bobby Milburn's been buyin' timber-land up about yore property, don't you?"

"I didn't know how much," answered Miller, "but I knew he had secured some."

"Fust and last in the neighborhood o' six thousand acres," affirmed Pole, "an' he's still on the war-path. What fust attracted my notice was findin' out that old Bobby hain't a dollar to his name. That made me suspicious, an' I went to work to investigate."

"Good boy!" said Uncle Abner, in an admiring undertone.

"Well, I found out he was usin' Wilson's money, an' secretly buyin' fer him; an' what's more, he seems to have unlimited authority, an' a big bank account to draw from."

There was a startled pause. It was broken by Miller, whose eyes were gleaming excitedly.

"It's blame good news," he said, eying Alan.

"Do you think so?" said Alan, who was still under his cloud of displeasure with his friend.

"Yes; it simply means that Wilson intends to build that road. He's been quiet, and pretending indifference, for two reasons. First, to bring us to closer terms, and next to secure more land. Alan, my boy, the plot thickens! I'm getting that fellow right where I want him. Pole, you have brought us a dandy Christmas gift, but I 'll be blamed if you get a thing for it. I don't intend to get shot."

Then they all went to find Bishop to tell him the news.

CHAPTER XXXI

IT was a cold, dry day about the middle of January. They were killing hogs at the farm. Seven or eight negroes, men and women, had gathered from all about in the neighborhood to assist in the work and get the parts of the meat usually given away in payment for such services.

Two hogsheads for hot water were half buried in the ground. A big iron pot with a fire beneath it was heating water and a long fire of logs heaped over with big stones was near by. When hot, the stones were to be put into the cooling water to raise the temperature, it being easier to do this than to replace the water in the pot. The hogs to be killed were grunting and squealing in a big pen near the barn.

Abner Daniel and old man Bishop were superintending these preparations when Alan came from the house to say that Rayburn Miller had just ridden out to see them on business. "I think it's the railroad," Alan informed his father, who always displayed signs of almost childish excitement when the subject came up. They found Miller in the parlor being entertained by Adele, who immediately left the room on their arrival. They all sat down before the cheerful fire. Miller showed certain signs of embarrassment at first, but gradually threw them off and got down to the matter in hand quite with his office manner.

"I've got a proposition to make to you, Mr. Bishop," he opened up, with a slight flush on his face. "I've been making some inquiries about Wilson, and I am more and more convinced that he intends to freeze us out—or you rather—by holding off till you are obliged to sell your property for a much lower figure than you now ask him for it."

"You think so," grunted Bishop, pulling a long face.

"Yes; but what I now want to do is to show him, indirectly, that we are independent of him."

"Huh!" ejaculated Bishop, even more dejectedly—"huh! I say!"

Alan was looking at Miller eagerly, as if trying to divine the point he was about to make. "I must confess," he smiled, "that I can' t well see how we can show independence right now."

"Well, I think I see a way," said Miller, the flush stealing over his face again. "You see, there is no doubt that Wilson is on his high horse simply because he thinks he could call on you for that twenty-five thousand dollars and put you to some trouble raising it without—without, I say, throwing your land on the market. I can' t blame him," Miller went on, smiling, "for it's only what any business man would do, who is out for profit, but we must not knuckle to him."

"Huh, huh!" Bishop grunted, in deeper despondency.

"How do you propose to get around the knuckling process?" asked Alan, who had caught the depression influencing his parent.

"I'd simply take up that note," said the lawyer. "You know, under the contract, we are privileged to pay it to-morrow if we wish. It would simply paralyze him. He's so confident that you can' t take it up that he has not even written to ask if you want to renew it or not. Yes; he's confident that he 'll rake in that security—so confident that he has been, as you know, secretly buying land near yours."

Old Bishop's eyes were wide open. In the somewhat darkened room the firelight reflected in them showed like illuminated blood-spots. He said nothing, but breathed heavily.

"But," exclaimed Alan, "Ray, you know we—father has invested that money, and the truth is, that he and mother have already had so much worry over the business that they would rather let the land go at what was raised on it than to—to run any more risks."

Bishop groaned out his approval of this elucidation of his condition and sat silently nodding his head. The very thought of further risks stunned and chilled him.

Miller's embarrassment now descended on him in full force.

"I was not thinking of having your father disturb his investments," he said. "The truth is, I have met with a little financial disappointment in a certain direction. For the last three months I have been raking and scraping among the dry bones of my investments to get up exactly twenty-five thousand dollars to secure a leading interest in a cotton mill at Darley, of which I was to be president. I managed to get the money together and only yesterday I learned that the Northern capital that was to guarantee the thing was only in the corner of a fellow's eye up in Boston—a man that had not a dollar on earth. Well, there you are! I've my twenty-five thousand dollars, and no place to put it. I thought, if you had just as soon owe me the money as Wilson, that you'd really be doing me a favor to let me take up the note. You see, it would actually floor him. He means business, and this would show him that we are not asking any favors of him. In fact, I have an idea it would scare him out of his skin. He'd think we had another opportunity of selling. I'm dying to do this, and I hope you 'll let me work it. Really, I think you ought to consent. I'd never drive you to the wall and—well—*he* might."

All eyes were on the speaker. Bishop had the dazed expression of a bewildered man trying to believe in sudden good luck. Abner Daniel lowered his head and shook with low, subdued laughter.

"You are a jim-dandy, young man," he said to Miller. "That's all there is about it. You take the rag off the bush. Oh, my Lord! They say in Alt's meeting-house that it's a sin to play poker with no stakes, but Alf's in a game with half the earth put up agin another feller's wad as big as a bale o' hay. Play down, Alf. Play down. You've got a full hand an' plenty to draw from."

"We couldn't let you do this, Ray," expostulated Alan.

"But I assure you it is merely a matter of business with me," declared the lawyer. "You know I'm interested myself, and I believe we shall come out all right. I'm simply itching to do it."

Bishop's face was ablaze. The assurance that a wise young business man would consider a purchase of his of sufficient value to put a large amount of money on pleased him, banished his fears, thrilled him.

"If you feel that way," he said, smiling at the corners of his mouth, "go ahead. I don't know but what you are plumb right. It will show Wilson that we ain't beholden to him, an' will set 'im to work ef anything will."

So it was finally settled, and no one seemed so well pleased with the arrangement as Miller himself. Adele entered the room with the air of one half fearful of intruding, and her three relatives quietly withdrew, leaving her to entertain the guest.

"I wonder what's the matter with your brother," Miller remarked, as his eyes followed Alan from the room.

"Oh, brother?" laughed Adele. "No one tries to keep up with his whims and fancies."

"But, really," said Miller, in a serious tone, "he has mystified me lately. I wonder if he has had bad news from Dolly. I've tried to get into a confidential chat with him several times of late, but he seems to get around it. Really, it seems to me, at times, that he treats me rather coldly."

"Oh, if you waste time noticing Al you 'll become a beggar," and Adele gave another amused laugh. "Take my advice and let him alone."

"I almost believe you know what ails him," said Miller, eying her closely.

"I know what he *thinks* ails him," the girl responded.

"And won't you tell me what—what he thinks ails him?"

"No, I couldn't do that," answered our young lady, with a knowing smile. "If you are ever any wiser on the subject you will have to get your wisdom from him."

She turned to the piano and began to arrange some scattered pieces of music, and he remained on the hearth, his back to the fire, his brow wrinkled in pleased perplexity.

"I 'll have to get my wisdom from him," repeated Miller, pronouncing each word with separate distinctness, as if one of them might prove the key to the mystery.

"Yes, I should think two wise men could settle a little thing like that. If not, you may call in the third—you know there were three of you, according to the Bible."

"Oh, so there were," smiled Miller; "but it's hard to tell when we three shall meet again. The last time I saw the other two they were having their sandals half-soled for a tramp across the desert. I came this way to build a railroad, and I believe I'm going to do it. That's linking ancient and modern times together with a coupling-pin, isn't it?"

She came from the piano and stood by him, looking down into the fire. "Ah," she said, seriously, "if you could *only* do it!"

"Would you like it very much?"

"Very, very much; it means the world to us—to Alan, to father and mother, and—yes, to me. I hunger for independence."

"Then it shall be done," he said, fervently.

CHAPTER XXXII

AS the elevator in the big building was taking Rayburn Miller up to the offices of the Southern Land and Timber Company, many reflections passed hurriedly through his mind.

"You are going to get the usual cold shoulder from Wilson," he mused; "but he 'll put it up against something about as warm as he's touched in many a day. If you don't make him squirm, it will be only because you don't want to."

Wilson was busy at his desk looking over bills of lading, receipts, and other papers, and now and then giving instructions to a typewriter in the corner of the room.

"Ahl how are you, Miller?" he said, indifferently, giving the caller his hand without rising. "Down to see the city again, eh?"

Rayburn leaned on the top of the desk, and knocked the ashes from his cigar with the tip of his little finger.

"Partly that and partly business," he returned, carelessly.

"Two birds, eh?"

"That's about it. I concluded you were not coming up our way soon, and so I decided to drop in on you."

"Yes, glad you did." Wilson glanced at the papers on his desk and frowned. "Wish I had more time at my disposal. I'd run up to the club with you and show you my Kentucky thoroughbreds, but I realty am rushed, to-day particularly."

"Oh, I haven't a bit of time to spare myself! I take the afternoon train home. The truth is, I came to see you for my clients, the Bishops."

"Ah, I see." Wilson's face clouded over by some mechanical arrangement known only to himself. "Well, I can' t realty report any progress in that matter," he said. "All the company think Bishop's figures are away out of reason, and the truth is, right now, we are over head and ears in operations in other quarters, and—well, you see how it is?"

Abner Daniel | 199

"Yes, I think I do." Miller smoked a moment. "In fact, I told my clients last month that the matter was not absorbing your attention, and so they gave up counting on you."

Wilson so far forgot his pose that he looked up in a startled sort of way and began to study Miller's smoke-wrapped profile.

"You say they are not—have not been counting on my company to—to buy their land?"

"Why, no," said Miller, in accents well resembling those of slow and genuine surprise. "Why, you have not shown the slightest interest in the matter since the day you made the loan, and naturally they ceased to think you wanted the land. The only reason I called was that the note is payable to-day, and—"

"Oh yes, by Jove! that was careless of me. The interest is due. I knew it would be all right, and I had no idea you would bother to run down for that. Why, my boy, we could have drawn for it, you know."

Miller smiled inwardly, as he looked calmly and fixedly through his smoke into the unsuspecting visage upturned to him.

"But the note itself is payable to-day," he said, closely on the alert for a facial collapse; "and, while you or I might take up a paper for twenty-five thousand dollars through a bank, old-fashioned people like Mr. and Mrs. Bishop would feel safer to have it done by an agent. That's why I came."

Miller, in silent satisfaction, saw the face of his antagonist fall to pieces like an artificial flower suddenly shattered.

"Pay the note?" gasped Wilson. "Why—"

Miller puffed at his cigar and gazed at his victim as if slightly surprised over the assumption that his clients had not, all along, intended to avail themselves of that condition in their contract.

"You mean that the Bishops are ready to—" Wilson began again on another breath—"to pay us the twenty-five thousand dollars?"

"And the interest for six months," quietly added Miller, reaching for a match on the desk. "I reckon you've got the note here. I don't want to miss my train."

Wilson was a good business man, but his Puritanical training in New England had not fitted him for wily diplomacy; besides, he had not expected to meet a diplomat that day, and did not, even now, realize that he was in the hands of one. He still believed that Miller was only a half-educated country lawyer who had barely enough brains and experience to succeed as a legal servant for mountain clients. Hence, he now made little effort to conceal his embarrassment into which the sudden turn of affairs had plunged him. In awkward silence he squirmed in his big chair.

"Of course, they can take up their note to-day if they wish," he said, with alarmed frankness. "I was not counting on it, though." He rose to his feet. Miller's watchful eye detected a certain trembling of his lower lip. He thrust his hands into his pockets nervously; and in a tone of open irritation he said to the young man at the typewriter: "Brown, I wish you'd let up on that infernal clicking; sometimes I can stand it, and then again I can' t. You can do those letters in the next room."

When the young man had gone out, carrying his machine, Wilson turned to Miller. "As I understand it, you, personally, have no interest in the Bishop property?"

"Oh, not a dollar!" smiled the lawyer. "I'm only acting for them."

"Then" — Wilson drove his hands into his pockets again — "perhaps you wouldn't mind telling me if the Bishops are on trade with other parties. Are they?"

Miller smiled and shook his head. "As their lawyer, Mr. Wilson, I simply couldn't answer that question."

The blow was well directed and it struck a vulnerable spot.

"I beg your pardon," Wilson stammered. "I did not mean to suggest that you would betray confidence." He reflected a moment, and then he said, in a flurried tone, "They have not actually sold out, have they?"

Miller was silent for a moment, then he answered: "I don't see any reason why I may not answer that question I don't think my clients would object to my saying that they have not yet accepted any offer."

A look of relief suffused itself over Wilson's broad face.

"Then they are still open to accept their offer to me?"

Miller laughed as if highly amused at the complication of the matter.

"They are bound, you remember, only so long as you hold their note."

"Then I tell you what to do," proposed Wilson. "Go back and tell them not to bother about payment, for a few days, anyway, and that we will soon tell them positively whether we will pay their price or not. That's fair, isn't it?"

"It might seem so to a man personally interested in the deal," admitted Miller, as the introduction to another of his blows from the shoulder; "but as lawyer for my clients I can only obey orders, like the boy who stood on the burning deck."

Wilson's face fell. The remote clicking of the typewriter seemed to grate upon his high-wrought nerves, and he went and slammed the partly opened door, muttering something like an oath. On that slight journey, however, he caught an idea.

"Suppose you wire them my proposition and wait here for a reply," he suggested.

Miller frowned. "That would do no good," he said. "I'm sorry I can' t explain fully, but the truth is this: I happen to know that they wish, for reasons of their own, to take up the note you hold, and that nothing else will suit them."

At this juncture Wilson lost his grip on all self-possession, and degenerated into the sullen anger of sharp and unexpected disappointment.

"I don't feel that we are being fairly treated," he said. "We most naturally assumed that your clients wanted to—to extend our option on the property for at least another six months. We assumed that from the fact that we had no notification from them that they would be ready to pay the note to-day. That's where we feel injured, Mr. Miller."

Rayburn threw his cigar into a cuspidor; his attitude of being a non-interested agent was simply a stroke of genius. Behind this plea he crouched, showing himself only to fire shots that played havoc with whatever they struck.

"I believe my clients *did* feel, I may say, honor bound to you to sell for the price they offered; but—now I may be mistaken—but I'm sure they were under the impression, as I was, too, that you only wanted the property provided you could build a railroad from Dar-ley to it, and—"

"Well, that's true," broke in Wilson. "That's quite true."

"And," finished Miller, still behind his inevitable fortification, "they tell me that you have certainly shown indifference to the project ever since the note was given. In fact, they asked me pointedly if I thought you meant business, and I was forced, conscientiously, to tell them that I thought you seemed to have other fish to fry."

Wilson glared at the lawyer as if he wanted to kick him for a stupid idiot who could not do two things at once—work for the interests of his clients and not wreck his plans also. It had been a long time since he had found himself in such a hot frying-pan.

"So you think the thing is off," he said, desperately, probably recalling several purchases of land he had made in the section he had expected to develop. "You think it's off?"

"I hardly know what to say," said Miller. "The old gentleman, Mr. Bishop, is a slow-going old-timer, but his son is rather up to date, full of energy and ambition. I think he's made up his mind to sell that property."

Wilson went to his desk, hovered over it like a dark, human cloud, and then reluctantly turned to the big iron safe against the wall, obviously to get the note. His disappointment was too great for concealment. With his fat, pink hand on the silver-plated combination-bolt he turned to Miller again.

"Would you mind sitting down till I telephone one or two of the directors?"

"Not at all," said Miller, "if you 'll get me a cigar and the *Constitution*. The Atlanta baseball team played Mobile yesterday, and I was wondering—"

"I don't keep track of such things," said Wilson, coming back to his desk, with an impatient frown, to ring his call-bell for the office-boy.

"Oh yes, I believe football is your national sport," said Miller, with a dry smile. "Well, it's only a difference between arms and legs—whole bones and casualties."

Wilson ordered the cigar and paper when the boy appeared, and, leaving the lawyer suddenly, he went into the room containing the telephone, closing the door after him.

In a few minutes he reappeared, standing before Miller, who was chewing a cold cigar and attentively reading. He looked up at Wilson abstractedly.

"Bully for Atlanta!" he said. "The boys made ten runs before the Mobiles had scored—"

"Oh, come down to business!" said the New-Eng-lander, with a ready-made smile. "Honestly, I don't believe you drowsy Southerners ever will get over your habit of sleeping during business hours. It seems to be bred in the bone."

Miller laughed misleadingly. "Try to down us at a horse-race and we 'll beat you in the middle of the night. Hang it all, man, you don't know human nature, that's all! How can you expect me, on my measly fees, to dance a breakdown over business I am transacting for other people?"

"Well, that may account for it," admitted Wilson, who seemed bent on being more agreeable in the light of some fresh hopes he had absorbed from the telephone-wires. "See here, I've got a rock-bottom proposal to make to your people. Now listen, and drop that damned paper for a minute. By Jove! if I had to send a man from your State to attend to legal business I'd pick one not full of mental morphine."

"Oh, you wouldn't?" Miller laid down the paper and assumed a posture indicative of attention roused from deep sleep. "Fire away. I'm listening."

"I already had authority to act for the company, but I thought it best to telephone some of the directors." Wilson sat down in his chair and leaned towards the lawyer. "Here's what we will do. The whole truth is, we are willing to plank down the required one hundred thousand for that property, provided we can lay our road there without incurring the expense of purchasing the right of way. Now if the citizens along the proposed line want their country developed bad enough to donate the right of way through their lands, we can trade."

There was a pause. Then Miller broke it by striking a match on the sole of his boot. He looked crosseyed at the flame as he applied it to his cigar. "Don't you think your people could stand whatever value is appraised by law in case of refusals along the line?"

"No," said Wilson. "The price for the land is too steep for that. Your clients have our ultimatum. What do you say? We can advertise a meeting of citizens at Springtown, which is about the centre of the territory involved, and if all agree to give the right of way it will be a trade. We can have the meeting set for to-day two weeks. How does that strike you?"

"I'd have to wire my clients."

"When can you get an answer?"

Miller looked at his watch. "By five o' clock this afternoon. The message would have to go into the country."

"Then send it off at once."

A few minutes after five o' clock Miller sauntered into the office. Wilson sat at his desk and looked up eagerly.

"Well?" he asked, almost under his breath.

The lawyer leaned on the top of the desk. "They are willing to grant you the two weeks' time, provided you sign an agreement for your firm that you will purchase their property at the price named at the expiration of that time."

"With the provision," interpolated Wilson, "that a right of way is donated."

"Yes, with that provision," Miller nodded.

"Then sit down here and write out your paper."

Miller complied as nonchalantly as if he were drawing up a bill of sale for a worn-out horse.

"There you are," he said, pushing the paper to Wilson when he had finished.

Wilson read it critically. "It certainly is binding," he said. "You people may sleep during business hours, but you have your eyes open when you draw up papers. However, I don't care; I want the Bishops to feel secure. They must get to work to secure the right of way. It will be no easy job, I 'll let you know. I've struck shrewd, obstinate people in my life, but those up there beat the world. Noah couldn't have driven them in the ark, even after the Flood set in."

"You know something about them, then?" said Miller, laughing to himself over the implied confession.

Wilson flushed, and then admitted that he had been up that way several times looking the situation over.

"How about the charter?" asked Miller, indifferently.

"That's fixed. I have already seen to that."

"Then it all depends on the right of way," remarked the lawyer as he drew a check from his pocket and handed it to Wilson. "Now get me that note," he said.

Wilson brought it from the safe.

"Turning this over cuts my option down to two weeks," he said. "But we 'll know at the meeting what can be done."

"Yes, we 'll know then what they can do with *you*," said Miller, significantly, as he put the cancelled note in his pocket and rose to go.

CHAPTER XXXIII

WHEN Miller's train reached Darley and he alighted in the car-shed, he was met by a blinding snow-storm. He could see the dim lantern of the hotel porter as he came towards him through the slanting feathery sheet and the yet dimmer lights of the hotel.

"Heer! Marse Miller!" shouted the darky; "look out fer dat plank er you 'll fall in er ditch. Marse Alan Bishop is at de hotel, an' he say tell you ter stop dar—dat you couldn't git home in dis sto'm no how."

"Oh, he's in town," said Miller. "Well, I was thinking of spending the night at the hotel, anyway."

In the office of the hotel, almost the only occupant of the room besides the clerk, sat Abner Daniel, at the red-hot coal stove.

"Why," exclaimed Miller, in surprise, "I didn't know you were in town."

"The fact is, we're all heer," smiled the old man, standing up and stretching himself. He looked as if he had been napping. "We fetched the women in to do some tradin', an' this storm blowed up. We could 'a' made it home all right," he laughed out impulsively, "but the last one of 'em wanted a excuse to stay over. They are et up with curiosity to know how yore trip come out. They are all up in Betsy an' Alf's room. Go up?"

"Yes, I reckon I'd better relieve their minds."

Abner offered to pilot him to the room in question, and when it was reached the old man opened the door without knocking. "Heer's the man you've been hankerin' to see all day," he announced, jovially. "I fetched 'im straight up."

They all rose from their seats around the big grate-fire and shook hands with the lawyer.

"He looks like he has news of some kind," said Adele, who was studying his face attentively. "Now, sir, sit down and tell us are we to be rich or poor, bankrupt or robber."

"Don't put the most likely word last," said Abner, dryly.

"Well," began Miller, as he sat down in the semicircle. "As it now stands, we've got a chance to gain our point. I have a signed agreement—and a good one—that your price will be paid if we can get the citizens through whose property the road passes to donate a right of way. That's the only thing that now stands between you and a cash sale."

"They 'll do it, I think," declared Alan, elatedly.

"I dunno about that," said Abner. "It's owin' to whose land is to be donated. Thar's some skunks over in them mountains that wouldn't let the gates o' heaven swing over the'r property except to let themselves through."

No one laughed at this remark save Abner himself. Mrs. Bishop was staring straight into the fire. Her husband leaned forward and twirled his stiff fingers slowly in front of him.

"Huh! So it depends on *that*," he said. "Well, it *does* look like mighty nigh anybody ud ruther see a railroad run out thar than not, but I'm no judge."

"Well, it is to be tested two weeks from now," Miller said. And then he went into a detailed and amusing account of how he had brought Wilson to terms.

"Well, that beats the Dutch!" laughed Abner. "I'd ruther 'a' been thar 'an to a circus. You worked 'im to a queen's taste—as fine as split silk. You 'n' Pole Baker'd make a good team—you to look after the bon-tons an' him to rake in the scum o' mankind. I don't know but Pole could dress up an' look after both ends, once in a while, ef you wanted to take a rest."

"I'm always sorry when I heer of it bein' necessary to resort to trickery," ventured Mrs. Bishop, in her mild way. "It don't look exactly right to me."

"I don't like it, nuther," said Bishop. "Ef the land's wuth the money, an'—"

"The trouble with Alf," broke in Abner, "is that with all his Bible readin' he never seems to git any practical benefit out'n it. Now, when I'm in doubt about whether a thing's right or wrong, I generally find some Scriptural sanction fer the side I want to win. Some'rs in the Bible thar was a big, rich king that sent a pore feller off to git 'im kilt in battle so he could add his woman to his collection. Now, no harm ever come to the king that I know of, an', fer my part, I don't think what you did to yank Wilson into line was nigh as bad, beca'se you was work-in' fer friends. Then Wilson was loaded fer bear his-se'f. War's over, I reckon, but when Wilson's sort comes down heer expectin' to ride rough-shod over us agin, I feel like givin' a war-whoop an' rammin' home a Minié ball."

"I sha 'n't worry about the morality of the thing," said Miller. "Wilson was dead set on crushing you to powder. I saw that. Besides, if he takes the property and builds the road, he 'll make a lot of money out of it."

After this the conversation languished, and, thinking that the old people might wish to retire, Miller bade them good-night and went to his own room.

A snow of sufficient thickness for sleighing in that locality was a rare occurrence, and the next morning an odd scene presented itself in front of the hotel. The young men of the near-by stores had hastily improvised sleds by taking the wheels from buggies and fastening the axles to rough wooden runners, and were making engagements to take the young ladies of the town sleighing.

"Have you ever ridden in a sleigh?" Miller asked Adele, as they stood at a window in the parlor witnessing these preparations.

"Never in my life," she said.

"Well, you shall," he said. "I 'll set a carpenter at work on my buggy, and be after you in an hour. Get your wraps. My pair of horses will make one of those sleds fairly spin."

About eleven o' clock that morning Alan saw them returning from their ride, and, much to his surprise, he noted that Dolly Barclay was with them. As they drew up at the entrance of the hotel, Alan doffed his hat and stepped forward to assist the ladies out of the sled.

"Miss Dolly won't stop," said Miller. "Get in and drive her around. She's hardly had a taste of it; we only picked her up as we passed her house."

Alan's heart bounded and then it sank. Miller was smiling at him knowingly. "Go ahead," he said, pushing him gently towards the sled. "It's all right."

Hardly knowing if he were acting wisely, Alan took the reins and sat down by Dolly.

Adele stepped up behind to say good-bye to Dolly, and they kissed each other. It was barely audible, and yet it reached the ears of the restive horses and they bounded away like the wind.

"A peculiar way to start horses," Alan laughed.

"A pleasant way," she said. "Your sister is a dear, dear girl."

Then he told her his fears in regard to what her father would think of his driving with her.

"He's out of town to-day," she answered, with a frank upward glance, "and mother wouldn't care."

"Then I'm going to enjoy it fully," he said. "I've been dying to see you, Dolly."

"And do you suppose I haven't wanted to see you? When Mr. Miller proposed this just now it fairly took my breath away. I was afraid you might happen not to be around the hotel. Oh, there is so much I want to say—and so little time."

"When I'm with you I can' t talk," he said. "It seems, in some way, to take up time like the ticking of a clock. I simply want to close my eyes, and—be with you, Dolly—*YOU*."

"I know, but we must be practical, and think of the future. Mr. Miller tells me there is a chance for your big scheme to succeed. Oh, if it only would!"

"Yes, a pretty good chance," he told her; "but even then your father—"

"He'd not hold out against you then," said Dolly, just for an impulsive moment clasping his arm as they shot through a snow-drift and turned a corner of the street leading into the country.

"Then it must succeed," he said, looking at her tenderly. "It *must*, Dolly."

"I shall pray for it—that and nothing else."

Feeling the slack reins on their backs, the horses slowed up till they were plodding along lazily. Suddenly the sled began to drag on the clay road where the wind had bared it of snow, and the horses stopped of their own accord, looking back at their increased burden inquiringly. Alan made no effort to start them on again. It was a sequestered spot, well hidden from the rest of the road by an old hedge of Osage orange bushes.

"We must not stop, *dear*," Dolly said, laying her hand again on his arm. "You know driving is—is different from this. As long as we are moving in any direction, I have no scruples, but to stop here in the road—no, it won't do."

"I was just wondering if we can start them," he said, a mischievous look in his laughing eye.

"Start them?" She extended her hand for the reins, but he held them out of her reach. "Why, what do you mean?"

"Why, you saw the way they were started at the hotel," he answered, in quite a serious tone. "Ray has trained them-that way. They won't budge an inch unless—"

"Oh, you silly boy!" Dolly was flushing charmingly.

"It's true," he said. "I'm sorry if you object, for it's absolutely the only available way."

She raised her full, trusting eyes to his.

"You make me want to kiss you, Alan, but—"

He did not let her finish. Putting his arm around her, he drew her close to him and kissed her on the lips. "Now, darling," he said, "you are mine."

"Yes, I am yours, Alan."

As they were nearing her house he told her that Wilson had agents out secretly buying land, and that she must not allow her father to dispose of his timbered interests until it was decided whether the railroad would be built.

She promised to keep an eye on the Colonel's transactions and do all she could to prevent him from taking a false step. "You may not know it," she said, "but I'm his chief adviser. He 'll be apt to mention any offer he gets to me."

"Well, don't tell him about the railroad unless you have to," he said, in parting with her at the gate. "But it would be glorious to have him profit by our scheme, and I think he will."

"We are going to hope for success, anyway, aren't we?" she said, leaning over the gate. "I have believed in you so much that I feel almost sure you are to be rewarded."

"Miller thinks the chances are good," he told her, "but father is afraid those men over there will do their best to ruin the whole thing."

Dolly waved her handkerchief to some one at a window of the house. "It's mother," she said. "She's shaking her finger at me."

"I reckon she's mad at me," said Alan, disconsolately.

"Not much," Dolly laughed. "She's simply crazy to come out and gossip with us. She would, too, if she wasn't afraid of father. Oh, young man, you 'll have a mother-in-law that will reverse the order of things! Instead of her keeping you straight, you 'll have to help us manage her. Father says she's 'as wild as a buck.'"

They both laughed from the fulness of their happiness. A buggy on runners dashed by. It contained a pair of lovers, who shouted and waved their hands. The sun was shining broadly. The snow would not last long. The crudest sled of all passed in the wake of the other. It was simply a plank about twelve inches wide and ten feet long to which a gaunt, limping horse was hitched. On the plank stood a triumphant lad balancing himself with the skill of a bareback rider. His face was flushed; he had never been so full of joy and ozone. From the other direction came a gigantic concern looking like a snow-plough or a metropolitan street-sweeper. It was a sliding road-wagon to which Frank Hillhouse had hitched four sturdy mules. The wagon was full of girls. Frank sat on the front seat cracking a whip and smoking. A little negro boy sat astride of the leading mule, digging his rag-clothed heels into the animal's side. Frank bowed as he passed, but his face was rigid.

"He didn't intend to ask me," said Dolly. "He hardly speaks to me since—"

"Since what?" Alan questioned.

"Since I asked him not to come to see me so often. I had to do it. He was making a fool of himself. It had to stop."

"You refused him?"

"Yes; but you must go now." Dolly was laughing again. "Mother will be out here in a minute; she can't curb her curiosity any longer. She'd make you take her riding, and I wouldn't have you do it for the world. Good-bye."

"Well, good-bye."

"Now, you must hope for the best, Alan."

"I'm going to. Good-bye."

CHAPTER XXXIV

DOLLY had the opportunity to warn her father in regard to his financial interests sooner than she expected. The very next morning, as she sat reading at a window in the sitting-room, she overheard the Colonel speaking to her mother about an offer he had just had for his mountain property.

"I believe it's a good chance for me to get rid of it," he was saying, as he stood at the mantel-piece dipping his pipe into his blue tobacco-jar.

"I never did see any sense in paying taxes on land you have never seen," said Mrs. Barclay, at her sewing-machine. "Surely you can put the money where it will bring in something."

"Milburn wants it because there is about a hundred acres that could be cleared for cultivation. I'm of the opinion that it won't make as good soil as he thinks, but I'm not going to tell him that."

"Would you be getting as much as it cost you?" asked Mrs. Barclay, smoothing down a white hem with her thumb-nail.

"About five hundred more," her husband chuckled. "People said when I bought it that I was as big a fool as old Bishop, but you see I've already struck a purchaser at a profit."

Then Dolly spoke up from behind her newspaper: "I wouldn't sell it, papa," she said, coloring under the task before her.

"Oh, you wouldn't?" sniffed her father. "And why?"

"Because it's going to be worth a good deal more money," she affirmed, coloring deeper and yet looking her parent fairly in the eyes.

Mrs. Barclay broke into a rippling titter as she bent over her work. "Alan Bishop put that in her head," she said. "They think, the Bishops do, that they've got a gold-mine over there."

"You must not sell it, papa," Dolly went on, ignoring her mother's thrust. "I can't tell you why I don't want you to, but you must not—you 'll be sorry if you do."

"I don't know how I'm to keep on paying your bills for flimflam frippery if I don't sell something," retorted the old man, almost and yet not quite angry. Indirectly he was pleased at her valuation of his property, for he had discovered that her judgment was good.

"And she won't let Frank Hillhouse help," put in Mrs. Barclay, teasingly. "Poor fellow! I'm afraid he'll never get over it. He's taken to running around with school-girls—that's always a bad sign."

"A girl ought to be made to listen to reason," fumed Barclay, goaded on to this attack by his wife, who well knew his sore spots, and liked to rasp them.

"A girl will listen to the right sort of reason," retorted Dolly, who was valiantly struggling against an outburst. "Mamma knows how I feel."

"I know that you are bent on marrying a man without a dollar to his name," said her father. "You want to get into that visionary gang that will spend all I leave you in their wild-cat investments, but I tell you I will cut you out of my property if you do. Now, remember that. I mean it."

Dolly crushed the newspaper in her lap and rose. "There is no good in quarrelling over this again," she said, coldly. "Some day you will understand the injustice you are doing Alan Bishop. I could make you see it now, but I have no right to explain." And with that she left the room.

Half an hour later, from the window of her room up-stairs, she saw old Bobby Milburn open the front gate. Under his slouch hat and big gray shawl he thumped up the gravelled walk and began to scrape his feet on the steps. There was a door-bell, with a handle like that of a coffee-mill, to be turned round, but old Bobby, like many of his kind, either did not know of its existence, or, knowing, dreaded the use of innovations that sometimes made even stoics like himself feel ridiculous. His method of announcing himself was by far more sensible, as it did not even require the removal of his hands from his pockets; and, at the same time, helped divest his boots of mud. He stamped on the floor of the veranda loudly and paused to listen for the approach of some one to admit him. Then, as no one appeared, he clattered along the veranda to the window of the sitting-room and peered in. Colonel Barclay saw him and opened the door, inviting the old fellow into the sitting-room. Old Bobby laid his hat on the floor beside his chair as he sat down, but he did not unpin his shawl.

"Well, I've come round to know what's yore lowest notch, Colonel," he said, gruffly, as he brushed his long, stringy hair back from his ears and side whiskers. "You see, it's jest this way. I kin git a patch o' land from Lank Buford that will do me, in a pinch, but I like yore'n a leetle grain better, beca'se it's nigher my line by a quarter or so; but, as I say, I kin make out with Buford's piece; an' ef we cayn't agree, I 'll have to ride over whar he is workin' in Springtown."

At this juncture Dolly came into the room. She shook hands with the visitor, who remained seated and mumbled out some sort of gruff greeting, and went to her chair near the window, taking up her paper again. Her eyes, however, were on her father's face.

"I hardly know what to say," answered Barclay, deliberately. "Your price the other day didn't strike me just right, and so I really haven't been thinking about it."

There was concession enough, Dolly thought, in Milburn's eye, if not in his voice, when he spoke. "Well," he said, carelessly, "bein' as me'n you are old friends, an' thar always was a sort o' neighborly feelin' betwixt us, I 'll agree, if we trade, to hire a lawyer an' a scribe to draw up the papers an' have 'em duly recorded. You know that's always done by the party sellin'."

"Oh, that's a *little* thing," said the Colonel; but his watchful daughter saw that the mere smallness of Milburn's raise in his offer had had a depressing effect on her father's rather doubtful valuation of the property in question. The truth was that Wilson had employed the shrewdest trader in all that part of the country, and one who worked all the more effectively for his plainness of dress and rough manner. "That's a little thing," went on the Colonel, "but here's what I 'll do—"

"Father," broke in Dolly, "don't make a proposition to Mr. Milburn. Please don't."

Milburn turned to her, his big brows contracting in surprise, but he controlled himself. "Heigho!" he laughed, "so you've turned trader, too, Miss Dolly? Now, I jest wish my gals had that much enterprise; they git beat ef they buy a spool o' thread."

The Colonel frowned and Mrs. Barclay turned to Dolly with a real tone of reproof. "Don't interfere in your father's business," she said. "He can attend to it."

The Colonel was not above making capital of the interruption, and he smiled down on the shaggy visitor.

"She's been deviling the life out of me not to part with that land. They say women have the intuition to look ahead better than men. I don't know but I ought to listen to her, but she ain't running me, and as I was about to say—"

"Wait just one minute, papa!" insisted Dolly, with a grim look of determination on her face. "Just let me speak to you a moment in the parlor, and then you can come back to Mr. Milburn."

The face of the Colonel darkened under impatience, but he was afraid failure to grant his daughter's request would look like over-anxiety to close with Mil-burn, and so he followed her into the parlor across the hallway.

"Now, what on earth is the matter with you?" he demanded, sternly. "I have never seen you conduct yourself like this before."

She faced him, touching his arms with her two hands.

"Father, don't be angry with me," she said, "but when you know what I do, you will be glad I stopped you just now. Mr. Milburn is not buying that land for his own use."

"He isn't?" exclaimed the Colonel.

"No; he's secretly employed by a concern worth over two million dollars—the Southern Land and Timber Company of Atlanta."

"What?" the word came out as suddenly as if some one had struck him on the breast.

"No," answered the girl, now pale and agitated. "To save Mr. Bishop from loss, Alan and Rayburn Miller have worked up a scheme to build a railroad from Darley to the Bishop property. All arrangements have been made. There can be no hitch in it unless the citizens refuse to grant a right of way. In a week from now a meeting is to be advertised. Of course, it is not a certainty, but you can see that the chance is good, and you ought not to sacrifice your land."

"Good Heavens!" ejaculated Barclay, his eyes distended, "is this a fact?"

"I am telling you what I have really no right to reveal," said Dolly, "but I promised Alan not to let you sell if I could help it."

The Colonel was staggered by the revelation; his face was working under strong excitement. "I thought that old rascal"—he meant Milburn—"was powerfully anxious to trade. Huh! Looky' here, daughter, this news is almost too good to be true. Why, another railroad would make my town-lots bound up like fury, and as for this mountain-land—whew! It may be as you say. Ray Miller certainly is a wheel-horse."

"It was not his idea," said Dolly, loyally. "In fact, he tried his best to discourage Alan at first—till he saw what could be done. Since then he's been secretly working at it night and day."

"Whew!" whistled the Colonel. "I don't care a cent *whose* idea it is; if it goes through it's a good one, and, now that I think of it, the necessary capital is all that is needed to make a big spec' over there."

"So you won't sell to Mr. Milburn, then?" asked Dolly, humbly grateful for her father's change of mood.

"Sell to that old dough-faced scamp?" snorted Barclay. "Well, he 'll think I won't in a minute! Do you reckon I don't want to have some sort o' finger in the pie? Whether the road's built or not, I want my chance."

"But remember I am giving away state secrets," said Dolly. "He must not know that you have heard about the road."

"I 'll not give that away," the old man promised, with a smile, and he turned to the door as if eager to face Milburn. "Huh! That old scamp coming here to do me one! The idea!"

The two men, as they faced each other a moment later, presented an interesting study of human forces held well in check. The Colonel leaned on the mantel-piece and looked down at the toe of his boot, with which he pushed a chunk of wood beneath the logs.

"You never can tell about a woman' s whims, Mil-burn," he said. "Dolly's set her heart on holding onto that land, and I reckon I'm too easily wriggled about by my women folks. I reckon we'd better call it off."

"Oh, all right—all right!" said Milburn, with a start and a sharp contraction of his brows. "I'm that away some myse'f. My gals git me into devilish scrapes sometimes, an' I'm always sayin' they got to stop it. A man loses too much by lettin' 'em dabble in his business. But I was jest goin' to say that I mought raise my bid fifty cents on the acre ruther than trapse away over to Springtown to see Buford."

There was silence through which several kinds of thoughts percolated. The raise really amounted to so much that it materially increased Barclay's growing conviction that the railroad was next to a certainty. "Huh!" he grunted, his eyes ablaze with the amusement of a winner. "I wouldn't listen to less than a dollar more on the acre." And as the gaze of Milburn went down reflectively the Colonel winked slyly, even triumphantly, at his smiling daughter and said: "Dolly thinks it will make good land for a peach-orchard. Lots of money is being made that way."

"Bosh!" grunted Milburn. "It don't lie right fer peaches. You kin git jest as much property nigh the railroad as you want fer peaches. You are a hard man to trade with, but I reckon I 'll have to take yore offer of—"

"Hold on, hold on!" laughed the Colonel, his hand upraised. "I didn't say I'd *take* that price. I just said I wouldn't listen to less than a dollar raise. I've listened to many a thing I didn't jump at, like a frog in muddy water, not knowing what he's going to butt against."

Under his big shawl Milburn rose like a tent blown upward by wind. He was getting angry as he saw his commission money taking wing and flitting out of sight. He had evidently counted on making an easy victim of Barclay. For a moment he stood twisting his heavy, home-knit gloves in his horny hands.

"Now if it's a fair question," he said, as the last resort of a man ready and willing to trade at any reasonable cost, "what *will* you take, cash down, on your honor between us—me to accept or decline?"

The Colonel's pleasure was of the bubbling, overflowing kind. Every move made by Milburn was adding fuel to his hopes of the proposed railroad, and to his determination to be nobody's victim.

"Look here," he said, "that land has been rising at such a rate since you came in that I'm actually afraid to let it go. By dinner-time it may make me rich. Dolly, I believe, on my word, Milburn has discovered gold over there. Haven't you, Milburn? Now, honor bright."

"It will be a long time before you find gold or anything else on that land," Milburn retorted, as he reached for his hat and heavily strode from the room.

"Well! I do declare," and Mrs. Barclay turned to Dolly and her father. "What on earth does this mean?" The Colonel laughed out, then slapped his hand over his mouth, as he peered from the window to see if Milburn was out of hearing. "It's just this way—"

"Mind, father!" cautioned Dolly. "Do you want it to be all over town by dinner-time?"

"Dolly!" cried Mrs. Barclay, "the idea of such a thing!"

Dolly smiled and patted her mother on the cheek.

"Don't tell her, papa," she said, with decision.

"The truth is," said the Colonel, "Dolly really wants to plant peaches. I don't think there's much in it, but she will have her way."

"Well, I call that *mean* of you," retorted Mrs. Barclay, dark with vexation. "Well, miss, I 'll bet you didn't tell your father who you went sleigh-riding with."

The old man frowned suddenly. "Not with Alan Bishop," he said, "after my positive orders?"

"He came to tell me about the—the"—Dolly glanced at her mother suddenly—"about the peaches, papa."

"Well"—the Colonel was waxing angry—"I won't have it—that's all. I won't have you—"

"Wait, papa," entreated the girl, sweetly, "wait till we see about the—peaches!" And, with a little teasing laugh, she left the room.

CHAPTER XXXV

THE mass-meeting at Springtown was a most important event. It was held in the court-house in the centre of the few straggling houses which made up the hamlet. The entire Bishop family, including the servants, attended. Pole Baker brought his wife and all the children in a new spring-wagon. Darley society was represented, as the Springtown *Gazette* afterwards put it, by the fairest of the fair, Miss Dolly Barclay, accompanied by her mother and father.

The court-house yard was alive with groups of men eagerly talking over the situation. Every individual whose land was to be touched by the proposed road was on hand to protect his rights. Pole Baker was ubiquitous, trying to ascertain the drift of matters. He was, however, rather unsuccessful. He discovered that many of the groups ceased to talk when he entered them. "Some 'n' s up," he told Alan and Miller in the big, bare-looking court-room. "I don't know what it is, but I smell a rat, an' it ain't no little one, nuther."

"Opposition," said Miller, gloomily. "I saw that as soon as I came. If they really were in favor of the road they'd be here talking it over with us."

"I'm afraid that's it," said Alan. "Joe Bartell is the most interested, and he seems to be a sort of ringleader. I don't like the way he looks. I saw him sneer at Wilson when he drove up just now. I wish Wilson hadn't put on so much style—kid gloves, plug hat, and a negro driver."

"No, that won't go down with this crowd," agreed Miller. "It might in the slums of Boston, but not with these lords of the mountains. As for Bartell, I think I know what ails him. He's going to run for the legislature and thinks he can make votes by opposing us—convincing his constituency that we represent moneyed oppression. Well, he may down us, but it's tough on human progress."

Alan caught Dolly's eye and bowed. She was seated near her father and mother, well towards the judge's stand. She seemed to have been observing the faces of the two friends, and to be affected by their serious expressions. Adele sat at the long wood stove, several yards from her parents, who appeared quite as if they were in church waiting for service to begin. Abner Daniel leaned in the doorway opening into one of the jury-rooms. Wilson had given him a fine cigar, which he seemed to be enjoying hugely.

At the hour appointed for the meeting, to open, a young man who held the office of bailiff in the county, and seemed proud of his stentorian voice, opened one of the windows and shouted:

"Come in to court! Come in to court!" and the motley loiterers below began to clatter up the broad stairs and fall into the seats. Joe Bartell, a short, thick-set man in the neighborhood of fifty, with a florid face and a shock of reddish hair, led about twenty men up the aisle to the jury-benches at the right of the stand. They were the land-owners whose consent to grant the right of way was asked. Stern opposition was clearly written on the leader's brow and more or less distinctly reflected on the varying faces of his followers.

"Ef we needed it, it ud be a different matter," Miller overheard him say in a sudden lull, as the big room settled down into sudden quiet, "but we kin do without it. We've got along so fur an' we kin furder. All of us has got good teams."

Wilson, in his crisp, brusque way, made the opening speech. He told his hearers just what his company proposed to do and in much the same cold-blooded way as he would have dictated a letter to his stenographer, correctly punctuating the text by pauses, and yet, in his own way, endeavoring to be eloquent. He and his capital were going to dispel darkness where it had reigned since the dawn of civilization; people living there now would not recognize the spot ten years from the day the first whistle of a locomotive shrilled through those rocky gorges and rebounded from those lofty peaks — silent fingers pointing to God and speaking of a past dead and gone. All that was needed, he finished, was the consent of the property-owners appealed to; who, he felt confident, would not stand in their own light. They looked like intelligent men, and he believed they did not deceive appearances.

He had hardly taken his seat when Joe Bartell stood up. Alan and Miller exchanged ominous glances. They had at once recognized the inappropriateness of Wilson's speech, and did not like the white, twitching sneer on Bartell's smooth-shaven face. It was as if Bartell had been for a long time seeking just such an opportunity to make himself felt in the community, and there was no doubt that Wilson's almost dictatorial speech had made a fine opening for him.

"Fellow-citizens, an' ladies an' gentlemen," he began, "we are glad to welcome amongst us a sort of a second savior in our Sodom an' Gomorry of cracker-dom. What the gentleman with the plug hat an' spike-toe shoes ain't a-goin' to do fer us the Lord couldn't. He looks nice an' talks nice, an', to use his words, I don't believe he deceives appearances. I 'll bet one thing, an' that is 'at he won't deceive us. Accordin' to him we need 'im every hour, as the Sunday-school song puts it. Yes, he's a-goin' to he'p us powerful an' right off. An', fellow-citizens, I'm heer to propose a vote o' thanks. He's from away up in Boston, whar, they tell me, a nigger sets an' eats at the same table with the whites. When his sort come this away durin' the war, with all the'r up-to-date impliments of slaughter, they laid waste to ever'thing they struck, shot us like rabbits in holes, an' then went back an' said they'd had a good hunt. But they've been livin' high up thar sence the war an' the'r timber is a-playin' out, an' they want some more now, an' they *want it bad*. So they send the'r representatives out to find it an' lay hold of it. How does he happen to come heer? As well as I kin make out, old Alf Bishop, a good man an' a Southern soldier—a man that I hain't got nothin' agin, except maybe he holds his head too high, made up his mind awhile back that lumber would be in demand some day, an' he set to work buyin' all the timber-land he could lay his hands on. Then, when he had more'n he could tote, an' was about to go under, he give this gentleman a' option on it. Well, so fur so good; but, gentlemen, what have *we* got to do with this trade? Nothin' as I kin see. But we are expected to yell an' holler, an' deed 'em a free right of way through our property so they kin ship the timber straight through to the North an' turn it into cold Yankee coin. We don't count in this shuffle, gentlemen. We git our pay fer our land in bein' glad an' heerin' car-bells an' steam-whistles in the middle o' the night when we want to sleep. The engynes will kill our hogs, cattle, an' hosses, an' now an' then break the neck o' some chap that wasn't hit in the war, but we mustn't forget to be glad an' bend the knee o' gratitude. Of course, we all know the law kin compel us to give the right of way, but it provides fer just and sufficient payment fer the property used; an', gentlemen, I'm agin donations. I'm agin' em tooth an' toe-nail."

There was thunderous and ominous applause when Bartell sat down. Wilson sat flushed and embarrassed, twirling his gloves in his hands. He had expected anything but this personal fusillade. He stared at Miller in surprise over that gentleman's easy, half-amused smile as he stood up.

"Gentlemen," he began, "and ladies," he added, with a bow to the right and left. "As many of you know, I pretend to practise law a little, and I want to say now that I'm glad Mr. Bartell ain't in the profession. A lawyer with his keen wit and eloquence could convict an innocent mother before a jury of her own children. [Laughter.] And that's the point, gentlemen; we are innocent of the charges against us. I am speaking now of my clients, the Bishops. They are deeply interested in the development of this section. The elder Bishop does hold his head high, and in this case he held it high enough to smell coming prosperity in the air. He believed it would come, and that is why he bought timber-lands extensively. As for the accused gentleman from the Hub of the Universe, I must say that I have known of him for several years and have never heard a word against his character. He is not a farmer, but a business man, and it would be unfair to judge him by any other standard. He is not only a business man, but a big one. He handles big things. This railroad is going to be a big thing for you and your children. Yes, Wilson is all right. He didn't fight in the late unpleasantness. He tells the women he was too young; but I believe he hadn't the heart to fight a cause as just as ours. His only offence is in the matter of wearing sharp-toed shoes. There is no law against 'em in Atlanta, and he's simply gotten careless. He is ignorant of our ideas of proper dress, as befitting a meek and lowly spirit, which, in spite of appearances, I happen to know Wilson possesses. However, I have heard him say that these mountains produce the best corn liquor that ever went down grade in his system. He's right. It's good. Pole Baker says it's good, and he ought to know. [Laughter, in which Pole joined good-naturedly.] That reminds me of a story," Miller went on. "They tell this of Baker. They say that a lot of fellows were talking of the different ways they would prefer to meet death if it had to come. One said drowning, another shooting, another poisoning, and so on; but Pole reserved his opinion to the last. When the crowd urged him to say what manner of death he would select, if he had to die and had his choice, he said: 'Well, boys, ef I had to go, I'd like to be melted up into puore corn whiskey an' poured through my throat tell thar wasn't a drap left of me.'[Laughter and prolonged applause.] And Wilson said further, gentlemen and ladies, that he believed the men and women of this secluded section were, in their own way, living nearer to God than the inhabitants of the crowded cities. Wilson is not bad, even if he has a hang-dog look. A speech like Bartell's just now would give a hang-dog look to a paling-fence. Wilson is here to build a railroad for your good and prosperity, and he can' t build one where there is nothing to haul out. If he buys up timber for his company, it is the only way to get them to back him in the enterprise. Now, gentlemen of the opposition, if there are any here to-day, don't let the thought of Wilson's possible profit rob you of this golden opportunity. I live at Darley, but, as many of you know, this is my father's native county, and I want to see it bloom in progress and blossom like the rose of prosperity. I want to see the vast mineral wealth buried in these mountains dug out for the benefit of mankind wherever God's sunlight falls."

Miller sat down amid much applause, a faint part of which came even from the ranks of Bartell's faction. After this a pause ensued in which no one seemed willing to speak. Colonel Barclay rose and came to Miller.

"That was a good talk," he whispered. "You understand how to touch 'em up. You set them to laughin'; that's the thing. I wonder if it would do any good for me to try my hand."

"Do they know you have any timber-land over here?" asked Miller.

"Oh yes, I guess they do," replied the Colonel.

"Then I don't believe I'd chip in," advised Miller. "Bartell would throw it up to you."

"I reckon you are right," said Barclay, "but for the Lord's sake do something. It never will do to let this thing fall through."

"I've done all I can," said Miller, dejectedly. "Bartell's got the whole gang hoodooed—the blasted blockhead! Wouldn't he make a fine representative in the legislature?"

The Colonel went back to his seat, and Wilson came to Miller, just as Alan approached.

"It's going to fall flatter than a pancake," said Wilson. "My company simply cannot afford to buy the right of way. Can' t you choke that illiterate fellow over there or—or buy him off?"

"He ain't that sort," said Miller, disconsolately.

Alan glanced at his father and mother. On their wrinkled faces lay ample evidences of dejection. The old man seemed scarcely to breathe. Up to Bartell's speech he had seemed buoyantly hopeful, but his horizon had changed; he looked as if he were wondering why he had treated himself to such a bright view of a thing which had no foundation at all.

At this juncture Abner Daniel rose from his seat near the stove and slowly walked forward till he stood facing the audience. Immediately quiet reigned, for he was a man who was invariably listened to.

"Gentlemen an' ladies," he began, clearing his throat and wiping his mouth with his long hand. "This ain't no put-in o' mine, gracious knows!

I hain't got nothin', an' I don't expect to lose or gain by what is done in this matter, but I want to do what I kin fer what I think is right an' proper. Fer my part, I don't think we kin do without a railroad much longer. Folks is a-pokin' fun at us, I tell you. It's God's truth. T'other day I was over at Darley a-walkin' along the railroad nigh the turnin'-table, whar they flirt engynes round like children on a flyin'-jinny, when all at once a big strappin' feller with a red flag in his hand run up an' knocked me off'n the track kerwhallop in a ditch. It was just in time to keep me from bein' run over by a switch-engyne. He was as mad as Tucker. 'Looky' heer,' ses he, 'did you think that thing was playin' tag with you an' ud tap you on the shoulder an' run an' hide behind a tree? Say, ain't you from Short Pine Destrict, this side o' the mountains?' I told 'im he'd guessed right, an' he said, 'I'lowed so, fer thar ain't no other spot on the whirlin' globe that produces folks as green as gourds.' Well, gentlemen, that floored me; it was bad enough to be jerked about like a rag doll, but it was tough to heer my section jeered at. 'What makes you say that?' I axed 'im, as I stood thar tryin' to git a passle o' wet glass out o' my hip-pocket without cuttin' my fingers. [Laughter, led by Pole Baker, who sensed the meaning of the reference.] 'Beca'se,' ses he, 'you moss-backs over thar don't know the war's over; a nigger from over thar come in town t'other day an' heerd fer the fust time that he was free. Two men over thar swapped wives without knowin' thar was a law agin it. Half o' you-uns never laid eyes on a railroad, an' wouldn't have one as a free gift.' I turned off an' left 'im an' went up on the main street. Up thar a barber ketched me by the arm an' said, ses he: 'Come in an' le' me cut that hair. You are from Short Pine, ain't you?' I axed him why he thought so, an' he said, ses he, 'beca'se you got a Short Pine hair-cut.'' What's that?' ses I. An' he laughed at a feller cocked up in a cheer an' said: 'It's a cut that is made by the women out yore way. They jest turn a saucer upside down on the men's heads an' trim around the edges. I could tell one a mile; they make a man look like a bob-tailed mule.'[Laughter, loud and prolonged.] Yes, as I said, they are a-pokin' all manner o' fun at us, an' it's chiefly beca'se we hain't got no railroad. The maddest I ever got on this line was down at Filmore's store one day. A little, slick chap come along sellin' maps of the United States of America. They was purty things on black sticks, an' I wanted one fer the wall o' my room. I was about to buy one, but I thought I'd fust make shore that our county was on it, so I axed the peddler to p'int it out to me. Well, after some s'arch, he put his knife-blade on what he called this county, but lo an' behold! it was mighty nigh kivered with round dots about the size of fly-specks. 'What's the matter with it?' I axed 'im. 'Oh, you mean them dots,' ses he, an' he turned to a lot o' reference words in the corner of the map. 'Them,' ses he, 'them's put thar to indicate the amount o' ignorance in a locality. You 'll find 'em in all places away from the railroads; a body kin say what they please agin railroads, but they fetch schools, an' books, an' enlightenment. You've got a good many specks' ses he, kinder comfortin' like, 'but some o' these days a railroad will shoot out this away, an' them brainy men amongst you will git the chance God intends to give 'em,' Gentlemen, I didn't buy no map. I wouldn't 'a' had the thing on my wall with them specks a-starin' me in the face. It wouldn't 'a' done any good to scrape 'em off, fer the'r traces would 'a' been left. No, friends, citizens, an' well-wishers, thar ain't but one scraper that will ever rake our specks off, an' that's the cow-catcher of a steam-engyne. I say let 'er come. Some objection has been raised on the score o' killin' cattle. That reminds me of a story they tell on old Burt Preston, who has a farm on the main line beyant Darley. He was always a-gittin' his stock killed so fast, an' a-puttin' in heavy claims fer damages, until folks begun to say he made his livin' by buyin' scrub cattle an' sellin' mashed beef to the corporation. One day the road sent out a detective to watch 'im, an' he seed Burt drive a spindlin' yeerlin' out o' the thicket on the track jest in time to get it knocked off by a through freight. The detective went back an' reported, an' they waited to see what Preston ud do. By the next mail they got a claim in which Preston said the yeerlin' weighed eight hundred pound an' was a fine four-gallon milch-cow. They threatened to jail 'im, an' Preston agreed to withdraw his claim. But he got down-hearted an' traded his place fer a farm on t'other railroad, an' the last I heerd o' him he was at his old trade agin. I reckon that's about the way we 'll be damaged by gettin' our stock killed. That's all I got to say, gentlemen. Let's git this road an' scrape our fly-specks off."

The big house shook with the applause that greeted this speech. Even the opposition seemed to be wavering. Only Bartell kept a rigid countenance. He rose and in a low voice invited his group to repair with him to one of the jury-rooms. They got up and followed him out. As he was about to close the door after them he nodded to Miller. "We 'll take a vote on it an' let you know," he said, coldly.

"He's going to talk to them," said Miller, aloud to Wilson. "Mr. Daniel's speech almost shook them out of their boots, and he saw he was losing ground. It looks squally."

"You are right," said Wilson, gloomily. "Our chances are very slim."

Miller caught Adele's eye and went to her.

"I'm bound to say the outlook is not so favorable," he said. "If we could have put it to a vote just after your uncle spoke we would have clinched them, but Bartell thinks his election depends on beating us today, and being the chief land-owner he has influence."

"It will break my heart," said the girl, tremulously. "Poor father and mother! They look as if they were on trial for their lives. Oh, I had so much hope as we drove over here this morning, but now—"

"I can' t bear to see you take it that way," said Miller, tenderly. "I did not intend to speak to you so soon about another matter, but I can' t put it off. You have become very, very dear to me, little girl. In fact, I never dreamed there was such a thing as genuine, unselfish love till I knew you. It seems to me that you were actually created for me. I want you to be my wife. Somehow I feel that you care for me, at least a little, and I believe when you realize how much I love you, and how devoted I shall be, you will love me as I do you."

To his surprise she averted her face and said nothing, though he remarked that she had paled a little and compressed her lips. He waited a moment, then said, anxiously:

"Haven't you something to say, Adele? Perhaps I have misread you all along and really have no right to hope. Oh, that would be hard to bear!"

"It is not that," she said, her breast heaving suddenly. "It is not that."

"Not that?" he repeated, his wondering eyes fixed on hers.

Then she turned to him.

"Alan has told me of some of your talks to him about love, and—"

"Oh, he has!" Miller laughed out uneasily. "But surely you wouldn't hold anything against me that I said before I met you in Atlanta and fell heels over head in love with you. Besides, I was simply stretching my imagination to save him from making a serious mistake. But I know what it is to care for a girl now, and I have wanted to tell him so, but simply could not face him with my confession—when—when his own sister was in question."

"I have tried to believe," Adele hesitated, "that you had changed in your ideas of love since—since we learned to know each other, and I confess I succeeded to some extent, but there was one thing that simply sticks and refuses to be eradicated. It sticks more right now than ever. I mean this morning, since—"

"Now you *do* surprise me," declared Miller. "Please explain. Don't you see I'm simply dying with impatience?"

"You pressed the point in one of those talks with brother," said Adele, quite firmly, "that it was impossible for two people of unequal fortune to be happy together, and—"

"Now you wouldn't surely hurl that rubbish at me," broke in Miller. "I never would have dreamed of saying such a thing if I had not thought Alan was about to butt his head against a stone wall in the hostility of Colonel Barclay. If he had been fairly well off and she had been without money I'd have said sail in and take her, but I knew what a mercenary old man Barclay is, and I thought I could save the boy from a good many heartaches."

"That—even as you now put it—would be hard for a girl in my position to forget," Adele told him. "For if this enterprise fails to-day, I shall—just think of it!—I shall not only be penniless, but my father will owe you a large amount of money that he never will be able to pay. Oh, I could not bear to go to you under such circumstances! I have always wanted my independence, and this grates on my very soul."

Their eyes met in a long, steady stare. "Oh, you must—you really must not see it that way," floundered the young man. "You will make me very miserable. I can' t live without you, Adele. Besides, I shall not lose by the loan I made to your father. The land will bring the money back sooner or later, and what will it matter? You will be my wife and your parents will be my parents. Already I love them as my own. Oh, darling, don't turn me down this way! Really I can' t help the turn matters have taken, and if you care for me you ought not to wreck our happiness for a silly whim like this."

She sat unmoved for a moment, avoiding the fervid glow of his passion-filled eyes.

"If this thing fails I shall be very unhappy," she finally said. "Its success would not make me rich, but it would remove a debt that has nearly killed me. I have never mentioned it, but it has been like a sword hanging over my happiness."

"Then it shall not fail," he told her. "It shall not fail! If those blockheads vote against it, I 'll buy the right of way, if it takes the last cent I've got."

This forced a smile to Adele's lips. "Then we'd be as deep in the mud as we now are in the mire," she said. Just then Pole Baker came to Miller.

"I don't want to make no break," he said, "but I've got a idea I'd like to work on them hill-Billies in the jury-room if you hain't no objections. I hain't got time to tell you about it, but as you are a-runnin' the shebang I thought I'd ax permission."

"Go and do what you think best, Pole," said Miller, recklessly. "We can trust to your head, and anything is better than nothing just now. I really think it's gone by the board."

"All right, thanky'," said Pole, as he shuffled away. He marched straight to the jury-room, and, without rapping, opened the door and went in, closing the door after him. He found the men all discussing the matter and was delighted to find that the strength of the opposition now rested chiefly in Bartell and a few men who seemed afraid to pull away from him. Pole slid up to Bartell and said, as he drew him to one side: "Say, Mr. Bartell, what on earth have you got agin Alan Bishop?"

"Why, nothin', Pole, as I know of," said Bartell, rather sheepishly. "Nothin' as I know of."

"Well, it looks to me like you got a mighty pore way o' showin' good-will. Why, he's the best friend you got, Mr. Bartell, an' totes more votes in his vest-pocket fer you than any man in this county."

"Huh! You don't say!" grunted Bartell, in slow surprise. "Well, he never told *me* about it."

"Beca'se you hain't announced yorese'f yet," said Pole, with a steady eye and a set face. "Why, he said t'other day to several of us at the log-rollin'—you remember you rid by on yore bay, leadin' a milch-cow by a rope. Well, after you passed Alan Bishop said: 'Boys, thar goes the only man in this county that has convictions an' the courage to stand by 'em. They say he's goin' to run fer the legislature an' ef he does, I 'll do all I kin to elect 'im. He 'll make the best representative that we ever had. He's got brains, *he* has.'"

"You don't say!" Bartell's face beamed, his eye kindled and flashed.

"That's jest what!"

"I hadn't the least idea he was fer me," said Bartell, drawing a deep breath. "In fact, I 'lowed he would be agin anybody but a town man."

"Alan never talks much," said Pole, in a tone of conviction; "he *acts* when the time comes fer it. But, la me, Mr. Bartell, this is agoin' to break him all to pieces. He's in love with old Barclay's gal, an' she is with him. Ef he puts this road through to-day he 'll git his daddy out o' debt an' Barclay will withdraw his opposition. I don't know how you feel, but I'd hate like smoke to bu'st a man all to flinders that thought as much o' me as Alan does o' you."

"I never knowed he was fer me," was Bartell's next tottering step in the right direction.

"Well, vote fer the right o' way, an' you kin ride to an' from Atlanta durin' session all rail. Me'n Alan will pull fer you like a yoke o' steers—me with the moonshiners, an' my mountain clan, that ain't dead yet, an' him with his gang. What you say? Put up or shet up."

"I 'll do what I kin," said Bartell, a new light on his face, as he turned to the others. "Gentlemen," he began, "listen to me a minute. I see a good many of you was affected by Ab Daniel's speech an' sort o' want the road, anyway, so if—"

"I don't exactly like them specks," broke in a fat, middle-aged man at a window. "By gum! I believe old Ab had us down about right. Ef we kin git sort o' opened up along with the rest o' creation, I say le's git in the game. Huh!"—the man finished, with a laughing shrug—"I don't like them fly-specks one bit."

"Me nuther," said a man beside him.

"Nur me!" came from some one else.

"Well, I'm willin' ef the rest are," announced Bar-tell. "All in favor hold up yore hands."

Pole Baker grinned broadly as he counted them. "All up—the last one," he said, then he sprang for the door and stood before the expectant audience.

"Toot! toot!" he cried, imitating the whistle of a locomotive. "All aboard! The road's a settled thing. They say they don't want no specks, an' they ain't agoin' to have 'em. Hooray!"

The audience was electrified by the announcement. For an instant there was a pause of incredulous astonishment, and then the floor resounded from the clatter of feet and glad shouts filled the air.

Alan, his face ablaze with startled triumph, came towards Adele and Miller. "Pole worked the rabbit-foot on them back there," he said. "I don't know what he did, but he did something."

"He told me he had a card left," laughed Miller. "I 'll bet he had it up his sleeve. There he is now. Oh, Pole, come here!"

The man thus addressed slouched down the aisle to them, his big, brown eyes flashing merrily under his heavy brows, his sun-browned face dark with the flush of triumph.

"Out with it, you rascal," said Alan. "What did you say to them? Whatever it was it knocked their props clean from under them."

"Ef you don't back me in it, I'm a gone dog," said Pole to Alan. "All I want you to do is to vote for Bartell, ef you kin possibly swallow the dose."

A light broke on the two men. "I 'll do it if you say so, Pole," said Alan. "Not only that, but I 'll work for him if you wish it."

Pole looked down and pulled at his heavy mustache. "Well," he smiled, "I reckon he won't harm us any more in the legislatur' than the road 'll do us good, so you'd better support 'im. I seed the bars down a minute ago, an' I didn't have no time to consult you. I'd 'a' told a bigger lie 'an that to clinch this thing." Abner Daniel joined them, smiling broadly, his eyes twinkling joyously.

"We've won, Uncle Ab," exclaimed Alan; "what do you think of that?"

The old jester stroked his face and swung his long body back and forth in the wind of his content. "I've always argued," said he, "that what is to be *will* be, an' it *will* be a sight sooner 'n most of us count on, ef we 'll jest keep our sperits up."

The others moved on, leaving Adele and Miller together.

"Oh, just look at mamma and papa," she said, in the round, full voice indicative of deep emotion. "They are so glad they are about to cry."

"What a dear, dear girl you are," said Miller, softly. "There is nothing to separate us now, is there?"

For a moment they met in a full look into each other's eyes. Adele's voice shook when she replied: "I believe I'm the happiest, proudest girl in all the world."

"Then you love me?"

"I believe I've loved you from the very minute I met you in Atlanta last summer."

Alan saw Dolly looking at him and waving her handkerchief, her face warm and flushed. He was tempted to go to her, but she still sat by her father and mother, and that fact checked him. Mrs. Barclay caught his eye, and, rising suddenly, came through the crowd to him. She extended her gloved hand.

"You and Dolly must stop your foolishness," she said. "I've been thinking of a plan to help you two out. If I were you I wouldn't say a word to her now, but next Sunday night come and take her to church just like you used to. I 'll attend to Colonel Barclay. He is just tickled to death over this thing and he won't make any fuss. He is as stubborn as a mule, though, and when he has to give in, it's better not to let him think you are gloating over him. He won't bother you any more; I 'll see to that."

Alan thanked her. He was so full of happiness that he was afraid to trust his voice to utterance. As Mrs. Barclay was going back to her husband and daughter, Pole Baker passed. Alan grasped him by the hand.

"Say, Pole," he said, his voice full and quavering, "I want to tell you that I think more of you than I do of any man alive."

"Well, Alan," said Pole, awkwardly, yet with an eye that did not waver, "I kin shore return the compliment. Ef it hadn't been fer you an' yore advice I'd 'a' been in hell long ago, an' as it is, I feel more like livin' a straight, honest life than I ever did. You never axed me but one thing that I didn't grant, an' that was to give up whiskey. I don't know whether I ever will be able to do it or not, but, by the great God above, I'm agoin' to keep on tryin', fer I know you want it jest fer my good. I don't want a dram to-day, fer a wonder, an' maybe in time I 'll git over my thirst."

As Alan was about to get into his buggy with his uncle, the Colonel and his wife and daughter passed. With a sheepish look on his face the old man bowed to the two men, but Dolly stopped before Alan and held out her hand.

"You were going away without even speaking to me," she said, a catch in her voice. "Think of it—to-day of all days to be treated like that!"

"But your mother told me—"

"Didn't I tell you she couldn't be relied on?" broke in Dolly, with a smile. "I have more influence with papa than she has. I know what she told you. I made her confess it just now. Are you going to town to-day?"

"Yes," he informed her; "we shall complete the arrangements there."

"Then come right down to see me as soon as you possibly can," Dolly said. "I'm dying to see you—to talk with you. Oh, Alan, I'm so—so happy!"

"So am I," he told her, as he pressed her hand tenderly. "Then I shall see you again to-day."

"Yes, to-day, sure," she said, and she moved on.

"She's all right," said Abner Daniel, as Alan climbed in the buggy beside him. "She's all wool an' a yard wide."

"I reckon you are satisfied with the way it come out, Uncle Ab," said his nephew, flushing over the compliment to Dolly.

"Jest want one thing more," said the old man, "an' I can't make out whether it's a sin or not. I want to face Perkins an' Abe Tompkins. I'd give my right arm to meet 'em an' watch the'r faces when they heer about the railroad, an' the price yore pa's land fetched."